I can never
remember whether it
snowed for six days
and six nights when
I was twelve
or whether it snowed
for twelve days and
twelve nights when
I was six

*A Child's Christmas in Wales*
Dylan Thomas

Books
light up Christmas
*at* Waterstone's

GRANTA 56, WINTER 1996

EDITOR Ian Jack
DEPUTY EDITOR Robert Winder
MANAGING EDITOR Claire Wrathall
EDITORIAL ASSISTANT Karen Whitfield

CONTRIBUTING EDITORS Neil Belton, Pete de Bolla, Frances Coady,
Ursula Doyle, Will Hobson, Liz Jobey, Blake Morrison, Andrew O'Hagan

Granta, 2–3 Hanover Yard, Noel Road, London N1 8BE
TEL 0171 704 9776, FAX 0171 704 0474
SUBSCRIPTIONS 0171 704 0470

FINANCE Geoffrey Gordon, ASSOCIATE PUBLISHER Sally Lewis,
SALES Kate Griffin, SUBSCRIPTIONS John Kirkby, Rhiannon Thomas,
PUBLISHING ASSISTANT Jack Arthurs

TO ADVERTISE CONTACT Jenny Shramenko 0171 704 9776

Granta US, 250 West 57th Street, Suite 1316, New York, NY 10107, USA

PUBLISHER Rea S. Hederman

SUBSCRIPTION DETAILS: a one-year subscription (four issues) costs £24.95 (UK),
£32.95 (rest of Europe) and £39.95 (rest of the world).

Granta is printed in the United States of America. The paper used in this publication
meets the minimum requirements of American National Standard for Information
Sciences—Permanence of Paper for Printed Library Materials, ANSI Z39.48-1984. ♾

Granta is published by Granta Publications Ltd and distributed in the United Kingdom
by Bloomsbury, 2 Soho Square, London W1V 5DE; and in the United States by Penguin
Books USA Inc, 375 Hudson Street, New York, NY 10014, USA. This selection
copyright © 1996 by Granta Publications Ltd.

Cover photographs: Peter Marlow/Magnum (front)
and Hulton Getty/MSI (back)
Cover design by The Senate

ISBN 0 903141 03 5

# Troilus and Cressida

**by William Shakespeare**

ROYAL
SHAKESPEARE
COMPANY

Sponsored by
ALLIED
DOMECQ

'Ian Judge has delivered an epic production…at once bold and funny, sexy and heroic.'
Daily Mail

In repertoire until 25 March 1997
Barbican Theatre
0171 638 8891

Funded by
THE
ARTS
COUNCIL
OF ENGLAND

Now in repertoire at the National

# Death of a
# SALESMAN

by Arthur Miller

"The best-made as well as the most
courageous and emotionally compelling
play to come from America since the war"
Daily Telegraph

Alun Armstrong,
Mark Strong
and Marjorie Yates
lead the cast in
David Thacker's
production of Miller's
Pulitzer Prize-winning play.

Arthur Miller. Photo: Dan Weiner

## NT Royal
National
Theatre

Also in repertoire this winter

In the Olivier

### Guys and Dolls
Music and lyrics by
Frank Loesser
Book by Jo Swerling and
Abe Burrows
(from 9 December - 29 March)
(Extremely limited availability at all
performances in December and
matinees in January)

In the Lyttelton

### John Gabriel Borkman
by Henrik Ibsen
in a new version
by Nicholas Wright
(ends 21 December)

### The Homecoming
by Harold Pinter
(from 17 January)
Booking opens 25 November

In the Cottesloe

### Fair Ladies at a
### Game of Poem Cards
a new verse play
by Peter Oswald
based on an original work
by Chikamatsu Monzaemon
(ends 29 January)

### The Cripple of
### Inishmaan
by Martin McDonagh
(from 2 January)
Booking opens 25 November

### Light Shining in
### Buckinghamshire
by Caryl Churchill
(from 9 January)
Booking opens 25 November

Royal National Theatre,
South Bank, London SE1 9PX

## Box Office
## 0171-928 2252

First Call
0171-420 0000

Reg'd Charity

Funded by
ARTS
COUNCIL
OF ENGLAND

# WHAT HAPPENED TO US?

'A remarkable achievement
of serious storytelling . . .
The ease, the fluidity, the
economy, the precision
of Tóibín's masterly prose
make this novel sheer
pleasure to read'

NORMAN THOMAS di GIOVANNI
*The Times*

# COLM TÓIBÍN

## The STORY of the NIGHT

A Novel

PICADOR  Out now in Hardback

# EDITORIAL

Quite suddenly, or so it seems, Britain has changed. To the outsider, it may still look like a place of peculiar and historic qualities— 'traditions'; this is the way it chooses to advertise itself. But many of the people who live in it can scarcely recognize their way of life from twenty years before. The change had been predicted for some time. Most of my life, certainly, has been lived under the shade of Dean Acheson's famous pronouncement that Britain had lost an empire but had not yet found a role, a foreign analysis that was translated domestically into the conventional wisdom that British politics were about the management of decline. But what did Britain imagine this would mean? I think we thought it meant shrinkage, a kind of autumn shrivelling that would leave the roots untouched. The leaves of imperial possessions might flutter to the ground, the branches of old industries might be hacked off, but there, half-buried in the soil, would still be the magical jewels: the monarchy, Parliament ('the oldest democracy in the world'), the BBC ('the least bad television in the world'), morning milk delivered to the doorstep, a people characterized by what George Orwell (who is never far away from such soft thoughts) called decency. The core of the old place would be much the same.

Remarkably few people, even ten years ago, saw it otherwise. The 1980s, in fact, were generally hailed as a time of British resurgence. British troops sailed to the South Atlantic and defeated Argentina; the monarchy acquired a beautiful princess; some people got poorer—there was anger and civil strife—but more got richer; Mrs Thatcher, who said she intended to put the 'Great' back into 'Britain', linked arms with Ronald Reagan. The twin leaders of the western world! What was it that Harold Macmillan told Jack Kennedy? That Britain would play Greece to America's Rome?

That time can now be recalled like a dream. Perhaps it was the Indian summer of Britain, the last fling of Britishness. No British institution survives as serenely as it did then. The list of disclosure is too long—political corruption, judicial incompetence, a small bribe here, a large lie there—but at its head sits the chief symbol, the monarchy. How odd that we never examined its absurdity before; how odd that it took its frail humanity—eating disorders, adultery—rather than its fake medievalism and expense to bring it so close to destruction. And how odd that we thought the periphery could shrink, and the centre stay unchanged.

Scepticism and satire have replaced Orwellian decency as leading British qualities. The most prominent British art form is stand-up comedy. Shrillness, not phlegmatism, is the temper of the place. Are we inside or outside Europe? For how much longer will the United

Kingdom—as opposed to England, Wales, Scotland and the six counties that now form Northern Ireland—exist? We have absolutely no idea how things will work out.

Writing in Britain has been affected in various ways. A small specialism has developed in national self-examination, the kind of 'what's-wrong-with-us?' book that has a steady popularity in the United States but in Britain comes in spasms. In Scotland, fiction has evolved its own language and dark identity and flourishes; mostly it describes the present. English fiction—that is, fiction from England—has begun to do something else.

As one of the judges for the 1996 Booker Prize, I was struck by how many new English novels (and new English novelists) were preoccupied with the past; not with history—they weren't historical novels by way of research and period detail—but with the country and people that seemed to be there a minute ago, before we blinked and turned away. Nor were they nostalgic or romantic or (thank God) illustrative, dynastic stories of English society, comparing and contrasting the life of Family X decade by decade. Many were fine novels using new devices. One of them, *Last Orders* by Graham Swift, an extract from which appeared in *Granta* 52, went on to win the prize. Another, by Shena Mackay, got as far as the shortlist. Others again—Tim Binding, Patrick McGrath, John Preston—were not far from it. The 1950s was a favourite period, casually and unsentimentally evoked.

How to describe this writing? Twenty years ago the Scottish writer Tom Nairn, who is mentioned elsewhere in this issue, invented a phrase for the novels of Walter Scott. Nairn quoted the Hungarian Georg Lukács to argue that Scott was not the Romantic he is usually taken for. He belonged to a newly industrializing society and a country—Britain—that was forging a unified identity; as a writer he used the fresh tool of realism to depict another way of life in another kind of country—pre-industrial, pre-British Scotland—that had only recently disappeared. He was, in Nairn's phrase, a valedictory realist.

Valedictory realism can't, of course, be confined to England or English writers; nor do writers fit neatly under such a label. In this issue the Irish writer John Banville has been inspired by a singular life—that of the English spy Sir Anthony Blunt, the keeper of the Queen's Pictures, who was publicly exposed and disgraced as a traitor during Mrs Thatcher's first year as prime minister. But that life grew among other lives (versions of Graham Greene and Guy Burgess are here as well as Blunt) in a different, patrician England. The surface shone; the rot was underneath.

When did we say goodbye to it? Oh, it seems only yesterday. This is the literature of farewell. IAN JACK

**GRANTA**

# JOHN BANVILLE
## THE ENEMY WITHIN

*Anthony Blunt at his press conference in 1979 after Mrs Thatcher revealed his career as a Soviet spy and the Queen stripped him of his knighthood*     HULTON GETTY

First day of the new life. Very strange. Feeling almost skittish all day. Exhausted now yet feverish also, like a child at the end of a party. Like a child, yes: as if I had suffered a grotesque form of rebirth. Yet this morning I realized for the first time that I am an old man. I was crossing Gower Street, my former stamping ground. I stepped off the path and something hindered me. Odd sensation, as if the air at my ankles had developed a flaw, seemed to turn—what is the word: viscid?—and resisted me, and I almost stumbled. Bus thundering past with a grinning blackamoor at the wheel. What did he see? Sandals, mac, my inveterate string bag, old rheumy eye wild with fright. If I had been run over, they would have said it was suicide, with relief all round. But I will not give them that satisfaction. I shall be seventy-two this year. Impossible to believe. Inside, an eternal twenty-two. I suppose that is how it is for everybody old. Brr.

Never kept a journal before. Fear of incrimination. Leave nothing in writing, Boy Bannister always said. Why have I started now? I just sat down and began to write, as if it were the most natural thing in the world, which of course it is not. My last testament. It is twilight, everything very still and poignant. The trees in the square are dripping. Tiny sound of birdsong. April. I do not like the spring, its antics and agitations; I fear that anguished seething in the heart, what it might make me do. What it might have made me do: one has to be scrupulous with tenses, at my age. I miss my children. Goodness, where did that come from? They are hardly what you could call children any more. Julian must be—well, he must be forty this year, which makes Blanche thirty-eight, is it? Compared to them I seem to myself hardly grown-up at all. Auden wrote somewhere that no matter what the age of the company, he was always convinced he was the youngest in the room; me, too. All the same, I thought they might have called. *Sorry to hear about your treachery, Daddums.* Yet I am not at all sure I would want to hear Blanche sniffling and Julian tightening his lips at me down the line. His mother's son. I suppose all fathers say that.

I mustn't ramble.

Public disgrace is a strange thing. Fluttery feeling in the region of the diaphragm and a sort of racing sensation all over, as of the blood like mercury slithering along heavily just under the skin.

Excitement mixed with fright makes for a heady brew. At first I could not think what this state reminded me of, then it came to me: those first nights on the prowl after I had finally admitted to myself it was my own kind that I wanted. The same hot shiver of mingled anticipation and fear, the same desperate grin trying not to break out. Wanting to be caught. To be set upon. To be manhandled. Well, past all that now. Past everything, really.

Switch on the lamp. My steady, little light. How neatly it defines this narrow bourn of desk and page in which I have always found my deepest joy, this lighted tent wherein I crouch in happy hiding from the world. For even the pictures were more a matter of mind than eye. Here there is everything that—

That was a call from Querell. Well, he certainly has nerve, I'll say that for him. The telephone ringing gave me a dreadful start. I have never got used to this machine, the way it crouches so malevolently, ready to start clamouring for attention when you least expect it, like a mad baby. My poor heart is still thudding in the most alarming way. Who did I think it would be? He was calling from Antibes. I thought I could hear the sea in the background and I felt envious and annoyed, but more likely it was just the noise of traffic passing by outside his flat, along the Corniche, is it?—or is that somewhere else? Heard the news on the World Service, so he said. 'Dreadful, old man, dreadful; what can I say?' He could not keep the eagerness out of his voice. Wanted all the dirty details. 'Was it sex they got you on?' How disingenuous— and yet how little he realizes, after all. Should I have challenged him, told him I know him for his perfidy? What would have been the point? Skryne reads his books, he is a real fan. 'That Querell, now,' he says, doing that peculiar whistle with his dentures, 'he has the measure of us all.' Not of me, he hasn't, my friend; not of me. At least, I hope not.

No one else has called. Well, I hardly expected that he would.

I shall miss old Skryne. No question now of having to deal with him any more; that is all over, along with so much else. I should feel relieved but, oddly, I do not. We had become a kind of double act at the end, he and I, a music-hall routine. *I say, I say, I say, Mr Skryne! Well, bless my soul, Mr Bones!* He was hardly the popular image of an interrogator. Hardy little fellow with a narrow

11

head and miniature features and a neat thatch of very dry stone-coloured hair. He reminds me of the fierce father of the madcap bride in those Hollywood comedies of the Thirties. Blue eyes, not piercing, even a little fogged (incipient cataracts?). The buffed brogues, the pipe he plays with, the old tweed jacket with elbow patches. Ageless. Might be anything from fifty to seventy-five. Nimble mind, though, you could practically hear the cogs whirring. And an amazing memory. 'Hold on a sec,' he would say, stabbing at me with his pipe-stem, 'let's run over that bit once more,' and I would have to unpack the delicate tissue of lies I had been spinning him, searching with frantic calmness as I did so for the flaw he had detected in the fabric. By now I was only lying for fun, for recreation, you might say, like a retired tennis pro knocking up with an old opponent. I had no fear that he would discover some new enormity—I had confessed to everything by now, or almost everything—but it seemed imperative to maintain consistency, for aesthetic reasons, I suppose, and in order to be consistent it was necessary to invent. Ironic, I know. He has the tenacity of the ferret: never let go. He is straight out of Dickens; I picture a crooked little house in Stepney or Hackney or wherever it is he lives, complete with termagant wife and a brood of cheeky nippers. It is another of my besetting weaknesses, to see people always as caricatures. Including myself.

Not that I recognize myself in the public version of me that is being put about now. I was listening to the wireless when our dear prime minister (I really do admire her; such firmness, such fixity of purpose, and so handsome, too, in a fascinatingly mannish way) stood up in the Commons and made the announcement, and for a moment I did not register my own name. I mean I thought she was speaking of someone else, someone whom I knew, but not well, and whom I had not seen for a long time. It was a very peculiar sensation. The Department had already alerted me of what was to come—terribly rude, the people they have in there now, not at all the easygoing types of my day—but it was still a shock. Then on the television news at midday they had some extraordinary blurred photographs of me, I do not know how or where they got them, and cannot even remember them being taken—apt verb, that, applied to photography: the savages are right, it is a part of one's soul that is being taken away. I looked like one of those preserved bodies they dig up from Scandinavian bogs, all jaw and sinewy throat and hooded eyeballs. Some writer fellow, I have forgotten or suppressed his name—a 'contemporary historian', whatever that may be—was about to identify me, but the government got in first, in what I must say was a clumsy attempt to save face; I was embarrassed for the PM, really I was. Now here I am, exposed again, and after all this time. Exposed!—what a shiversome, naked-sounding word. Oh Querell, Querell. I know it was you. It is the kind of thing you would do, to settle old score. Is there no end to life's turbulences? Except the obvious one, I mean.

What is my purpose here? I may say, *I just sat down to write,* but I am not deceived. I have never done anything in my life that did not have a purpose, usually hidden, sometimes even from myself. Am I, like Querell, out to settle old scores? Or is it perhaps my intention to justify my deeds, to offer extenuations? I hope not. On the other hand, neither do I want to fashion for myself yet another burnished mask . . . Having pondered for a moment, I realize that the metaphor is obvious: attribution, verification, restoration. I shall strip away layer after layer of grime—the toffee-coloured varnish and caked soot left by a lifetime of dissembling—until I come to the very thing itself and know it for what it is. My soul. My self. (When I laugh out loud like this, the room seems to start back in surprise and dismay, with hand to lip. I have lived decorously here, I must not now turn into a shrieking hysteric.)

I kept my nerve in face of that pack of jackals from the newspapers today. *Did men die because of you?* Yes, dearie, swooned quite away. But no, no, I was superb, if I do say so myself. Cool, dry, balanced, every inch the Stoic: Coriolanus to the general. I am a great actor, that is the secret of my success (*Must not anyone who wants to move the crowd be an actor who impersonates himself?*—Nietzsche). I dressed the part to perfection: old but good houndstooth jacket, Jermyn Street shirt and Charvet tie—red, just to be mischievous—corduroy slacks, socks the colour and texture of porridge, that pair of scuffed brothel-creepers I had not worn in thirty years. Might have just come up from a weekend at Cliveden. I toyed with the idea of a tobacco pipe *à la* Skryne, but that would have been to overdo it, and besides, it requires years of practice to be a plausible pipeman—never take on cover that you can't do naturally, that was another of Boy's dicta. I believe it was a nice piece of strategy on my part to invite the gentlepersons of the press into my lovely home. They crowded in almost sheepishly, jostling each other's notebooks and holding their cameras protectively above their heads. Rather touching, really; so eager, so awkward. I felt as if I were back at the Institute, about to deliver a lecture on Poussin.

Midnight. My leg has gone to sleep. Wish the rest of me would go with it. Yet it is not unpleasant to be awake like this, awake and alert, like a nocturnal predator, or, better yet, the guardian of the tribe's resting place. I used to fear the night, its dreads and dreams, but lately I have begun to enjoy it, almost. Something soft and yielding comes over the world when darkness falls. On the threshold of my second childhood, I suppose I am remembering the nursery, with its woolly warmth and wide-eyed vigils. Even as a babe I was already solitary. It was not so much my mother's kiss that I Proustianly craved as the having done with it, so that I could be alone with my self, this strange soft breathing body in which my spinning consciousness was darkly trapped, like a dynamo in a sack. I can still see her dim form retreating and the yellow fan of light from the hall folding across the nursery floor as she lingeringly closed the door and stepped backwards in silence out of my life. I was not quite five when she died. Her death was not a cause of suffering to me, as I recall. I was old enough to register the loss but too young to find it more than merely puzzling. My father in his well-meaning way took to sleeping on a camp bed in the nursery to keep me company, and for weeks I had to listen to him thrashing all night long in the toils of his grief, mumbling and muttering and calling on his God, heaving long, shuddering sighs that made the camp bed crack its knuckles in exasperation. I would lie there intently, trying to listen beyond him to the wind in the trees that ringed the house like sentinels, and, farther off, the boxy collapses of waves on Carrick strand and the drawn-out hiss of waters receding over the shingle. I would not lie on my right side because that way I could feel my heart beating and I was convinced that if I were going to die I would feel it stop before the terrifying final darkness came down. Tomorrow. Dear God, how can I face a tomorrow?

Well, I am everywhere. Pages and pages of me. This must be how it feels to be the leading man on the morning after a stupendously disastrous first night. I went to a number of newsagents, for the sake of decency, though it got increasingly awkward as the bundle of newspapers under my arm steadily thickened. Some of the people behind the counters recognized me and curled a contemptuous lip; reactionaries to a man, shopkeepers, I have noticed it before. One chap, though, gave me a sort of sad, underhand smile. He was a Pakistani. What company I shall be in from now on. Old lags. Child molesters. Outcasts. The lost ones.

It has been confirmed: the knighthood is to be revoked. I mind. I am surprised how much I mind. Just Doctor again, if even that; maybe just plain Mister. At least they have not taken away my bus pass.

That writer chap telephoned, requesting an interview. What effrontery. Well-spoken, however, and not at all embarrassed. Brisk tone, faintly amused, with a hint almost of fondness: after all, I am his ticket to fame, or notoriety, at least. I asked him to say who it was that betrayed me. That provoked a chuckle. Said even a journalist would go to jail rather than reveal a source. They love to trot out that particular hobby horse. I might have said to him, *My dear fellow, I have been in jail for the best part of thirty years.* Instead, I rang off.

The *Telegraph* sent a photographer to Carrickdrum, site of my bourgeois beginnings in Ireland. The house is no longer the bishop's residence, and is owned, the paper tells me, by a man who deals in scrap metal. The sentinel trees are gone—the scrap merchant must have wanted more light—and the brickwork has been covered with a new facing, painted white. I am tempted to work up a metaphor for change and loss, but I must beware turning into a sentimental old ass, if I am not one already. St Nicholas's (*St Nicholas's!—I never made the connection before*) was a grim and gloomy pile, and a bit of stucco and white paint can only be an improvement.

To take possession of a city of which you are not a native you must first of all fall in love there. I had always known London; my family, although they hardly ever went there, considered it our capital, not dour Belfast, with its rain-coloured buildings and bellowing shipyard sirens. It was in that summer I spent in London with Nick, however, that the place came fully alive for me. I say I spent the summer with him but that is wishful exaggeration. He was working—another exaggeration—for his father at the publishers Brevoort & Klein, and had moved down from Oxford to a flat above a newsagent's shop off the Fulham Road. I remember that flat with remarkable clarity. There was a small living room at the front with two peaked mansard windows that made an incongruously ecclesiastical effect; the first time Boy Bannister came there he clapped his hands and cried: 'Fetch me my surplice, we must have a black mass!' The flat was known as the Eyrie, a word neither Nick nor I was sure how to pronounce, but it suited, for certainly it was eerie—Nick favoured tall candles and Piranesi prints—and airy, too, especially in spring, when the windows were filled with flying sky, and the timbers creaked like the spars of a sailing ship. Nick, who was by nature a unique mix of the aesthete and the hearty, let the place run to appalling squalor: I still shudder when I think of the lavatory. At the back was a poky bedroom with a sharply canted ceiling in which there was wedged skew-ways an enormous brass bed Nick claimed to have won in a poker game in a gambling den behind Paddington Station. It was one of Nick's stories.

He did not often sleep at the flat. His girls refused to stay there because of the filth, and anyway in those times girls rarely stayed overnight, at least not the sort of girl Nick consorted with. Mostly it was a place to throw parties in, and to recover in from the resulting hangovers. On these occasions he would take to his bed for two or three days, surrounded by an accumulating clutter of books and boxes of sweets and bottles of champagne, supplied by a succession of friends whom he would summon to him by telephone. I can still hear his voice on the line, an exaggeratedly anguished whisper: 'I say, old man, do you think you could come round? I do believe I'm dying.' Usually when I arrived a small crowd would have already assembled, another party in embryo, sitting about on that vast raft of a bed eating Nick's chocolates and drinking champagne from tooth-glasses and kitchen cups, with Nick in his nightshirt propped against a bank of pillows, pale as ivory, his black hair standing on end, all eyes and angles, a figure out of Schiele. Boy would be there, of course, and Leo Rothenstein, and girls called Daphne and Brenda and Daisy, in silks and cloche hats. Sometimes Querell would come round, tall, thin, sardonic, standing with his back against the wall and smoking a cigarette, somehow crooked, like the villain in a cautionary tale, one eyebrow arched, the corners of his mouth turned down, and a hand in the pocket of his tightly buttoned jacket that I always thought could be holding a gun. He had the look of a man who knew something damaging about everyone in the room.

Those parties: did anyone really enjoy them? What I chiefly recall is the air of suppressed desperation that pervaded them. We drank a lot, but drink seemed only to make us frightened, or despairing, so that we had to shriek all the louder, as if to scare demons. What was it that we feared? Another war, yes, the worldwide economic crisis, the threat of Fascism; there was no end of things to be afraid of. We felt such deep resentments! We blamed all our ills on the Great War and the old men who had forced the young to fight in it, and perhaps Flanders really did destroy us as a *nation*, but—But there I go, falling into the role of amateur sociologist that I despise. I never thought in terms of *us*, or the nation; none of us did, I am convinced of it. We talked in those terms, of course—we never *stopped* talking thus—but it was all no more than a striking of attitudes to make ourselves feel more serious, more weighty, more authentic. Deep down—if we did indeed have deeps—we cared about ourselves and, intermittently, one or two others; isn't that how it always is? *Why did you do it?* that girl reporter asked me yesterday, and I replied with parables of philosophy and art, and she went away dissatisfied. But what other reply could I have given? *I* am the answer to her question, the totality of what I am; nothing less will suffice. In the public mind, for the brief period it will entertain, and be entertained by, the thought of me, I am a figure with a single salient feature. Even for those who thought they knew me intimately, everything else I have done or not done has faded to insignificance before the fact

17

of my so-called treachery. While in reality all that I am is all of a piece: all of a piece, and yet broken up into a myriad selves. Does that make sense?

So what we were frightened of, then, was ourselves, each one his own demon.

Querell when he phoned the other day had the grace not to pretend to be shocked. He knows all about betrayal, the large variety and the small; he is a connoisseur in that department. When he was at the height of his fame (he has slipped somewhat from the headlines, since he is old and no longer the hellion he once was), I used to chuckle over newspaper photographs of him hobnobbing with the Pope, since I knew that the lips with which he kissed the papal ring had most likely been between some woman's thighs a half-hour previously. But Querell too is in danger of being shown up for what he really is, whatever that might be. That fishy look he always had is becoming more pronounced with age. In yet another interview recently—where did he ever get the reputation for shunning publicity?—he made one of those seemingly deep but in fact banal observations that have become his trademark. 'I don't know about God,' he told the interviewer, 'but certainly I believe in the Devil.' Oh yes, one always needed a long spoon to sup with Querell.

He was genuinely curious about people—the sure mark of the second-rate novelist. At those parties in the Eyrie he would stand for a long time leaning with his back against the wall, diabolical trickles of smoke issuing from the corners of his mouth, watching and listening as the party took on the air of monkey-house hysteria. He drank as much as the rest of us, but it seemed to have no effect on him except to make those unnervingly pale-blue eyes of his shine with a kind of malicious merriment. Usually he would slip away early, with a girl in tow; you would glance at the spot where he had been standing and find him gone, and seem to see a shadowy after-image of him, like the paler shadow left on a wall when a picture is removed. So I was surprised when during a party one August afternoon he accosted me in the corridor.

'Listen, Maskell,' he said, in that insinuatingly truculent way of his, 'I can't take much more of this filthy wine—let's go and have a real drink.'

My head felt as if it were stuffed with cotton wool, and the sunlight in the mansard windows had taken on the colour of urine, and for once I was content to leave. A girl was standing weeping in the bedroom doorway, her face in her hands; Nick was not to be seen. Querell and I walked in silence down the clattery stairs. The air in the street was blued with exhaust fumes; strange to think of a time when one still noticed the smell of petrol. We went to a pub—was it Finch's then, or had it another name?—and Querell ordered gin and water, 'the tart's tipple', as he said with a snicker. It was just after opening time, and there were few customers. Querell sat with one foot hooked on the rung of his stool and the other delicately braced *en pointe* on the floor; he did not undo the buttons of his jacket. I noticed the frayed shirt cuffs, the shine on the knees of his trousers. We were of an age, but I felt a generation younger than him. He had a job on the *Express*, or perhaps it was the *Telegraph*, writing juicy tidbits for the gossip column, and as we drank, he recounted office anecdotes, drolly describing the eccentricities of his fellow journalists and the public-school asininity of the editor of the day in what were obviously pre-prepared paragraphs of admirable fluency and precision.

He came to the end of his stories, and we were silent for a while. He ordered more drinks, and when I tried to pay for them he waved my money away with that matter-of-fact assumption of superiority that was another of his characteristics. I don't know why he should have assumed I was broke; on the contrary, I was comparatively well-off at the time, thanks to my column for the *Spectator* and occasional lectures.

'You're pretty fond of Nick, aren't you,' he said.

It was said with such studied casualness that I grew wary, despite the gin.

'I haven't known him for very long,' I said.

He nodded. 'Of course, you were a Cambridge man. Not that I saw a great deal of him at Oxford.' Nick had said to me of Querell that in their college days he had been too busy whoring to bother much with friendships. Despite rumours to the contrary, Querell was an incorrigible hetero, whose fascination with women ran almost to the level of the gynaecological. I thought he always *smelt* faintly of sex. I hear he is still chasing girls, in his seventies, down there on the Côte d'Azur.

'Quite a boy, Nick,' he said, and paused, and then gave me a peculiar, sidelong look and asked, 'Do you trust him?' I didn't know what to answer and mumbled something about not being sure that I thought anyone was really to be trusted. He nodded again, seemingly satisfied, and dropped the subject and began to talk instead about a fellow he had bumped into recently, whom he had known at Oxford.

'He'd interest you,' he said. 'He's a red-hot Sinn Feiner.'

I laughed.

'I'm from the other side of the fence, you know,' I said. 'My people are black Protestants.'

'Oh, Protestants in Ireland are all Catholics, really.'

'Rather the opposite, I should have thought. Or we're all just plain pagans, perhaps.'

'Well, anyway, the place is interesting, isn't it? I mean the politics.'

I wonder—good Lord, I wonder if he was putting out feelers with a view to recruiting me even then. That was the summer of '31; was he already with the Department, that early? Or maybe it was just the question of religion that interested him. Although none of us knew it, he was already taking instruction at Farm Street. (Querell's Catholicism, by the way, has always seemed to me far more of an anachronism than my Marxism.) And in fact now he dropped the subject of politics and went on to talk about religion, in his usual oblique way, telling me a story about Gerard Manley Hopkins preaching at some sort of women's gathering in Dublin and scandalizing the congregation by comparing the Church to a sow with seven teats representing the seven sacraments. I laughed and said what a sad poor fool Hopkins was, trying for the common touch like that and failing ridiculously, but Querell gave me another long, measuring look and said: 'Yes, he made the mistake of thinking that the way to be convincing is to put on a false front,' and I felt obscurely confounded.

R eading over these pages, I am struck by how little I impinge on them. The personal pronoun is everywhere, of course, propping up the edifice I am erecting, but what is there to be seen behind this slender capital? Yet I must have made a stronger impression than I remember; there were people who hated me, and a few even who claimed to have loved me. My dry jokes were appreciated—I know I was considered quite a wag in some quarters, and I once overheard myself described as an Irish wit (though I am not entirely sure it was meant to be complimentary). Why then am I not more vividly present to myself in these recollections I am setting down here with such finicking attention to detail? After a long pause for thought (funny there is no mark in prose to indicate lengthy lapses of time: whole days could pass in the space of a full stop—whole years) I have come to the conclusion that my early espousal of the Stoic philosophy had the inevitable consequence of forcing me to sacrifice an essential vitality of spirit. Have I lived at all? Sometimes the chill thought strikes me that the risks I took, the dangers I exposed myself to (after all, it is not far-fetched to think that I might have been bumped off at any time), were only a substitute for some more simple, much more authentic form of living that was beyond me. Yet if I had not stepped into the spate of history, what would I have been? A dried-up scholar, fussing over nice questions of attribution and what to have for supper ('Shivershanks' was Boy's nickname for me in later years). That's all true; all the same, these kinds of rationalization do not satisfy me.

Let me try another tack. Perhaps it was not the philosophy by which I lived, but the double life itself—which at first seemed to so many of us a source of strength—that acted upon me as a debilitating force. I know this has always been said of us, that the lying and the secrecy inevitably corrupted us, sapped our moral strength and blinded us to the actual nature of things, but I never believed it could be true. We were latter-day Gnostics, keepers of a secret knowledge, for whom the world of appearances was only a gross manifestation of an infinitely subtler, more real reality known only to the chosen few, but the iron, ineluctable laws of which were everywhere at work. This gnosis was, on the material level, the equivalent of the Freudian conception of the unconscious, that unacknowledged and irresistible legislator, that spy in the heart. Thus, for us, everything was itself and at the same time something else. So we could rag about the place and drink all night and laugh ourselves silly, because behind all our frivolity there operated the stern conviction that the world must

21

be changed and that we were the ones who would do it. At our lightest we seemed to ourselves possessed of a seriousness far more deep, partly because it was hidden, than anything our parents could manage, with their vaguenesses and lack of any certainty, any rigour, above all, their contemptibly feeble efforts at being good. Let the whole sham fortress fall, we said, and if we can give it a good hard shove, we will. *Destruam et aedificabo*, as Proudhon was wont to cry.

It was all selfishness, of course; we did not care a damn about the world, much as we might shout about freedom and justice and the plight of the masses. All selfishness.

And then, for me, there were other forces at work, ambiguous, ecstatic, anguished: the obsession with art, for instance; the tricky question of nationality, that constant drone note in the bagpipe music of my life; and, deeper again than any of these, the murk and slither of sex. *The Queer Irish Spy*; it sounds like the title of one of those tunes the Catholics used to play on melodeons in their pubs when I was a child. Did I call it a *double* life? Quadruple—quintuple—more like.

The newspapers all this week have portrayed me, rather flatteringly, I confess, as an ice-cold theoretician, a sort of philosopher-spy, the one real intellectual in our circle and the guardian of ideological purity. The fact is, the majority of us had no more than the sketchiest grasp of theory. We did not bother to read the texts; we had others to do that for us. The working-class comrades were the great readers—Communism could not have survived without autodidacts. I knew one or two of the shorter pieces—the *Manifesto*, of course, that great ringing shout of wishful thinking—and had made a determined start on *Kapital*—the dropping of the definite article was de rigueur for us smart young men, so long as the pronunciation was *echt deutsch*—but soon got bored. Besides, I had scholarly reading to do, and that was quite enough. Politics was not books, anyway; politics was action. Beyond the thickets of dry theory milled the ranks of the People, the final, authentic touchstone, waiting for us to liberate them into collectivity. We saw no contradiction between liberation and the collective. Holistic social engineering, as that old reactionary Popper calls it, was the logical and necessary means to achieve freedom—an orderly freedom, that is. Why should there not be order in human affairs? Throughout history the tyranny of the individual had brought nothing but chaos and butchery. The People must be united, must be melded into a single, vast, breathing being! We were like those Jacobin mobs in the early days of the French Revolution, who would go surging through the streets of Paris in a rage for fraternity, clasping the Common Man to their breasts so fiercely they knocked the stuffing out of him.

Anyway, of all our ideological exemplars, I always secretly preferred Bakunin, so impetuous, disreputable, fierce and irresponsible compared to stolid, hairy-handed Marx. I once went so far as to copy out by hand Bakunin's elegantly vitriolic description of his rival: 'M. Marx is by origin a Jew. He unites in himself all the qualities and defects of that gifted race. Nervous, some say, to the point of cowardice, he is so immensely malicious, vain, quarrelsome, as intolerant and autocratic as Jehovah, the God of his fathers, and like Him, insanely vindictive.' Not that Marx was any less ferocious than Bakunin, in his way; I admired in particular his intellectual annihilation of Proudhon, whose *petit-bourgeois* post-Hegelianism and country-bumpkin faith in the essential goodness of the little man Marx held up to cruel and exhaustive ridicule. The spectacle of Marx mercilessly destroying his unfortunate predecessor is horribly exciting, like watching a great beast of the jungle plunging its jaws into the ripped-open belly of some still-thrashing delicate-limbed herbivore. Violence by proxy, that is the thing: stimulating, satisfying, safe.

How they do bring one back to the days of youth, these ancient battles for the soul of man. I feel quite excited, here at my desk, in these last, unbearably expectant days of spring. Time for a gin, I think.

It will seem strange—it seems strange to me—but Boy was the most ideologically driven of the lot of us. God, how he would talk! On and on, superstructure and substructure and the division of labour and all the rest of it, endlessly. Mind you, there was more to Boy than talk. He was quite the activist. At Cambridge he had set about organizing the gyps and bedders into a union, and

23

joined in strike protests by bus drivers and sewerage workers in the town. Oh yes, he put us all to shame. I can see him still, marching down King's Parade on the way to a strike meeting, shirt collar open, dirty old trousers held up with a workman's broad belt, a figure straight out of a Moscow mural. I was jealous of his energy, his boldness, his freedom from that self-consciousness which froze me solid when it came to practical activism, I mean the activism of the streets. But in my heart I despised him, too, for what I could not but think of as his crassness in seeking to turn theory into action, in the same way that I despised the Cambridge physicists of my day for translating pure mathematics into applied science. This is what I marvel at still, that I could have given myself over to such an essentially *vulgar* ideology.

Boy. I miss him, despite everything. Oh, I know, he was a clown, cruel, dishonest, slovenly, careless of himself and others, but for all that he maintained a curious kind of—what shall I call it?—a kind of grace. Yes, a kind of splendorous grace; it is not too much to say.

Odd, but I cannot remember when I first met him. It must have been at Cambridge, yet he seems to have been always present in my life, a constant force, even in childhood. Singular though he may have seemed, I suppose he was of a type: the toddler who pinches the little girls and makes them cry, the boy at the back of the class showing off his erection under the desk, the unabashed queer who can spot instantly the queer streak in others. Despite what people may think, he and I did not have an affair. There was a drunken scuffle one night in my rooms at Trinity in the early Thirties, long before I had 'come out', as they say now, that left me shaking with embarrassment and fright, though Boy shrugged it off with his usual insouciance; I recall him going down the ill-lit stairs with half his shirt-tail hanging out and smiling back at me knowingly and wagging a playful, minatory finger. While revelling in its privileges, he held the world of his parents and their circle in jocular contempt. At home he subsisted mainly on a horrible gruel-like stuff—I can smell it still—that he boiled up from oatmeal and crushed garlic, but when he went out it was always the Ritz or the Savoy, after which he would lumber into a taxi and make his raucous way down to the docks or the East End to trawl through the pubs for what with a smacking of those big lips he referred to as 'likely meat'.

He could be subtle, if subtlety was what was needed. When we joined with Alastair Sykes in the putsch on the Apostles in the summer term of 1932, Boy turned out to be not only the most energetic activist of the three of us but also the smoothest plotter. He was skilled too at curbing Alastair's more hair-raising flights of enthusiasm. 'Look here, Psyche,' he would say with cheerful firmness, 'you just belt up now, like a good chap, and let Victor and me do the talking.' And Alastair, after a moment's hesitation during which the tips of his ears would turn bright pink while his pipe belched smoke and sparks like a steam train, would meekly do as he was told, although he was the senior man. He got the credit for packing the society with our people, but I am sure it was really Boy's doing. Boy's charm, at once sunny and sinister, was hard to resist. (Not much is known publicly, even still, about the Apostles, that absurd boys' club, to which only the most gilded of Cambridge's golden youth were admitted; being Irish and not yet queer, I had to work hard and scheme long before I managed to worm my way in.)

The Apostles' meetings that term were held in Alastair's rooms; as a senior Fellow he had ampler quarters than any of the rest of us. I had met him my first year up. Those were the days when I still thought I had it in me to be a mathematician. The discipline held a deep appeal for me. Its procedures had the mark of an arcane ritual, another secret doctrine like that which I was soon to discover in Marxism. I relished the thought of being privy to a specialized language which even in its most rarefied form is an exact—well, plausible—expression of empirical reality. Mathematics speaks the world, as Alastair put it, with an uncharacteristic rhetorical flourish. Seeing the work that Alastair could do was what convinced me, more than my poor showing in the exams, that my future must lie in scholarship and not science. Alastair had the purest, most elegant intellect I have ever encountered. His father had been a docker in Liverpool, and Alastair had come up to Cambridge on a scholarship. In appearance he was a fierce, choleric little fellow with big teeth and a spiky bush of black hair standing straight up from his forehead

25

like the bristles of a yard-brush. He favoured hobnailed boots and shapeless jackets made from a peculiar kind of stiff, hairy tweed that might have been run up specially for him. That first year we were inseparable. It was a strange liaison, I suppose; what we shared most deeply, though we would never dream of speaking of it openly, was that we both felt keenly the insecurity of being outsiders. One of the wits dubbed us Jekyll and Hyde, and no doubt we did look an ill-assorted pair, I the gangling youth with pointed nose and already pronounced stoop loping across Great Court pursued by the little man in the boots, his stumpy legs going like a pair of blunt scissors and tobacco pipe fuming. It was the theoretical side of mathematics that interested me, but Alastair had a genius for application. He adored gadgets. At Bletchley Park during the war he found his true and perfect place. 'It was like coming home,' he told me afterwards, his eyes shiny with misery. That was in the Fifties, the last time I saw him. He had fallen into an enticement trap in the gents in Piccadilly Circus and was due in court the following week. The heavies from the Department had been tormenting him, he knew he could expect no mercy. He would not go to prison: on the eve of his court appearance he injected cyanide into an apple (a Cox's orange pippin, the report said; very scrupulous, the heavies) and ate it. Another uncharacteristic flourish. I wonder where he got the poison, not to mention the needle? I had not even known that he was queer. Perhaps he had not known it himself, before that jug-eared copper with his trousers round his ankles beckoned to him from his stall. Poor Psyche. I imagine him in the weeks before he died, lying between army-surplus blankets in that dreary bedsit he had off the Cromwell Road, miserably turning over the ruins of his life. He had broken some of the most difficult of the German army's codes, thus saving God knows how many Allied lives, yet they hounded him to death. And they call me a traitor. Could I have done something for him, pulled a few strings, put a word in with the internal security people? The thought gnaws at me.

Alastair, now, Alastair had read the sacred texts. Whatever scraps of theory I knew, I learned from him. The cause of Ireland was his great enthusiasm. His Irish mother had made him into a Sinn Feiner. Like me, he regretted that it was in Russia the

Revolution had occurred, but I could not agree with him that Ireland would have been a more congenial battleground; the notion seemed to me utterly risible. He had even taught himself the Irish language and could swear in it—though to my ears, I confess, the language in general sounds like a string of softly vehement oaths strung haphazardly together. He berated me for my lack of patriotism and called me a dirty Unionist, not wholly in jest. However, when I asked him one day for specific details of his knowledge of my country he grew evasive, and when I pressed him he blushed—those reddening ears—and admitted that in fact he had never set foot in Ireland.

He did not much care for the company of the majority of the Apostles, with their plush accents and aesthete manners. 'You could be speaking in bloody code, you lot, when you get started,' he complained, digging a blackened thumb into the burning dottle of his pipe. 'Bloody public schoolboys.' I used to laugh at him, with not much malice, but Boy gave him an awful time, mimicking perfectly his Scouse accent and bullying him into drinking too much beer. Alastair thought Boy was not sufficiently serious about the cause, and considered him—with remarkable prescience, as it turned out—to be a security risk. 'That Bannister,' he would mutter darkly, 'he'll get us all shopped.'

Here is a snapshot from the bulging album I keep in my head. It is sometime in the Thirties. Tea, thick sandwiches and thin beer, the sun of April on Trinity court. A dozen Apostles—some Fellows, such as Alastair and myself, a couple of nondescript dons, one or two earnest postgraduate scholars, every one of us a devout Marxist—are sitting about in Alastair's big gloomy living room. We favoured dark jackets and fawn bags and open-necked white shirts, except for Leo Rothenstein, always suavely magnificent in his Savile Row suits. Boy was more flamboyant: I recall crimson ties and purple waistcoats and, on this occasion, plus fours in a bright-green check. He is pacing up and down the room, dropping cigarette ash on the threadbare carpet, telling us, as I have heard him tell many times before, of the event that, so he insisted, had made him a homosexual.

'God, it was frightful! There she was, poor Mother, flat on her back with her legs in the air, shrieking, and my huge father lying naked on top of her, dead as a doornail. I had the hell of a job getting him off her. The smells! Twelve years old, I was. Haven't been able to look at a woman since without seeing Mater's big white breasts, colour of a fish's belly. The paps that gave me suck. In dreams those nipples still stare up at me cock-eyed. No Oedipus I, or Hamlet, either, that's certain. When she threw off her widow's weeds and remarried I felt only relief.'

I used to divide people into two sorts, those who were shocked by Boy's stories and those who were not, though I could never decide which was the more reprehensible half. Alastair had begun to huff and puff. 'Look here, we've got a motion before us which we should consider. Spain is going to be the next theatre of operations'—Alastair, who had never heard a shot fired in anger, had a great fondness for military jargon—'and we've got to decide where we stand.'

Leo Rothenstein laughed. 'That's obvious, surely? We're hardly in favour of the Fascists.' At the age of twenty-one Leo had come into an inheritance of two million pounds, along with Maule Park and a mansion in Portman Square.

Alastair fussed with his pipe; he disliked Leo and was at pains to hide the fact, afraid of being thought an anti-Semite.

'But the point is,' he said, 'will we fight?'

It strikes me how much talk of fighting there was throughout the Thirties, among our set, at least. Did the appeasers talk about appeasement with the same passion, I wonder?

'Don't be a fathead,' Boy said. 'Uncle Joe won't let it come to that.'

A chap called Wilkins, I've forgotten his first name, weedy type with glasses and a bad case of psoriasis, who was to die at El Alamein in command of a tank, turned from the window with a glass of beer in his fist and said: 'According to a man I spoke to the other day who's been over there, Uncle Joe has too much of a job on his hands trying to feed the masses at home to think of sending aid abroad.'

A silence followed. Bad form on Wilkins's part: we did not speak of the comrades' difficulties. Doubt was a bourgeois self-indulgence. Then Boy gave a nasty little laugh. 'Surprising,' he said, 'how some of us can't recognize propaganda when we hear it,' and

Wilkins threw him a baleful look and turned back to the window.

Spain, the kulaks, the machinations of the Trotskyites, racial violence in the East End—how antique it all seems now, almost quaint, and yet how seriously we took ourselves and our place on the world stage. I often have the idea that what drove those of us who went on to become active agents was the burden of deep—of intolerable—embarrassment that the talk-drunk Thirties left us with. The beer, the sandwiches, the sunlight on the cobbles, the aimless walks in shadowed lanes, the sudden, always amazing fact of sex—a whole world of privilege and assurance, all going on, while elsewhere millions were preparing to die. How could we have borne the thought of all that and not—

But no. It will not do. These fine sentiments will not do. I have told myself already, I must not attempt to impose retrospective significance on what we were and did. Is it that I believed in something then and now believe in nothing? Or that even then I only believed in the belief, out of longing, out of necessity? The latter, surely. The wave of history rolled over us, as it rolled over so many others of our kind, leaving us quite dry.

'Oh, Uncle Joe is sound,' Boy was saying. 'Quite sound.'

They are all dead: Boy the outrageous, Leo and his millions, Wilkins the sceptic, burnt to a cinder in his sardine tin in the desert. I ask again: Have I lived at all?

I often think how differently things might have gone for me if I had not encountered Felix Hartmann when I did. Naturally, I fell a little in love with him. You will not have heard of this person. He was one of Moscow's most impressive people, both an ideologue and a dedicated activist (dear me, how easily one falls into the jargon of the Sunday papers!). His front was a fur-trading business in the vicinity of Brick Lane, or some such insalubrious place, which gave him frequent opportunities for travel, both within the country and abroad. He was a Hungarian national of German and Slav extraction: father a soldier, mother a Serb, or a Slovenian, something like that. It was said, though I do not know where the story originated (it may even be true), that he had been ordained a Catholic priest and had served in the Great War as a chaplain in the Austro-Hungarian army; when I asked him once about this period of his life he would say nothing and only gave me one of his studiedly enigmatic smiles. He had suffered a shrapnel wound—'in a skirmish in the Carpathians'—which had left him with an attractive Byronic limp. He was tall, straight-backed, with glossy blue-black hair, soft eyes, an engaging, if somewhat laboured, ironical smile. He could have been one of those Prussian princes out of the last century, all gold braid and duelling scars, so beloved of operetta composers. He claimed he had been captured in battle by the Russian army, and when the Revolution came had joined the Reds and fought in the civil war. All this gave him the faintly preposterous air of fortitude and self-importance of the Man Who Has Seen Action. In his own eyes, I suspect, he was not the Student Prince, but one of those tormented warrior priests of the Counter-Reformation, trailing his bloodied sword through the smoking ruins of sacked towns.

It was Alastair Sykes who introduced me to him. Summer of 1936. I had travelled up to Cambridge in the middle of August—I still had rooms at Trinity—to finish work on a long essay on the drawings of Poussin. The weather was hot, and London impossible, and I had a deadline from my publisher. War had broken out in Spain, and people were excitedly preparing to go off and fight. I must say it never occurred to me to join them. Not that I was afraid—as I was later to discover, I was physically not uncourageous—or that I did not appreciate the significance of what was happening in Spain. It is just that I have never been one for the grand gesture. The John Cornford type of manufactured hero struck me as self-regarding and, if I may be allowed the oxymoron, profoundly frivolous. For an Englishman to rush out and get his head shot off in some *arroyo* in Seville or wherever seemed to me merely an extreme form of rhetoric, excessive, wasteful, futile. The man of action would despise me for such sentiments—I would not have dreamed of expressing them to Felix Hartmann, for example—but I have a different definition of what constitutes effective action. The worm in the bud is more thorough than the wind that shakes the bough. This is what the spy knows. It is what I know.

Alastair, of course, was in a high state of excitement over the events in Spain. The remarkable thing about the Spanish war—

about all ideological wars, I suppose—was the fiery single-mindedness, not to say simple-mindedness, that it produced in otherwise quite sophisticated people. All doubts were banished, all questions answered, all quibbling done with. Franco was Moloch, and the Popular Front were the children in white whom the West was offering to the fiend in heartless and craven sacrifice. The fact that Stalin, while flying to the aid of the Spanish Loyalists, was at the same time systematically exterminating all opposition to his rule at home, was conveniently ignored. I was a Marxist, yes, but I never had anything other than contempt for the Iron Man; such an unappetizing person.

'Come on, Victor!' Alastair said, wrenching the stem of his pipe from its socket and shaking dribbles of black goo out of it. 'These are dangerous times. The Revolution has to be protected.'

I sighed and smiled.

'The city must be destroyed in order to save it, is that what you mean?'

We were sitting in deckchairs in the sun in the little back garden below the windows of his rooms in Trinity. Alastair tended the garden himself and was touchingly proud of it. There were roses and snapdragons, and the lawn was as smooth as a billiard table. He poured out tea from a blue pot, daintily holding the lid in place with a fingertip, and slowly, gloomily, shook his head.

'Sometimes I wonder about your commitment to the cause, Victor.'

'Yes,' I said, 'and if we were in Moscow you could denounce me to the secret police.' He gave me a wounded look. 'Oh, Alastair,' I said wearily, 'for goodness' sake, you know as well as I what's going on over there. We're not blind, we're not fools.'

He poured tea into his saucer and slurped it up through exaggeratedly pouted lips; it was one of his ways of demonstrating class solidarity; it struck me as ostentatious and, I'm afraid, slightly repulsive.

'Yes, but what we are is believers,' he said, and smacked his lips and smiled, and leaned back on the faded striped canvas of the deckchair, balancing the cup and saucer on the shelf of his little pot belly. He looked so smug, in his sleeveless Fair Isle pullover and brown boots, that I wanted to hit him.

31

'You sound like a priest,' I said.

He grinned at me, showing the gap between his rabbity front teeth. 'Funny you should say that,' he said. 'There's a chap coming round shortly who used to be a priest. You'll like him.'

'You forget,' I said sourly, 'I come from a family of clergymen.'

'Well, you'll have a lot to talk about then, won't you.'

Presently Alastair's gyp appeared, a cringing, forelock-pulling semi-dwarf—God, how I despised those people!—to announce that there was a visitor. Felix Hartmann wore black: black suit, black shirt, and, remarkably in the surroundings, a pair of narrow, patent-leather black shoes as delicate as dancing pumps. As he crossed the lawn to meet us I noticed how he tried to hide his limp. Alastair introduced us, and we shook hands. I should like to be able to say that a spark of excited recognition of each other's potential passed between us, but I suspect that significant first encounters only take on their aura of significance in retrospect. His handshake, a brief pressure quickly released, communicated nothing other than a mild and not wholly impolite indifference. (Yet what a strange ceremony it is, shaking hands; I always see it in heraldic terms: solemn, antiquated, a little ridiculous, slightly indecent, and yet, for all that, peculiarly affecting.) Felix's soft, Slavic eyes, the colour of toffee, rested on my face a moment, and then he turned them vaguely aside. It was one of his tactics to seem always just a bit distracted; he would pause for a second in the middle of a sentence and frown, then give himself a sort of infinitesimal shake, and go on again. He had a habit also, when being spoken to, no matter how earnestly, of turning very slowly on his heel and limping a little way away, head bowed, and then stopping to stand with his back turned and hands clasped behind him, so that one could never be sure that he was still listening to what one was saying, or had sunk into altogether more profound communings with himself. I could never finally decide whether these mannerisms were genuine, or if he was merely trying things out, rehearsing in mid-play, as it were, like an actor walking into the wings to have a quick practice of a particularly tricky passage while the rest of the cast went on with the drama. 'Felix is in furs,' Alastair said, and giggled. Hartmann smiled wanly. 'You are such a wit, Alastair,' he said. We stood about awkwardly on the grass, the three of us, there being only two deckchairs, and Felix Hartmann studied the glossy toes of his shoes. Alastair, squinting in the sunlight, was still holding his cup and saucer at chest level. I seemed to have heard Hartmann's name before. I thought perhaps Boy had mentioned him, and assumed he must be one of his doubtful friends—but if so, what was he doing in Alastair's garden on a summer Sunday morning, for Boy and Psyche moved in very different social worlds? Now Alastair put down his cup and muttered something about fetching another chair, and scuttled off. Hartmann shifted his gaze to the roses and sighed. We listened to the buzz of summer about us. 'You are the art critic?' he said.

'More an historian.'

'But of art?'

'Yes.'

He nodded, looking now in the vicinity of my knees. 'I know something of art,' he said.

'Oh, yes?' I waited, but he offered nothing more. 'I have a great fondness for the German baroque,' I said, speaking over-loudly. 'Do you know that style at all?'

He shook his head.

'I am not German,' he said, with a lugubrious intonation, frowning to one side.

And we were silent again. I wondered if I had offended him somehow, or if I were being a bore, and I felt faintly annoyed; we cannot all be winged in skirmishes in the Carpathians. Alastair came back with a third deckchair and set it up with much struggling and cursing, pinching his thumb badly in the process. He offered to make a fresh pot of tea, but Hartmann silently declined, with a throwaway motion of his left hand. We sat down. Alastair heaved a happy sigh; gardeners have a particularly irritating way of sighing when they contemplate their handiwork.

'Hard to think of Spain and a war starting,' he said, 'while we sit here in the sun.' He touched the sleeve of Felix's black suit. 'Aren't you hot, old chap?'

'Yes,' Hartmann said, nodding again with that peculiar mixture of indifference and frowning solemnity.

33

Pause. The bells of King's began to chime, the bronzen strokes beating thickly high up through the dense blue air.

'Alastair thinks we should all go to Spain and fight Franco,' I said lightly, and was startled and even a little unnerved when Hartmann lifted his gaze and fixed it on me briefly, with a positively theatrical intensity.

'And perhaps he is right?' he said.

If not a Hun, I thought, then Austrian, surely—somewhere German-speaking, at any rate; all that gloom and soulfulness could only be the result of an upbringing among compound words.

Alastair sat forward earnestly and clasped his hands between his knees, putting on that look, like that of a constipated bulldog, that always heralded an attack of polemics. Before he could get started, however, Hartmann said: 'Your theory of art: what is it?'

Strange now to think how natural a question like that seemed then. In those days we were constantly asking each other such things, demanding explanations, justifications; challenging; defending; attacking. Everything was gloriously open to question. Even the most dogmatic Marxists among us knew the giddy and intoxicating excitement of exposing to doubt all that we were supposed to believe in, of taking our essential faith, like some delicate and fantastically intricate piece of spun glass, and letting it drop into the slippery and possibly malevolent hands of a fellow ideologue. It fed the illusion that words are actions. We were young.

'Oh, don't get him started,' said Alastair. 'We'll have significant form and the autonomy of the object until the cows come home. His only belief is in the uselessness of art.'

'I prefer the word inutility,' I said. 'And anyway, my position has shifted on that, as on much else.'

There was a beat of silence and the atmosphere thickened briefly. I glanced from one of them to the other, seeming to detect an invisible something passing between them, not so much a signal as a sort of silent token, like one of those almost impalpable acknowledgements that adulterers exchange when they are in company. The phenomenon was strange to me still but would become increasingly familiar the deeper I penetrated into the secret world. It marks that moment when a group of initiates, in the midst of the usual prattle, begin to go to work on a potential recruit. It was always the same: the pause, the brief tumescence in the air, then the smooth resumption of whatever the subject was, though all, even the target, were aware that in fact the subject had been irretrievably changed. Later, when I was an initiate myself, this little secret flurry of speculative activity always stirred me deeply. Nothing so tentative, nothing so thrilling, excepting, of course, certain manoeuvres in the sexual chase.

I knew what was going on; I knew I was being recruited. It was exciting and alarming and slightly ludicrous, like being summoned from the sideline to play in the senior-school game. It was *amusing*. This word no longer carries the weight that it did for us. Amusement was not amusement, but a test of the authenticity of a thing, a verification of its worth. The most serious matters amused us. This was something the Felix Hartmanns never understood.

'Yes,' I said, 'it is the case that I did once argue for the primacy of pure form. So much in art is merely anecdotal, which is what attracts the bourgeois sentimentalist. I wanted something harsh and studied, the truly lifelike: Poussin, Cézanne, Picasso. But these new movements—this surrealism, these arid abstractions— what do they have to do with the actual world, in which men live and work and die?'

Alastair did a soundless slow handclap. Hartmann, frowning thoughtfully at my ankle, ignored him.

'Bonnard?' he said. Bonnard was all the rage just then.

'Domestic bliss. Saturday-night sex.'

'Matisse?'

'Hand-tinted postcards.'

'Diego Rivera?'

'A true painter of the people, of course. A great painter.'

He ignored the lip-biting little smile I could not suppress.

'As great as . . . Poussin?' he said.

I shrugged. So he knew my interests. Someone had been talking to him. I looked at Alastair, but he was engrossed in examining his sore thumb.

'The question does not arise,' I said. 'Comparative criticism is essentially Fascist. Our task'—how gently I applied the pressure on that *our*—'is to emphasize the progressive elements in art. In times such as this, surely that is the critic's first and most important duty.'

There followed another significant silence, while Alastair sucked his thumb, and Hartmann sat and nodded to himself, and I gazed off, showing him my profile, all proletarian modesty and firmness of resolve, looking, I felt sure, like one of those figures in fanned-out relief on the pedestal of a socialist-realist monument. It is odd how the small dishonesties are the ones that snag in the silk of the mind. Diego Rivera—God! Alastair was watching me now with a sly grin.

'More to the point,' he said to Hartmann, 'Victor's looking forward to being made Minister of Culture when the Revolution comes, so he can ransack the stately homes of England.'

'Indeed,' I said, prim as a postmistress, 'I see no reason why masterpieces pillaged by our hunting fathers in successive European wars should not be taken back for the people and housed in a central gallery.'

Alastair heaved himself forward again, his deckchair groaning, and tapped Hartmann on the knee. 'You see?' he said happily. It was obvious he was referring to something more than my curatorial ambitions; Alastair prided himself on his talent-spotting abilities. Hartmann frowned, a pained little frown like that of a great singer when his accompanist hits a wrong note, and this time made a point of paying him no heed.

'So, then,' he said to me slowly, with a judicious tilt of the head, 'you are opposed to the bourgeois interpretation of art as luxury—'

'Bitterly opposed.'

'—and consider the artist to have a clear political duty.'

'Like the rest of us,' I said, 'the artist must contribute to the great forward movement of history.'

Oh, I was shameless; like a hoyden set on losing her virginity.

'Or . . . ?' he said.

'Or he becomes redundant, and his art descends to the level of mere decoration and self-indulgent reverie . . .'

Everything went still then, subsided softly to a stop, and I was left hanging in vague consternation; I had thought we were in the middle and not at the end of this interesting discussion. Hartmann was looking at me directly for what seemed the first time, and I realized two things: first, that he had not for a moment been taken in by my stout declarations of political rectitude, and, second, that instead of being disappointed or offended, he was on the contrary gratified that I had lied to him, or at least that I had offered a carefully tinted version of what might be the truth. Now, this is difficult; this is the nub of the matter, in a way. It is hard for anyone who has not given himself wholeheartedly to a belief to appreciate how the believer's conscious mind can separate itself into many compartments containing many, conflicting, dogmas. These are not sealed compartments; they are like the cells of a battery (I think this is how a battery works), over which the electrical charge plays, leaping from one cell to another, gathering force and direction as it goes. You put in the acid of world-historical necessity and the distilled water of pure theory and connect up your points and with a flash and a shudder the patched-together monster of commitment, sutures straining and ape brow clenched, rises in jerky slow motion from Dr Diabolo's operating table. That is how it is, for the likes of us—I mean the likes of Felix Hartmann and me, though not, perhaps, Alastair, who was essentially an innocent, with an innocent's faith in the justice and inevitability of the cause. So when Hartmann looked at me that day, in the lemon-and-blue light of Psyche's sun-dazzled garden in Cambridge, as the Falangist guns were firing five hundred miles to the south of us, he saw that I was exactly what was required: harder than Alastair, more biddable than Boy, a casuist who would split an ideological hair to an infinitesimal extreme of thinness—in other words, a man in need of a faith (*No one more devout than a sceptic on his knees*—Querell *dixit*), and so there was nothing left to say. Hartmann distrusted words, and made it a point of pride never to use more of them than the occasion required.

Alastair suddenly stood up and began fussily gathering the teacups, making a great show of not treading on our toes, and walked off, muttering, with a sort of resentful flounce, bearing the tea tray aloft before him like a grievance: I suppose he too was a little in love with Felix—more than a little, probably—and was jealous, now that his matchmaking exercise had proved so successful so quickly. Hartmann, however, seemed hardly to notice his going. He was leaning forward intently, head bowed, with his elbows on his knees and his hands clasped (it must be a mark of true grace to be able to sit in a deckchair without looking like a discommoded frog). After a moment he glanced up at me sideways with a crooked, oddly feral smile.

'You know Boy Bannister, of course,' he said.

'Of course; everyone knows Boy.'

He nodded, still with that fierce leer, an eye-tooth glinting.

'He is going to make a journey to Russia,' he said. 'It's time for him to become disenchanted with the Soviet system.' By now his look was positively wolfish. 'Perhaps you would care to accompany him? I could arrange it. We—they—have many art treasures. In public galleries, of course.'

We both laughed at once, which left me feeling uneasy. It will sound strange, coming from me, but the complicity suggested by that kind of thing—the soft laugh exchanged, the quick pressure of the hand, the covert wink—always strikes me as faintly improper, and shaming, a small conspiracy got up against a world altogether more open and decent than I or my accomplice in intimacy could ever hope to be.

I smiled back into Felix Hartmann's face and with an insouciance I did not fully feel said that yes, a couple of weeks in the arms of great Mother Rus might be just the thing to harden up my ideological position and strengthen my ties of solidarity with the proletariat. At this his look turned wary—the comrades never were very strong in the irony department—and he frowned again at his shiny toecaps and began to speak earnestly of his experiences in the war against the Whites: the burnt villages, the raped children, the old man he had come upon one rainy evening somewhere in the Crimea, crucified on his own barn door, and still alive.

'I shot him through the heart,' he said, making a pistol of finger and thumb and silently firing it. 'There was nothing else to do for him. I see his eyes still in my dreams.'

I nodded and I too looked grimly at my shoes, to show how thoroughly ashamed I was of that facetious reference to Holy Mother Russia; but just below the lid of my sobriety there was squeezed a cackle of disgraceful laughter, as if there were an evil, merry little elf curled up inside me, hand clapped to mouth and cheeks bulging and weasel eyes malignantly aglitter. It was not that I thought the horrors of war were funny, or Hartmann completely ridiculous; that was not the sort of laughter that was threatening to break out. Perhaps laughter is the wrong word. What I felt at moments such as this—and there would be many such: solemn, silent, fraught with portent—was a kind of hysteria, made up of equal parts of disgust and shame and appalling mirth. I cannot explain it—or could, perhaps, but do not want to. (One can know too much about oneself, that is a thing I have learned.) Someone has written somewhere, I wish I could remember who, of the sensation of gleeful anticipatory horror he experiences in the concert hall when in the middle of a movement the orchestra grinds to a halt and the virtuoso draws back his arm preparatory to plunging his bow into the quivering heart of the cadenza. Although the writer is a cynic, and as a Marxist (am I a Marxist, still?) I should disapprove of him, I know exactly what he means and secretly applaud his baleful honesty. Belief is hard, and the abyss is always there, under one's feet.

Alastair came back. Seeing Hartmann and me sunk in what must have looked like silent communion, and perhaps was, he grew more cross than ever.

'Well,' he said, 'have you decided the future of art?'

When neither of us responded—Hartmann looked up at him with a vacant frown as if trying to remember who he was—he threw himself down on the deckchair, which gave a loud, pained grunt of protest, and clamped his stubby arms across his chest and glared at a bush of shell-pink roses.

'What do you think, Alastair?' I said. 'Mr Hartmann—'

'Felix,' Hartmann said smoothly, 'please.'

'—has offered me a trip to Russia.'

There was something about Alastair—the combination of that not quite convincing bulldog ferocity and an almost girlish tentativeness, not to mention the hobnailed boots and hairy tweeds—that made it impossible to resist being cruel to him.

'Oh?' he said. He would not look at me, but folded his arms more tightly still, while under his glare the roses seemed to blush a deeper shade of pink. 'How interesting for you.'

'Yes,' I said blithely, 'Boy and I are going to go.'

'And one or two others,' Hartmann murmured, looking at his fingernails.

'Boy, eh?' Alastair said, and essayed a nasty little laugh. 'He'll probably get you both arrested on your first night in Moscow.'

'Yes,' I said, faltering a little (others?—what others?), 'I'm sure we'll have some amusing times.'

Hartmann was still examining his nails.

'Of course, we shall arrange guides for you, and so on,' he said.

Yes, Comrade Hartmann, I'm sure you will.

'Your ship will sail in three weeks' time from London port,' he said. 'Amsterdam, Helsinki, Leningrad. She is called the *Liberation*. A good name, don't you think?'

A good name, but a poor thing. The *Liberation* was a blunt-ended, low-slung merchant vessel carrying a cargo of pig-iron destined for the People's smelters. The North Sea was rough, a jostling waste of clay-coloured waves, each one half the size of a house, through which the little ship snuffled and heaved, like an iron pig, indeed, going along with its snout rising and falling in the troughs and tail invisibly twirling behind us. Our captain was a black-bearded Dutchman of vast girth who had spent the early years of his career in the East Indies engaged in activities which from his colourful but deliberately vague descriptions of them sounded to me suspiciously like the slave trade. He spoke of the Soviet Union with jovial detestation. His crew, made up of a medley of races, were a slovenly, furtive, piratical-looking bunch. Boy could hardly believe his luck; he spent most of the voyage below decks, changing bunks and partners with each watch. We would catch the noise of drunken revels rising from the bowels of the ship, with Boy's voice dominant, singing sea shanties and roaring for rum. 'What a filthy gang!' he would croak happily, emerging red-eyed and barefoot on to the passenger deck in search of cigarettes and something to eat. 'Talk about close quarters!' It always baffled me, how Boy could get away with so much. Despite his disgraceful doings on that voyage, he remained a favourite at Captain Kloos's table, and even when a complaint was lodged against him by one of the younger crewmen, a Friesian Islander pining for his girl, the matter was hushed up.

'It's that famous charm of his,' Archie Fletcher said sourly. 'Some day it will let him down, when he's old and fat and clapped-out.'

Fletcher, himself a charmless hetero, was disapproving of our party in general, considering it far too frolicsome for a delegation handpicked by the Comintern to be the spearhead of its English undercover drive. There were also a couple of Cambridge dons—pipes, dandruff, woollen mufflers—whom I knew slightly; Bill Darling, a sociologist from the London School of Economics, who even then I could see was too neurotic and excitable to be a spy; and a rather pompous young aristo named Belvoir, the same Toby Belvoir who in the Sixties would renounce his title to serve in a Labour cabinet, for which piece of Socialist good faith he was rewarded with a junior ministry in charge of sport or some such. So there we were, a boatload of superannuated boys, bucketing through autumn storms along the Skagerrak and down into the Baltic, on our way to encounter the future at first hand. Needless to say, what I see is a *Ship of Fools* by one of the anonymous medieval masters, with curly whitecaps and a stylized porpoise bustling through the waves, and our party, in robes and funny hats, crowded on the poop deck, peering eastwards, an emblem of hope and fortitude and, yes, innocence.

I know that this, my first and last visit to Russia, should have been, and perhaps was, one of the formative experiences of my life, yet my recollections of it are curiously blurred, like the features of a weather-worn statue; the form is still there, the impression of significance and stony weight: only the details are largely gone.

Leningrad was an astonishment, of course. I had the sense, looking down those noble prospects, of a flare of trumpets sounding all around me, announcing the commencement of some grand imperial venture: the declaration of a war, the inauguration of a peace. Years later, when the comrades were urging me to defect, I passed a sleepless night weighing in the scales the losing of the Louvre against the gaining of the Hermitage, and the choice, I can tell you, was not as straightforward as I might have expected.

In Moscow there were few architectural magnificences to distract one's attention from the people passing by in those impossibly wide, sleet-grey streets. The weather was unseasonably cold, with a wind in which one could feel already the glassy edge of winter. We had been warned of shortages, and although the worst of the famines in the countryside were over by then, even the most enthusiastic among our party found it hard, in contemplating those hunched crowds, not to recognize the marks of deprivation and dull fear. Stalin's Russia was a horrible place. But we understood that what was happening here was only a start, you see. The temporal factor is what you must always keep in mind if you wish to understand us and our politics. The present we could forgive for the sake of the future. And then, it was a matter of choosing; as we trooped past the glorious monuments of Peter's northern Venice, or tossed in our lumpy beds in a Moscow hotel, or stared in a bored stupor through the grimy windows of a rattling railway carriage at mile after mile of empty fields on the way south to Kiev, we could hear in our mind's ear, off to the west, faintly but with unignorable distinctness, the stamp and rattle of drilling armies. Hitler or Stalin: could life be simpler?

And there was art. Here, I told myself, here, for the first time since the Italian Renaissance, art had become a public medium, available to all, a lamp to illumine even the humblest of lives. By art, I need not tell you, I meant the art of the past: socialist realism I passed over in tactful silence. (An aphorism: kitsch is to art as physics is to mathematics—its technology.) But can you imagine my excitement at the possibilities that seemed to open before me in Russia? Art liberated for the populace—Poussin for the Proletariat! Here was being built a society which would apply to its own workings the rules of order and harmony by which art operates; a society in which the artist would no longer be dilettante or romantic rebel, pariah or parasite; a society whose art would be more deeply rooted in ordinary life than any since medieval times. What a prospect, for a sensibility as hungry for certainties as mine was!

I recall a discussion on the topic that I had with Boy on the last night before we docked in Leningrad. I say discussion, but really it was one of Boy's lectures, for he was drunk and in hectoring mood as he expounded what he grandly called his Theory of the Decline of Art under Bourgeois Values, which I had heard many times before, and which I think was largely filched anyway from a refugee Czech professor of aesthetics whom he had heard giving a talk on the BBC. It was hardly original, consisting mainly of sweeping generalizations on the glory of the Renaissance and the humanistic self-delusions of the Enlightenment, and all boiled down in the end to the thesis that in our time only the totalitarian state could legitimately assume the role of patron of the arts. I believed it, of course—I still do, surprising as it may seem—but that night, stimulated, I suppose, by Hollands gin and the needle-sharp northern air, I thought it a lot of fatuous twaddle, and said so. Really, I was not prepared to be lectured to by the likes of Boy Bannister, especially on art. He stopped, and glared at me. He had taken on that bulbous, froggy look—thick lips thicker than ever, eyes bulging and slightly crossed—that the combination of drink and polemics always produced in him. He was sitting cross-legged on the end of my bunk in shirtsleeves, his braces loosed and his flies half unbuttoned; his big feet were bare and crusted with dirt.

'Trespassing on your territory, am I?' he said, all scowl and slur. 'Touchy old Vic.'

'You don't know what you're talking about, that's the trouble,' I said.

As so often when he was stood up to, he chose not to fight. The bloodshot scowl slackened and slid.

'America,' he said after a while, nodding ponderously. 'America is the real bloody enemy. Art, culture, all that: nothing. America will sweep it all away, into the trashcan. You'll see.'

We were silent for a time, nursing our tooth-glasses of gin, then Boy, in a tone that was too casual, said: 'Have you a contact in Moscow?'

'No,' I answered, immediately on the alert. 'What do you mean?'

He shrugged again. 'Oh, I just wondered if Hartmann had given you a name, or something. You know: a contact. Nothing like that?'

'No.'

'Hmm.'

He brooded glumly. Boy adored the trappings of the secret

world, the code names and letter-drops and the rest. Brought up on Buchan and Henty, he saw his life in the lurid terms of an old-fashioned thriller and himself dashing through the preposterous plot heedless of all perils. In this fantasy he was always the hero, of course, never the villain in the pay of a foreign power.

He need not have felt cast down. No sooner had we arrived in the capital—tank-grey sky, great sloping spaces spectrally peopled with ugly, disproportionate statuary, and always that constant, icy wind cutting into one's face like a flung handful of ground glass—than he disappeared for an afternoon, and turned up at dinner time looking insufferably pleased with himself. When I asked where he had been, he only grinned and tapped a finger along the side of his nose and peered in happy horror at his plate and said loudly: 'Good Christ, is this to eat, or has it been eaten already?'

My turn came to be singled out. It was on our last night in Moscow. I was walking back to the hotel, having been at the Kremlin for most of the day. As always after a long time spent among pictures (or an hour in bed with a boy), I felt light-headed and tottery, and at first did not register the motor car chugging along beside me at walking speed. (Really, that is the kind of thing they did; I suspect they got it from Hollywood movies, of which they were depressingly fond.) Then, with the car still moving, the door opened, and a tall, thin young man in a tightly belted, ankle-length black leather overcoat stepped nimbly on to the pavement and approached me rapidly at a sort of stiff-armed march, his heels coming down so violently on the pavement it seemed they must strike sparks from the stone. He addressed me in a harsh growl—all Russians sounded like drunks to me—and I began flusteredly to protest that I did not understand the language, but then realized that he was speaking in English, or an approximation of it. Would I please to come with him.

'This is my hotel,' I said in a loud, foolish voice. 'I am staying here.' I pointed to the marble entryway, where the doorman, a blue-chinned heavy in a dirty brown uniform, stood looking on with knowing amusement. I do not know what sort of sanctuary I thought I was claiming. 'My passport is in my room,' I said; it sounded as if I were reading from a phrase book. 'I can fetch it if you wish.'

The man in the leather coat laughed. Now, I must say something about this laugh, which was peculiar to Soviet officialdom, and especially prevalent among the security establishment. There was real, if bleak, amusement in it, almost, one might say, a kind of attenuated delight; here's another one, it seemed to say, another poor dolt who thinks he has some weight in the world. The chief ingredient was a sort of bored weariness. The one who laughed had seen everything, every form of bluster and bombast, every failed attempt at cajoling and ingratiation; had seen it, and then had seen the abasements, the tears, had heard the cries for mercy and the heels clattering backwards over the flagstones and the cell doors banging shut. I exaggerate. I mean, I am exaggerating my perspicacity. It is only with hindsight that I am able to dismantle this laugh into its component parts.

We drew to a lurching stop in a crooked courtyard. I glanced upwards, past the high, dark-windowed walls of the surrounding buildings that seemed to lean inwards at their tops, and saw the sky, delicate, pale and depthless, where a solitary crystalline star, like a star on a Christmas card, like the star of Bethlehem itself, stood with its stiletto point poised on an onion dome, and in that moment I realized with a sharp, precise shock that I was about to step out of one life and into another. Then a richly accented voice said warmly, 'Professor Maskell, please!' and I turned to find a short, dapper, balding man in an ill-fitting, tightly buttoned three-piece suit approaching me from the doorway with both stubby little hands outstretched. He was a dead ringer for the older Martin Heidegger, with a smudge of moustache and a sinisterly avuncular smile and little black eyes shiny as marbles. Never taking those eyes off mine, he fumbled for my hand and pressed it fervently between both of his. 'Welcome, comrade, welcome,' he said breathily, 'welcome to the Kremlin!' And I was ushered inside, and felt a tingling sensation in the middle of my back, as if that star had dropped out of the sky and stabbed me between the shoulder blades.

Mouldy corridors, ill lit, with someone standing in every other doorway—sag-suited officials, clerks in drooping cardigans, secretary-looking middle-aged women—all smiling the same worrying smile as Heidegger, and nodding mute greetings and encouragement, as if I had won a prize and was on my way to be presented with it. He walked at my side, gripping my arm above the elbow and murmuring rapidly in my ear. Although his English was faultless—another mark of the sinister—his accent was so thick I could not properly understand what he was saying, and in my agitation and apprehensiveness was hardly listening anyway. We arrived at another pair of tall double doors—I was, I realized, nervously humming a snatch of Mussorgsky in my head—and Leathercoat, who had been loping nonchalantly behind us with his hat in his hand, stepped forward quickly and, like a harem guard, shoulders and head down and both arms thrust out stiffly, pushed them open on a vast, high-ceilinged, brown-painted room hung with an enormous chandelier that was a kind of monstrous, multiple parody of the star I had seen outside in the square.

I was led off to one side of the room, where a door that I had taken for a part of the panelling opened, and here was another ill-lit corridor, and suddenly my heart was in my mouth as I realized with incontrovertible certainty that it was Him I was about to meet. But I was wrong. At the end of the corridor was an office, or study—big desk with green-shaded lamp, shelves of books no one had ever read, a ticker-tape machine, inactive but tense with potential, on a stand in the corner—the kind of room that in films the important man slips away to, leaving his sleek wife to entertain the guests while he makes a vital telephone call, standing silk-suited, sombre and cigaretted in the light from a half-open doorway (yes, I used to go to the pictures a lot, when they were still in black-and-white). I thought the room was empty until there stepped forward from the shadows another plumpish, balding little man, who might be Heidegger's older brother. He was dressed in one of those square, shiny pinstripe suits that Soviet officials seem to have exclusively made for them, and wore spectacles, which, remembering them, he whipped off quickly and slipped into his jacket pocket, as if they were a shameful sign of weakness and decadence. He must have been a man of some consequence, for I could feel Heidegger trembling faintly beside me in reigned-in excitement, like a steeplechaser waiting for the off. There was no introduction, and Comrade Pinstripe did not offer to shake hands, but smiled the kind of rapidly nodding,

46

excessively enthusiastic smile that told me he did not speak English. Then he delivered himself, in a rolling, rapid voice, of a lengthy and, I guess, elaborately embellished address. I noticed again how Russians, when they spoke, seemed not only drunk but at the same time looked as if they were juggling a hot potato in their mouths. This is true also of working people in the part of Ireland where I was brought up; for a mad moment I wondered if I might mention this—to me, interesting—correspondence, perhaps offering it as evidence of an essential class solidarity stretching from the glens of Antrim to the slopes of the Urals. Ending his peroration with a sort of trilled verbal flourish, Pinstripe made a stiff little bow and stepped one pace backwards, smugly, like a star pupil at a school speech day. There followed an awful silence. My stomach pinged and rumbled; Heidegger's shoes creaked. Pinstripe, with eyebrows lifted, was smiling and nodding again, with some impatience. I realized with a start that he was awaiting a reply.

'Ah,' I said stumblingly, 'yes, well, ah.' Then paused. 'I am—' My voice was too high-pitched; I adjusted it to a rumbling baritone. 'I am extremely proud and honoured to be here, in this historic place, seat of so many of our hopes. Of the hopes of so many of us.' I was doing quite well; I began to relax. 'The Kremlin—'

Here Heidegger silenced me by putting a hand on my arm and giving it a not unfriendly but definitely admonitory squeeze. He said something in Russian, at which Pinstripe looked a little piqued, though he went to the desk and from a drawer took out a vodka bottle and three tiny glasses, which he lined up on the desktop and with tremulous care filled to the brim. I ventured a cautious sip and winced as the cold, silvery fire slithered down my oesophagus. The two Russians, however, gave a sort of shout and in unison knocked back their shots with a quick toss of the head, their neck tendons cracking. On the third round Heidegger turned to me and with a roguish smile cried out, 'King George Six!', and I choked on my drink and had to have my back slapped. Then the audience was at an end. The vodka bottle was put away, along with the glasses, unwashed, and Pinstripe bowed to me once more and retreated backwards out of the lamplight as if on castors.

The return trip was a far jollier affair than the voyage out. It did not start auspiciously: we were flown to Leningrad by military transport, and then went on by train to Helsinki. Finland smelt of fish and fir trees. I felt wretched. We joined an English cruise ship which had been visiting the Baltic ports. There was a jazz band on board. Boy sat in the bar propositioning the waiters and arguing politics with young Lord Belvoir, whose strongest impression of Russia had been a distinct sense of the shadow of the guillotine, with a consequent falling-off in his enthusiasm for the cause. This placed Boy in a quandary; normally he would have countered any sign of apostasy with a storm of argument and exhortation, but since on Felix Hartmann's advice he was himself supposed to be displaying signs of disenchantment with the Soviet system he had to perform an elaborate game of verbal hide-and-seek, and the strain was showing.

'What the hell is Bannister playing at?' Archie Fletcher wanted to know, his little pink face pinched with outrage.

'It's the shock,' I said. 'You know what they say: you should never wake a sleepwalker.'

'What? What the hell is that supposed to mean?' Archie had always disliked me.

'The dream has ended for him. He has seen the future, and it doesn't work. Don't you feel that, too?'

'No, I damn well don't.'

Archie gave me an apoplectic stare and strode off. Boy, sweating in desperation, winked at me miserably over young Belvoir's shoulder.

I never did discover the identity of Heidegger or his big brother. Year after year I scanned the newspaper photographs of Politburo members on their balcony at the May Day parades, but in vain. Certain gaps along the rows of squat heads and daintily waving hands gave me pause: had Pinstripe stood there, before he was airbrushed out? Whenever I thought of that mysterious pair, in the years when I was active as an agent, I experienced a faint tremor of apprehension, like the flat smack caused in the air by an unheard, distant explosion.

I arrived back from Russia into a smoky English autumn and went straight to Cambridge. The weather on the fens was gloomy and wet; fine rain fell over the town like drifts of silver webbing. My white-walled rooms wore a pursed, disapproving aspect, seeming to hunch a cold shoulder against me, as if they knew where I had been and what I had been up to. I had always liked this time of year, with its sense of quickening expectation, so much more manageable than spring's false alarms, but now the prospect of winter was suddenly dispiriting. I had finished my long essay on the Poussin drawings and could not disguise from myself the fact that it was a poor, dry thing. I often ask myself whether my decision to pursue a life of scholarship—if decision is the word—was the result of an essential poverty of the soul, or if the desiccation which I sometimes suspect is the one truly distinguishing mark of my scholarship was an inevitable consequence of that decision. What I mean to say is, did the pursuit of accuracy and what I call the right knowledge of things quench the fires of passion in me? The fires of passion: there sounds the voice of a spoiled romantic.

I suppose that is what I meant when I was first asked why I became a spy and I answered, before I had given myself time to think, that it was essentially a frivolous impulse: a flight from ennui and a search for diversion. The life of action, heedless, mind-numbing action, that is what I had always hankered after. Yet I had not succeeded in defining what, for me, might constitute action, until Felix Hartmann turned up and solved the question for me.

'Think of it,' he said smoothly, 'as another form of academic work. You are trained in research; well, research for us.'

We were in The Fox in Roundleigh. He had motored up from London in the afternoon and picked me up at my rooms. I had not invited him in, from a combination of shyness and distrust—distrust of myself, that is. The little world with which I had surrounded myself—my books, my prints—was a delicate construct, and I feared it might not bear without injury the weight of Felix's scrutiny. His car was an unexpectedly fancy model, low and sleek with spoked wheels and worryingly eager-looking globe headlights, over the chrome cheeks of which, as we approached, our curved reflections slid, rippling amid a speckle of raindrops. The back seat was piled with mink coats, the polished fur agleam and somehow sinister; they looked like a large dead soft brown bloodless beast thrown there. Hartmann saw me looking at them, and sighed sepulchrally and said, 'Business.' The bucket seat clasped me in a muscular embrace. There was a warm, womanly afterbreath of perfume; Hartmann's love life was as covert as his spying. He drove through the rain-smeared streets at a sustained forty—that was terrifically fast in those days—skidding on the cobbles, and almost ran down one of my graduate students who was crossing the road outside Peterhouse. Beyond the town the fields were retreating into a sodden twilight. Suddenly, as I looked out at the rain and the crepuscular bundles of shadow falling away on either side of our steadily strengthening, burrowing headlights, a wave of homesickness rose up and drenched me in an extravagant wash of sorrow.

Hartmann that day was in a strange mood, a sort of slow-burning, troubled euphoria—lately, with so much talk of drugs, I have wondered if he may have been an addict—and was avid for details of my pilgrimage to Russia. I tried to sound enthusiastic, but I could tell I was disappointing him. As I spoke, he grew increasingly restless, fiddling with the gearstick and drumming his fingers on the steering wheel. We came to a crossroads, and he pulled the car to a lurching stop and got out and stamped into the middle of the road and stood looking in all directions, as if in desperate search of an escape route, with his fists in his overcoat pockets and his lips moving, billowed about by dark-silver wraiths of rain. Because of his bad leg he leaned at a slight angle, so that he seemed to be canted sideways against a strong wind. I waited with misgiving, not knowing quite what to do. When he came back he sat for a long moment staring through the windscreen, suddenly haggard and hollow-seeming. A tracery of raindrops fine as lace was delicately draped across the shoulders of his coat. I could smell the wetted wool. He began to speak in a gabbling way about the risks he was taking, the pressures he was under, stopping abruptly every so often and sighing angrily and staring out at the rain. This was not at all like him.

'I can trust no one,' he muttered. 'No one.'

'I don't think you need fear any of us,' I said mildly, 'Boy or
Alastair, Leo or me.'

He went on looking out at the deepening dark as if he had
not heard me, then stirred.

'What? No, no, I don't mean you. I mean'—he gestured—
'over there.' I thought of Leathercoat and of his faceless driver.
Hartmann gave a brief laugh that sounded like a cough. 'Perhaps I
should defect,' he said, 'what do you think?' It did not seem
entirely a joke.

We drove on then to Roundleigh and parked in the village
square. It was fully dark by now, and the lamps under the trees
stood glowing whitely in the fine rain, like big, streaming seed-
heads. The Fox in those days—I wonder if it is still there?—was a
tall, teetering, crooked place, with a public bar and a chophouse,
and rooms upstairs where travelling salesmen and illicit couples
sometimes stayed. The ceilings, stained by centuries of tobacco
smoke, were a wonderfully delicate, honeysuckle shade of yellowy-
brown. There were fish mounted in glass cases on the wall, and a
stuffed fox cub under a bell jar. Hartmann, I could see, found it
all irresistibly charming; he had a weakness for English kitsch—
they all had.

'But tell me what it is I'm expected to do,' I said to Hartmann,
when we had settled ourselves with our halves of bitter on high-
backed benches facing each other on either side of the coke fire.
(Coke: that is something else that has gone; if I try, I can still smell
the fumes and feel their acid prickle at the back of my palate.)

'Do?' he said, putting on an arch, amused expression; his
earlier, violent mood had subsided and he was his smooth self
again. 'You do not do anything, really.' He took a draught of
beer and with relish licked the fringe of foam from his upper lip.
His blue-black oiled hair was combed starkly back from his
forehead, giving him the pert, suave look of a raptor. He had
rubber galoshes on over his dancer's dainty shoes. It was said that
he wore a hairnet in bed. 'Your value for us is that you are at the
heart of the English establishment—'

'I am?'

'—and from the information you and the others supply to us
we shall be able to build a picture of the power bases of this

country.' He loved these expositions, the setting out of aims and objectives, the homilies on strategy; every spy is part priest, part pedant. 'It is like—what is it called . . . ?'

'A jigsaw puzzle?'

'Yes!' He frowned. 'How did you know that was what I meant?'

'Oh, just a guess.'

I sipped my beer; I only ever drank beer when I was with the comrades—class solidarity and all that; I was as bad as Alastair, in my way. A miniature but distinctly detailed horned red devil was glowing and grinning at me from the pulsing heart of the fire.

'So,' I said, 'I am to be a sort of social diarist, am I? The Kremlin's answer to William Hickey.'

At mention of the Kremlin he flinched, and glanced over at the bar, where the landlord was polishing a glass and whistling silently, his puckered big lips swivelled to one side.

'Please,' Hartmann whispered, 'who is William Hickey?'

'A joke,' I said wearily, 'just a joke. I had rather thought I would be required to do more than pass on cocktail-party gossip. Where is my code book, my cyanide pill? Sorry—another joke.'

He frowned and began to say something but thought better of it, and instead smiled his crookedest, most winning smile, and did his exaggerated European shrug.

'Everything,' he said, 'must go so slowly in this strange business of ours. In Vienna once I had the task of watching one man for a year—a whole year! Then it turned out he was the wrong man. So you see.'

I laughed, which I should not have done, and he gave me a reproachful look. Then he began to speak very earnestly of how the English aristocracy was riddled with Fascist sympathizers, and passed me a list of the names of a number of people in whom Moscow was particularly interested. I glanced down the list and stopped myself from laughing again.

'Felix,' I said, 'these people are of no consequence. They're just common-or-garden reactionaries; cranks; dinner-party speech-makers.'

He shrugged and said nothing and looked away. I felt a familiar depression descending upon me. Espionage has something of the quality of a dream. In the spy's world, as in dreams, the terrain is always uncertain. You put your foot on what looks like solid ground, and it gives way under you, and you go into a kind of free fall, turning slowly tail over tip and clutching on to things that are themselves falling. This instability, this myriadness that the world takes on, is both the attraction and the terror of being a spy. Attraction, because in the midst of such uncertainty you are never required to be yourself; whatever you do, there is another, alternative you standing invisibly to one side, observing, evaluating, remembering. This is the secret power of the spy, different from the power that orders armies into battle; it is purely personal; it is the power to be and not be, to detach oneself from oneself, to be oneself and at the same time another. The trouble is, if I were always at least two versions of myself, so all others must be similarly twinned with themselves in this awful, slippery way. And so, laughable as it seemed, it was not impossible that the people on Felix's list might be not only the society hostesses and double-barrelled bores whom I thought I knew, but a ruthless and efficient ring of Fascists poised to wrest power from the elected government and set an abdicated king back on a swastika-draped throne. And there lay the fascination, and the fear—not of plots and pacts and royal shenanigans (I could never take the Duke or that awful Simpson woman seriously), but of the possibility that nothing, absolutely nothing, is as it seems.

'Look here, Felix,' I said, 'are you seriously proposing that I should spend my time attending dinners and going to weekend house parties so that I can report back to you on what I overheard Fruity Metcalfe telling Nancy Astor about the German armaments industry? Do you have any idea what conversations are like on these occasions?'

He considered his beer glass. Light from the fire lay along his jaw like a polished, dark-pink scar. This evening his eyes had a distinctly Slavic cast; did mine look Irish, to him, I wonder?

'No, I do not know what these occasions are like,' he said stiffly. 'A fur trader from the East End of London is not likely to be invited for weekends to Cliveden.'

'It's Clivden,' I said absently. 'It's pronounced Clivden.'

'Thank you.'

We supped the last of our warm beer in silence, me irritated and Hartmann bridling. A few locals had come in and sat about lumpily in the reddish gloom, their ovine, steamy smell insinuating itself amid the coke fumes. The early-evening murmur in English public houses, so wan and weary, so circumspect, always depresses me. Not that I go into public houses very often, nowadays.

'Tell me, Victor,' Hartmann said, and I could tell, by the breathy, consonantal way he uttered my name ('Vikh-torr . . . '), that he was about to shift into the realm of the personal, 'why do you do this?'

I sighed. I had thought he would ask it, sooner or later.

'Oh, the rottenness of the system,' I said gaily. 'Miners' wages, children with rickets—you know. Here, let me buy you a whiskey; this beer is so dreary.'

He held up his glass to the weak light and contemplated it solemnly.

'Yes,' he said, with a mournful catch. 'But it reminds me of home.'

Dear me; I could almost hear the twang of a phantom zither. When I brought back the whiskey he looked at it doubtfully, sipped, and winced; no doubt he would have preferred plum brandy, or whatever it is they drink on rainy autumn nights on the shores of Lake Balaton. He drank again, more deeply this time, and huddled tightly into himself, elbows pressed to his ribs and his legs twined about each other corkscrew fashion with one slender foot tucked behind an ankle like a cocked trigger. They do love a cosy chat, these international spies.

'And you,' I said, 'why do you do it?'

'England is not my country—'

'Nor mine.'

He shrugged grumpily.

'But it is your home,' he said, with a stubborn set of the jaw. 'This is where you live, where your friends are. Cambridge, London . . . ' He made a sweeping gesture with his glass, and the measure of whiskey tilted and in its depths a sulphurous gemlike fire flashed. 'Home.'

Another phantom slither of strings. I sighed.

'Do you get homesick?' I asked.

He shook his head.

'I have no home.'

'No,' I said, 'I suppose you haven't. I should have thought that would make you feel quite . . . free?'

He leaned back on the bench seat, his face sinking into darkness. 'Boy Bannister gives us information that he gets from his father,' he said.

'Boy's father? Boy's father is dead.'

'His stepfather, then.'

'Retired, surely?'

'He still has contacts at the Admiralty.' He paused. 'Would you,' softly, 'would you do that?'

'Betray my father? I doubt if the secrets of the bishopric of Down and Dromore would be of great interest to our masters.'

'But would you?'

The upper part of his torso was swallowed in shadow, so that all I could see were his corkscrewed legs and one hand resting on his thigh with a cigarette clipped between thumb and middle fingers. He took a sip of whiskey, and the rim of the glass clinked tinily against his teeth.

'Of course I would,' I said, 'if it were necessary. Wouldn't you?'

When we left the pub the rain had stopped. The night was blowy and bad-tempered, and the vast, wet darkness felt hollowed out by the wind. Sodden sycamore leaves lolloped about the road like injured toads. Hartmann turned up the collar of his coat and shivered. 'Ach, this weather!' He was on his way back to London, to catch the sleeper to Paris. He liked trains. I imagined him on the Blue Train with a gun in his hand and a girl in his bunk. Our footsteps plashed on the pavement, and as we walked from the light of one lamp to another our shadows stood up hastily to meet us and then collapsed on their backs behind us.

'Felix,' I said. 'I'm not at all adventurous, you know; you mustn't expect heroics.'

We reached the car. An overhanging tree gave itself a doggy shake and a random splatter of raindrops fell on me, rattling on the brim of my hat. I suddenly saw the Back Road in Carrickdrum, and remembered myself walking with my father one

wet November night like this when I was a boy: the steamy light
of the infrequent gas lamps, and the undersides of the dark trees
thrashing in what seemed an anguish of their own, and the
sudden, inexplicable swelling of ardour inside me that made me
want to howl in ecstatic sorrow, yearning for something nameless,
which must have been the future, I suppose.

Anyway. Thus began my career as a working spy. I recalled
Felix Hartmann's hope that we scions of the loftier classes
would provide Moscow with a completed jigsaw-puzzle picture of
the English establishment. Diligently I began to accept the dinner
invitations that previously I would have declined with a shudder,
and found myself discussing watercolours and the price of poultry
with the moustached, slightly mad-eyed wife of a Cabinet minister,
or listening, befuddled with brandy and cigar smoke, while a peer
of the realm with brick-red jowls and a monocle, gesturing
expansively, expounded to the table on the devilishly clever
methods the Jews and Freemasons had employed to infiltrate
every level of government, to the point where they were now ready
to seize power and murder the King. I wrote up exhaustive
accounts of these occasions—discovering, by the way, an
unexpected flair for narrative; some of these early reports were
positively racy, if somewhat over-coloured—and passed them on.
What Moscow considered to be my greatest early triumph was the
long and, to me, extremely tedious conversation I had at a Trinity
Feast with a Private Secretary at the War Office, a portly, sleek-
headed man with a small moustache, who as he prattled on
reminded me of those blithe gaffe-makers in the Bateman
cartoons; as the night ground along he became increasingly,
solemnly, comically drunk—his dicky kept flying up, as in a
music-hall farce—and told me, in indiscreet detail, how
unprepared for war our armed forces were, that the armaments
industry was a joke and that the government had not the will or
the means to do anything to rectify the situation. I could see that
Hartmann, sitting at a low table in a corner of the Hare and
Hounds in Highbury, crouched intently over my report, could not
decide whether he should be appalled or jubilant at the
implications for Europe in general, and Russia in particular, of

what he was reading. What he seemed unaware of was that every newsboy in the country already knew how scandalously ill-equipped we were for war, and how spineless the government was.

This naivety on the part of Moscow and its emissaries was a cause of deep misgiving to all of us on our side; much of what passed with them for intelligence was freely available to the public. Didn't they ever, I asked Felix Hartmann in exasperation, read the papers or listen to the ten o'clock news on the wireless? 'What do your people do at the embassy all day, apart from issuing laughable communiqués about Russia's industrial output and refusing entry visas to defence correspondents of the *Daily Express*?' He smiled, and shrugged, and looked at the sky and began to whistle through his teeth. We were walking by the frozen Serpentine. It was January, the air was dense with mauve-white frost-smoke, and the ducks were waddling unsteadily about on the ice, baffled and disgruntled by this inexplicable solidification of their liquid world.

'Life at the embassy is somewhat . . . subdued, just now,' Hartmann said. He stopped and looked across the iron-coloured ice, rocking back and forth on his heels, his hands thrust deep in the pockets of his long overcoat.

'Moscow has gone silent,' he said. 'I send my messages along the usual channels, but nothing comes back. I am like a person who has survived an accident. Or like a person waiting for an accident to happen. It is a very strange sensation.'

On the bank near us a small boy attended by a black-stockinged nurse was throwing crusts of bread to the ducks; the child laughed throatily in delight to see the birds ignominiously slipping and slithering, their wings thrashing, as they chased the wildly skidding morsels. We turned and walked on. At the other side of the lake, on Rotten Row, a group of riders was jostling along untidily amid white bursts of horse breath. In silence we reached the bridge, and there we stopped. Distant behind the tops of the black trees around us the blue-grey, shrouded forms of London loomed. Hartmann, dreamily smiling, stood with his head tilted to one side, as if listening for some small, expected sound.

'I am going back,' he said. 'They have told me I must come back.'

High up in the frozen mist, above the spires and the chimney pots, I seemed to see something hover for a second, a giant figure, all silver and gold and dully ashine. I heard myself swallow.

'I say, old man,' I said, 'is that wise, do you think? They tell me the climate over there is not at all congenial, these days. Quite the coldest it's been for a long time.'

He turned away from me and glanced skyward, as if he too had sensed some hovering portent.

'Oh, it will be all right,' he said absently. 'They say they want me to make a personal report, that's all.'

I nodded. Strange, how like incipient laughter dismay can feel. We set off across the bridge.

'You could always stay here,' I said. 'I mean, they can't make you go, can they?'

He laughed, and linked his arm through mine.

'This is what I like about you,' he said, 'all of you. Matters are so simple.' Our footsteps rang on the bridge like axe-blows. He pressed my arm against his ribs. 'I must go,' he said. 'Otherwise there is . . . nothing. Do you see?'

We left the bridge still arm in arm and stood on the brow of the park's gentle rise and surveyed the city crouched before us motionless in the mist.

'I shall miss London,' Hartmann said. 'Kensington Gore, the Brompton Road, Tooting Bec—is there really a place called Tooting Bec? And Beauchamp Place, which only yesterday I at last learned how to pronounce in the correct way. Such a waste, all this valuable knowledge.'

He squeezed my arm again and glanced quickly at me sidewise, and I felt something in him falter, as if a part of an inner mechanism had suddenly, finally run down.

'Listen,' I said, 'the thing is, you mustn't go; we won't let you, you know.'

He only smiled, and turned and limped away, back in the direction we had come, over the bridge, under the massy black mist-draped trees, and I never saw him again.  □

GRANTA

# FINTAN O'TOOLE
## IMAGINING SCOTLAND

*Mel Gibson as William Wallace*

TWENTIETH CENTURY FOX

On 25 August 1996 a team of archaeologists digging in the grounds of Melrose Abbey in Scotland's border country found a lead cylinder measuring seven inches in diameter and twelve inches long. A few days later, newspaper and radio journalists and television crews were invited by Scottish Heritage, the public body entrusted with marketing Scotland's past, to attend an event in a laboratory in Edinburgh. There they found a man and a woman dressed in face masks, rubber gloves and white coats standing behind a white table on which were placed an assortment of tools—tiny electric drills, screwdrivers, hacksaws, a fibre-optic cable with a miniature camera at its head—and the cylinder. As the couple in the white coats began to drill into the cylinder, the television lights made the sweat trickle round the edge of their masks. This had been confected as a powerful, national moment; it would be on that night's news broadcasts and appear on the front pages of the next day's newspapers as a moment of discovery—not a re-enactment but the real thing, before your very eyes! Scotland had found the heart of Robert the Bruce.

The timing of the find seemed auspicious and, to a few sceptics, suspicious. Robert the Bruce was the Scottish king who defeated the English at the Battle of Bannockburn in 1314 and secured Scottish independence for the next four centuries. Recently, along with his contemporary and sometime ally William Wallace, he had been given new and vivid life in the Hollywood film *Braveheart*, directed by Mel Gibson, who also played Wallace. In Scotland, the film was an astonishing success. Bruce and Wallace have always been legendary heroes, but now, with a kilted Gibson on horseback and waving his sword at the English, they had been taken from dim history and stamped with the seal of international (or at least American) approval.

Nobody knows, or will ever know, where the remnants of Wallace are buried. He was disembowelled and beheaded in London by the English enemy, who then displayed his head on London Bridge and distributed his limbs among four towns in the kingdom to advertise the penalty for what the English deemed sedition. Bruce, on the other hand, died of leprosy. His body is thought to be buried in the abbey of Dunfermline, once one of the seats of the Scottish monarchy. According to legend, however, his heart was extracted as a kind of talisman and (in one version) eventually buried in Melrose.

In the Edinburgh laboratory, holes were bored and the fibrescope inserted, and another, even more exciting, possibility seemed to offer itself. Through the lens of the tiny camera could be seen a piece of folded parchment. Might the cylinder contain not just the heart of mythic Scotland but a message from the past, some words to posterity, some exhortation that might point the way out of present confusions towards a new horizon of nationhood? They cut through the cylinder, unfolded the parchment and found a small copper plaque. Engraved on it in a bold hand were the words: 'The enclosed leaden casket, containing a heart, was found beneath Chapter House, March 1921, and reburied by His Majesty's Office of Works.'

The cylinder had lain under the soil, not for six centuries, but a mere seventy-five years. True, the casket inside it looked much older, but it seemed that its discovery in 1921 was so unremarkable that hardly anyone had remembered it. The inscription from His Britannic Majesty's Office of Works did not mention Bruce, and the evidence that the heart in the casket ever beat in the Bruce's chest is at best circumstantial. The archaeologists decided to leave this inner casket unbroken and unbored; it was, they said, too fragile to be explored. It would be reburied inside a new container in an unmarked spot at Melrose Abbey.

Nonetheless the news went out: Bruce's heart found! It was not scrupulous reporting, it was not rigorous history (when has nationalism, any nationalism, gone in for that approach?), but it did mark a significant shift in Scotland's sense of itself. In 1921 the same event was barely noticed. Scotland was then still a senior partner in the British Empire. Though its industrial might had passed its peak, it was still a place of coal and steel, of textile factories and engineering works, still recognizably the country that had, during some good years in the nineteenth century, built eighty per cent of the world's ships. Scottish nationalism barely existed as a political force, and all the indications were that Scotland would become more and more integrated with England. The discovery of what might be the Bruce's heart would have been a politically meaningless act.

In 1996, when the heart was found again, it had acquired a meaning. The old Empire and the old industries have gone, and with them much of what has tied Scotland to Great Britain since 1707, when the Scottish parliament voted to dissolve itself and unite the country with England and Wales. In the general election of 1992 three out of every four voters in Scotland supported parties which were campaigning either for complete independence (the Scottish National Party) or for a Scottish parliament with substantial powers devolved from London (Labour and the Liberal Democrats). More recent tests of opinion show that about a quarter of the population want independence, and that a further third want more autonomy within the United Kingdom in the shape of a powerful Scottish parliament. Bruce embodies the dream of an independent Scotland that has found in recent years an ever-larger place in Scottish minds. His unearthed heart would be, literally and metaphorically, the heart of the nation.

I was in Glasgow when news of Bruce's heart appeared on the newspaper placards. I'd recently arrived in Scotland from Dublin, my home, and at first I thought that the Bruce business was a piece of light comedy, something to fill media time and space in the summer season. Growing up in Ireland in the 1960s and 1970s had taught me to be wary of the myths of nationalism; the consequences of their bloody competition across the border in Northern Ireland, where Irish Republicanism clashed with British Unionism, were all too plain. At that time I saw Scotland as a country that confirmed the uselessness of romantic nationalism. Going there in the 1970s, I found a place where the apparent similarities to Ireland served only to underline the extraordinary differences. Scotland, like Ireland, had a sectarian divide, and people in Glasgow would ask, 'Are you a Protestant or a Catholic?' with a directness that was unthinkable even in Belfast. Like Ireland, it was a small nation (five million people compared with the Republic of Ireland's three and a half million) whose history had been shaped by a fraught relationship with a big, expansionist neighbour—England. Scots, like Irish people, liked to affect a mixture of pity and scorn when they talked about the English. And Scottish culture was just as distinctive as Ireland's. Its manners, accents, music, literature, football, all described its unEnglishness.

The difference between Scotland and Ireland lay in the way people described their political future and their political past. Martyrs in Scotland were difficult to come by; it was hard to imagine Scots singing sentimental songs about pure young Scottish heroes gunned down by their English oppressors. When people in Scotland talked about politics, the arguments were about jobs and houses, poverty and wealth. Even when the discussion was about the proposals for a Scottish assembly with powers devolved from London—the devolution debate—they were framed in these mundane terms. Would the place be better managed? Would people be better off? Could Scots get their hands on the vast reserves of oil and gas off the Scottish coast? I come from a country where the dominance of nationalism allowed its rulers to talk in mystical abstractions. I envied the Scots this ability to believe that politics was about the ordinary realities of the here and now.

But that was then. Now, I noticed, the oil under the North Sea was hardly mentioned—Scotland's view of itself as a cold Saudi Arabia had declined after the frantic extraction rates of the 1980s and the shrinking figures for the exploitable oil that remains. Now, I also noticed, the arguments had a more pronounced anti-English strain. It wasn't hard to see why. Since my visits in the 1970s, Scotland had been governed for seventeen years by a succession of Conservative governments in London. In 1979, when Mrs Thatcher became the prime minister, her party won less than a third of the Scottish vote. Three general elections later, it holds only fifteen per cent of Scottish seats in Parliament. Quite simply, people in Scotland have been governed for nearly two decades by a party that most of them dislike and few support. Still, the new popularity of Scottish nationalism cannot purely be explained as an inverse reaction to an unpopular London government, even though Mrs Thatcher would appear in Glasgow pantomimes as the Wicked Witch of the South. An old idea of Britain is being questioned, with results that have been quantified in polls and surveys to show a sharp decline in an inclusive British identity. The most recent reports that thirty-seven per cent of people in Scotland say they are 'Scottish not British'; twenty-seven per cent that they are 'more Scottish than British'; twenty-five per cent 'equally Scottish and British'. Only ten per cent define themselves as either 'more British than Scottish' or 'British not Scottish'. Even among those who voted for the Conservative Party, the one political party committed to resisting any form of Scottish autonomy, only fifteen per cent regard themselves as more British than Scottish.

In Edinburgh, I went to see George Rosie, a journalist and playwright who has watched the growth of Scottish nationalist sentiment over three generations. He remembered his time at school in Edinburgh in the 1950s. 'There was one guy who would take a nationalist line in arguments. It was a really eccentric position, and he used to get beaten up regularly for it. The older folk, my father's generation, who fought in the Second World War, who sat in convoy ships and Lancaster bombers with Welsh guys from Cardiff and English guys from Peckham and Somerset, that generation feels very British. But my daughter's generation don't feel British at all.' His own emotions are typical of an earlier generation's confusion: 'I guess I feel more Scottish than British, but if the day ever comes when they lower the Union flag from Edinburgh Castle, I guess I'll have a tear in my eye.'

How could such mixed feelings ever be embodied in the static, unequivocal symbols of nationhood?

# For want of an Easter Rising

I first realized how difficult it is for Scots to answer such a question in 1991, during the seventy-fifth anniversary of the Easter Rising in Dublin. At the time I was working at the Abbey Theatre. My colleagues and I thought the Abbey, as Ireland's national theatre, ought to mark the event in some way. The Rising had given birth to the independent Irish state. It had been, in my view, a violent and doomed expression of romantic nationalism, but for most people in the Irish Republic it also evoked an odd mixture of boredom and fear. When I was growing up in the 1960s, the Rising had been so thoroughly mythologized, so tightly wrapped in the pieties of official commemorations, that the only thing to do was to make jokes about it. And yet, because it seemed to sanction violence for the cause of Irish independence, it was, for an Irish state now trying to suppress a violent nationalist movement, both dangerous and embarrassing.

We decided to put on a play by Tom Murphy called *The Patriot Game* which replayed the events and rhetoric of 1916 through the eyes of a group of modern teenagers. It was a lively and thoughtful piece, powerfully acted, but it played to very small audiences. Hardly anyone in the capital city of the first country to break free of the British Empire wanted to know. If people felt anything at all about the leaders of the Rising, it was either gratitude that they had brought the whole messy business of nationalism to a head long before our time, or a rueful realization that after you dream a nation into being, you then wake up in a land of mundane disappointments. Watching an especially nasty ethnic and national conflict grind on across the border in Northern Ireland, we were glad to live in a place where, because a previous generation had devoted their lives to the idea of the nation, we didn't have to waste our time on nationalism.

The play, to the great indifference of the Dublin public, reached the end of its run. But we knew that this failure was to have a dreadful sequel. We had agreed, months before, to send it to Scotland, where it would play at the Tramway theatre, a huge auditorium in a converted Glasgow tram shed. On the opening night, my shame at having been partly responsible for sending a group of young actors to a big space in a foreign city with a play that had not worked in its own country was made more acute by the sight of a large and eager audience. And yet, almost from the moment it began, the play was transformed. The revolutionaries' rhetoric of nation and freedom, of defiance and resurrection, seemed to be lifted up by the intensity of the audience's reaction. Instead of being about the past, it began, in a way that was impossible in Dublin, to address the present. When the play ended, and the lights came up, I noticed that the woman beside me had tears running down her face. I asked her if it was the executions of the Rising's leaders at the end of the play that had moved her. Not really, she said. What she felt wasn't so much sadness or anger as jealousy. She just wished that Scotland had something like that in its recent past; that some simple, heroic gesture had cut through the complexities and contradictions of being Scottish.

This, I discovered, is a common hankering among nationalists in Scotland; not for armed revolt—Scottish nationalism is a remarkably pacific and law-abiding movement—but for some grand, resonant assertion of identity that has occurred in living memory. The best it can offer so far is the seizing of the Stone of Destiny in 1950, when some students stole from beneath the Coronation Chair in Westminster Abbey the literal touchstone of Scottish sovereignty, the stone on which Scotland's kings had been crowned until (in 1296) the English king Edward I hauled it south to London. In 1950 the students took it back north again in the boot of a car, an act of historic restitution that produced satisfying amounts of publicity until the stone was discovered four months later and taken back to London. A jape then, which over the next forty years slowly sank into the recesses of Scottish memory. Then, in 1996, the British Government announced that the Stone of Destiny would be returned to Scotland permanently and officially; a student escapade would be repeated as a solemn act of reconciliation, a final assuagement of a Scottish sense of grievance that seems to English Conservatives increasingly perverse and unfathomable. As Tom Nairn, the leading theoretician of Scottish nationalism, describes it: 'The message is—here is your sacred stone. Go and worship at your will and folk-dance in front of it. What do you need politics for?'

It might work. The stone's restitution has become a serious business. During my stay in Scotland, the newspapers were filled with argument, claim and counter-claim. Several towns and cities wanted it to embroider their histories and attract more tourists. Edinburgh, Perth, Arbroath, Stirling—each of them could produce a historical case and a present need. Then, more troublingly, came questions about the stone itself. Was the stone that Edward I took to London in 1296 the real thing? There is a persistent tradition that an ordinary lump of sandstone was substituted for the real one, and that rival Stones of Destiny litter the Scottish landscape. Or was the stone that was returned to Westminster Abbey in 1951 the one the students had taken from it? A sculptor who was involved in the affair claimed ten years later that he had made at least two replicas, and that, though he could not be certain, it was a copy that had been found and returned to London. In 1968 another of the 1950 conspirators returned to Westminster Abbey and slipped a cardboard sign through the iron railings that now guarded the stone: 'This is not the original Stone of Destiny. The real Stone is of black basalt marked with hieroglyphics and is inside a hill in Scotland.'

With its multiplying stories, the Stone of Destiny may not, in the end, be a bad symbol for Scottish nationhood—not in its mute fixity, but in the very variety of definitions that it offers. Which best represents the essence of the nation? A lump of rock over which generations of English monarchs have sat at coronations? A dark hieroglyphic hidden in an unknown hill? Or, perhaps most appropriately, a clever forgery that has become indistinguishable from the original?

# Scotland: where is it?

During my days in Edinburgh, I read about the search for Brigadoon in a book by Forsyth Hardy, who was once the film critic of the *Scotsman* newspaper. In 1953, Hardy wrote, he was visited by a Hollywood producer who was looking for a location in which to film the musical *Brigadoon*, which is set in a Highland village and would be directed by Vincente Minnelli and star Gene Kelly and Cyd Charisse. The producer wanted somewhere pretty, changeless and *Scottish*. Hardy took him to some likely places: Culross in Fife, Dunkeld and Comrie in Perthshire, Braemar in the Highlands, Inveraray in Argyll. None lived up to the image the producer had brought with him. He decided instead to build his Brigadoon in California. 'I went to Scotland,' he said, 'but I could find nothing that looked like Scotland.'

The same kind of story is told in all small countries whose culture has been seen, at one time or another, as an example of the exotic. What is remarkable about Scotland, though, is not that outsiders have made a dreamland of it but that Scots themselves sometimes see it in the same way. From Edinburgh I made the forty-mile journey to Scotland's largest city, Glasgow, and one of the largest post-war housing estates in Europe—Easterhouse—which was filled in the 1950s by working-class people who had been moved—the official word is 'decanted'—from the Victorian

67

slums of the inner city. In Easterhouse, I met Cathy McCormack, who has lived there for forty years and survives, like many people in her locality, on state benefits. 'People spoke about culture,' she said, 'and I didn't understand. What does culture mean? Until I discovered it was growing in my house, I didn't know.' The new houses were damp and cold, and the walls were infested with moulds and fungal cultures that made the children sick. And so when she hears the word culture, she reaches for her fungicide; the time she campaigned for properly heated homes, she said, was when she became 'active on the culture scene'.

She spoke with the kind of angry irony that is typical of Glasgow, but what she said next contained no irony at all. Recently a 'community development group' had taken her round the country on a study tour. She visited, for the first time, the countryside and the small towns, the kinds of places that appear in books and movies. 'What was interesting,' she said, 'was that it was really the first time I'd been in Scotland.' She was born and brought up in the suburbs of Glasgow; she had lived there all her life. But it seemed to her that she had never been in Scotland.

Who and what lives in this imagined country? A sociologist, David McCrone, has summarized its constituents as 'tartan; kilts; heather; haggis; misty landscapes; couthy (and slightly weird) natives; Jekyll and Hyde; Scottish soldiers; Mary, Queen of Scots; Bonnie Prince Charlie; Balmorality; Harry Lauder'. A kitsch list—so satirized over the past twenty years by Scots themselves that it should have vanished, ridiculed into oblivion. But the old romance is stubborn. Historic Scotland, the state agency that is in charge of historic buildings and monuments, gives in its advertising brochure this definition of the country whose culture it helps to define and preserve: 'Scotland is a land of castles. Mighty fortresses on rocky heights, isolated keeps, elegant homes for great families and grim strongholds set on towering sea cliffs.' In other words, a particular place (the Highlands and Islands) at a particular time (before industrial modernity).

The difficulty is not that most people in Scotland live in the central Lowlands rather than among the bens, glens and grim sea-girt strongholds. Nor does it lie in the vast gulf between the reality and the image invented by movies, tourism and the heritage industry—what country doesn't have such a gulf? The problem for political nationalism is that romantic notions of the country have become a crucial constituent of the way Scotland sees itself (often profitably: tourism is worth £2 billion a year to the Scottish economy, and with 180,000 workers it is by far Scotland's largest employer) and can't easily be evicted in favour of more modern ideas. If, that is, more modern ideas could be found.

George Kerevan, a key figure in the cultural politics of Edinburgh in the past decade as head of the regional council's economic development committee, believes that 'Scotland has never been a modern country in the sense of adopting European modernism. There was no cultural modernism—it failed entirely. So Scotland is conservative not just in social values, but in its cultural values. There is no good modern architecture. You go back to the first decade of the twentieth century—Scotland was one of the richest, most powerful industrial places in the entire globe. Where were the skyscrapers? Where was the film industry? If you take Czechoslovakia or Austria or the smaller industrialized European states, they embraced modernism at some stage. We don't even know what modernism is. We had the technology—we were making the steel, we had the engineers—but we didn't have the imagination.'

The failure, he said, persists: 'Even with the recent flowering of culture in Scotland, the cultural boundaries are very traditional. They're all about challenging London, about challenging Scottish dependency. But they will wake up some day to realize that when you are independent, you have to develop a culture that isn't merely reactive. Outside popular culture, there's no real understanding of what that might be.'

There was once. Critics of the kitsch images of Scotland used to call for the grit of urban realism, for truthful images of the shipyards and slums. But now those images are themselves suffused with nostalgia. They represent a world that is as dead as the Highland culture whose collapse in the eighteenth century gave rise to the elegiac romanticism that created tartanry. In the three years after Mrs Thatcher came to power in 1979, Scotland lost more than one-fifth of its manufacturing jobs and a tenth of its industrial output. In 1979 there were 600,000 people working in

Scottish manufacturing industries. In 1994 there were only 350,000, and they were much more likely to be assembling computers than building ships. The wearers of cloth caps are as much a lost tribe at the end of the twentieth century as the wearers of kilts were at the end of the eighteenth.

# Something wrong with the plot

If you grow up, as I did, in a small nation, you learn that nationalism needs a story to tell itself, preferably a simple narrative of conquest and resurrection. In the Golden Age, this story says, we were free and happy. Then the foreigners came and took our freedom. Now we must throw off the foreign yoke, and the Golden Age will come again. In this story, the future will be a version of the past, a transformation that is at heart a restoration.

At first glance Scotland has all the elements of this plot. It is a small nation with a big neighbour, a country of five million people beside a country of fifty million. It was for a very long time a separate state, preserving its independence by heroic deeds. It lost its independence and is governed by its bigger neighbour. It can be imagined as another Ireland, about to follow Ireland's example and restore its rightful freedom. In this kind of story, Robert the Bruce's heart could be a powerful metaphor, a fragment of the Golden Age dropping into the fallen present and heralding the rebirth of an ancient spirit.

The problem is that Scotland's Golden Age—the time of its greatest influence upon the world—occurred long after it lost its independence. It occurred in the nineteenth century—the supreme *British* century—in the era of Queen Victoria and David Livingstone, of industry and empire. A hundred years ago it was at the heart of one of the most aggressive colonial enterprises the world had ever seen. In the 1870s Scottish financiers pioneered investment trusts that bought and developed land, mines and railways in the Americas, Asia and Australia. In the 1880s Scots investors financed two-thirds of the cattle ranches in the American West. In the 1890s Nyasaland was virtually a Scots colony. In 1914 the United Kingdom as a whole had £4 billion invested abroad, an average of £90 per head of population. Scottish investors accounted for £500 million of this, an average of £110 per head of population. Even Scottish nationalists are now prepared to acknowledge this as the best of times. As Alex Salmond, leader of the Scottish National Party, has said: 'A hundred years ago, we were among the most prosperous nations of the world, a powerhouse of industry, providing manufacturing muscle at the centre of a major empire. Now we often appear to be a social and economic backwater, perched on the fringes of a third-rate, badly focused and perpetually wrong-footed power.'

Two things are notable about this complaint. First, that it is not the lost time of independence with which the present is unfavourably compared, but the heyday of the British Empire—a strange kind of nationalist nostalgia. Second, it is not the foreigner's might that fuels a sense of grievance, but the foreigner's current weakness. Irish nationalism used to draw on the image of Ireland as an innocent maiden violated by a cruel invader. A truthful Scottish nationalism finds that kind of outrage unattainable. Scotland is not Ireland. Rather than virgins and rapists, the more appropriate image for Scotland is of a contemptuous woman married to a husband who has gone to seed. England, shrivelled and pot-bellied, is no longer good company to step out with on the world stage. Old industries, blessings of Pax Britannica, have gone. New industries have their headquarters elsewhere. Today seventy per cent of Scotlands's industry is owned and controlled outside Scotland.

There is nostalgia and complaint; nationalism reflects both. But it is impossible for Scotland to cast itself as an oppressed and colonized nation and at the same time to locate its golden age in a time when it was most profoundly at one with its supposed oppressor. It needs a different story. Atavism perhaps—the appeal to race, blood and soil that has fuelled so many nationalist movements in other parts of Europe? Nationalist intellectuals think not; ethnic emotions in Scotland are split by sectarianism—Catholic and Protestant—and the divide that still exists between Lowlands and Highlands. The chastening example of Northern Ireland can be seen on a clear day from the west coast.

What remains—a belief rather than a story—is what the SNP and the Scottish intelligentsia call 'civic nationalism', the well-behaved, enlightened appeal to ideas of pluralist democracy. But even this kind of nationalism draws on a rather embarrassing reality, which is the extraordinary amount of independence that persisted after the Union with England. Scotland has its own church, entirely separate legal and educational systems, and a national administration—the Scottish Office—which employs 13,500 civil servants and has as its political head a minister in the UK Cabinet. Nine out of ten daily newspapers bought in Scotland are published in Scotland for a specifically Scottish market. 'The overwhelming majority of Scottish daily existence,' Tom Nairn said, 'is actually regulated by autonomous institutions which are almost entirely run by Scots. There are no English lawyers practising Scots law. There are virtually no English ministers preaching in the Church of Scotland. The education system is almost overwhelmingly native, except at the university level.'

Some nationalists make a counter-argument and demonstrate a 'colonial' effect by pointing to the domination of Scottish cultural and intellectual institutions by English people. The title of a television film made eight years ago and written by George Rosie has given a catchy name to this argument: *The Englishing of Scotland*. The programme listed the institutions run by what it euphemistically called 'non-Scots': the National Museums of Scotland, the National Galleries of Scotland, the National Library of Scotland, Scottish Opera, Scottish Ballet, the Scottish Arts Council, the Edinburgh International Festival, Glasgow Mayfest, five of the eight Scottish universities, the National Trust for Scotland and many others. A few people think that this is deliberate government policy, but George Kerevan, who left the Labour party for the Scottish Nationalists in 1996, disagrees. 'I think that's terribly exaggerated,' he said. 'Yes, there are a very large number of non-Scots in positions of cultural management in Scotland. But what is often forgotten is that far from being English fifth columnists, as it were, an awful lot of these people have come north to flee the English cultural wreckage of the past seventeen years. It's an extreme view to think that this is a form of imperialism. Only a very small number of people approach Scottish culture as something that's hermetically sealed, and get panicky when they see outsiders.'

Kerevan is probably right, though I thought his 'small number of people' too easily discounted a submerged strain of anti-Englishness that becomes audible to outsiders mainly at football matches. What struck me about this debate, however, was the *modernity* of the fear of English cultural invasion. If the Englishing of Scotland is a new phenomenon, then it acknowledges that Scotland was, until very recently, Scottish. If Scotland has been a colony of England since 1707, why has it taken so long for Scots to start worrying about English influence on native institutions?

According to Tom Nairn, 'The basis of cultural difference had been maintained by the existence of separate institutions. The place where it's most visible is in the areas just this side of the border with England. It's astonishing—a frontier without a single bit of barbed wire, no watchtowers or checkpoints, no fighting for centuries, and yet the separate distinctness of the places, the people, the accents, is still extraordinary.'

What makes people in, say, Eyemouth Scottish, and people a few miles away in Berwick-on-Tweed English is, he said, the fact that they go to different kinds of schools. 'The school system very effectively maintains a kind of cultural boundary which is not really an ethnic boundary. It can be made to have the appearance of an ethnic boundary, but it isn't. It is institutionally maintained. And that is what Scottish political nationalism is inevitably about: repoliticizing this difference. And that is an oddly difficult thing to do, in some ways more awkward and complicated than violent ethnic or religious confrontation.'

From the nationalist perspective, this is the nub of the Scottish problem. What makes Scottish nationalism so admirable and so amiable—its devotion to peaceful, democratic politics and its reluctance to play on racial and ethnic differences—may be the greatest handicap to its popularity. Scotland, in the words of Tom Nairn, 'is a society absolutely imbued with militarism', and yet violence has played an insignificant part in its nationalism. The efforts of the Scottish National Party have been almost exclusively concentrated on winning a majority of Scottish seats in the Westminster parliament; and at the last general election, in 1992, it won twenty-one per cent of the vote but only three seats. It can marshal rational arguments: that the industrial and imperial ties that once bound England to Scotland have broken and that there is now in England a specifically English rather than British nationalism; that Scotland's economic ties to Europe are much stronger than England's (Scotland exports a higher proportion of its output—mostly whisky and electronics—to Europe than does the UK as a whole); that Scotland misses out on the direct relationship with its European partners that, say, Ireland has by virtue of its independence; and that the growing anti-European feeling in English politics and the English media work against Scotland's desires and economic needs. But it lacks the tragic sense of destiny that has given urgency to national movements elsewhere. No sense of disaster—either in the recent past or in the foreseeable future—hangs over Scotland. In Nairn's analysis: 'The problem with Scottish nationalism is that it is devoted, not just to being good, but to being too good—to doing everything according to rules that we haven't set. This is the tremendous weakness of civic nationalism: it's hard to mobilize. The essentially military metaphor of mobilization is quite easy to translate into ethnic terms, but actually very difficult to translate into civic terms.'

# Enter a small actor on a horse

By the lights of its 'civic nationalism', therefore, the Scottish National Party should have been able to resist *Braveheart*. Instead it looked at Mel Gibson's shapely knees flashing under his kilt and crumbled; civic nationalism versus kilts, crags, broadswords and Anglophobia was not, as it turned out, an even contest. The SNP put pictures of Gibson on the cover of its recruitment leaflets and handed them out in cinema queues (later in 1996 young members of the party used *Trainspotting*, the film of Irvine Welsh's novel, in a similar way; leaflets reprinted the film's only overtly political dialogue, which included the view that the English were 'wankers'). *Braveheart*'s nationalism was not only ethnic and militaristic, it was also racist. The English were not just evil invaders, they were also sexual perverts. The Scots were noble savages and (though only with women) also good in bed. But the film offered the SNP a story of colonial aggression and native resistance which cut through the complexities of the past two hundred years.

For George Kerevan, *Braveheart* was 'just a nice western in kilts', made by an Australian living in the United States. For him, the film that will signal an independent Scotland will be about love and not war. 'There's never been one erotic Scottish movie. Scots are incapable of making erotic movies, or writing about eroticism, or producing erotic plays. They can't cope with it because it's not an erotic culture, it's a romantic culture. The first time somebody can make a serious erotic movie in Scotland, the culture will have changed, because Scots will have grown up. I've been saying this for ten years, and people can't understand what I mean. They think it's a joke. But I think it is the test of whether we're ready for independence.'

Meanwhile, the swirl of the kilt and the skirl of the pipes maintain the strongest appeal, which non-nationalist politicians ignore at their peril. *Braveheart* concludes with the Battle of Bannockburn, Robert the Bruce's epic victory over the English, the emotional lodestar of Scottish independence. In 1993 the *Scotsman* asked leading public figures to say what event they would most like to have attended. Ian Lang, then the British Government's Secretary of State for Scotland and as devoutly unionist as his party, replied: 'I would like to have been on the field of Bannockburn on 23 to 24 June 1314, to see the most decisive battle in Scottish history: the victory of Robert the Bruce's Scots over Edward II's English army.' Bannockburn, his argument ran, had secured for Scotland an independence that allowed it to become not a colony of England but an equal partner in a voluntary union: 'From then on, as a nation, we have never looked back.' A historical narrative that begins with *Braveheart* can end up anywhere, or anywhere except, perhaps, the real Bannockburn.

I went to the plain of Stirling to see the place. Today the battlefield is surrounded by housing estates—plain post-war terraces and semi-detached houses—which are such a typical feature of Scotland's urban landscape. The sacred site is marked by a flagstaff (erected in 1889), a memorial (erected in 1957) and a statue of Robert the Bruce (erected in 1964). Beyond lies that 'invisible' country of ordinariness: schools, small factories, hills in the distance, a hump where a coal mine once worked. Some years ago, when the Scottish Tourist Board commissioned Arthur

Young International to conduct a 'Heritage Attractions Study', the consultants were appalled by what they found. The site was too mundane, it did not offer 'the battle experience'. It lacked, they said, 'the magic of the real'. Scottish reality, in other words; not quite yet real enough to be magical.

When I was eight, my school, like all schools in Ireland, prepared to celebrate the fiftieth anniversary of the Easter Rising in 1916. A framed copy of the Proclamation of Independence was hung in the hallway, and the classrooms were festooned with crêpe hangings in the national colours: green, white and orange. We rehearsed a pageant: I would sing about a 'young Irish hero' cruelly shot down by an English soldier, in front of a dumbshow depicting the event. The audience would see the martyr raise himself up on his elbow and hear (in my voice) his dying words—a vision of the holy, happy land that was about to be born.

It should have been magnificent. But when the night of the performance arrived, and the fat boy playing the hero was shot, he fell with a graceless thud, and I could hear titters from the audience. As the scrawny pall-bearers struggled to hoist his flag-draped body on to their shoulders, the laughter began to undermine my tearful lyrics. And when, in despair, they gave up trying to lift him and dragged him off by the heels, guffaws drowned out the visionary climax of the song.

It was a terrible humiliation but it also broke a spell. A few years later civil conflict broke out in Northern Ireland, and stories about Irish martyrs and English soldiers moved out of sentimental songs and on to television screens. To be worth killing and dying for, nationalism needs sacred symbols and holy history, but we began to see that it was one thing to have great moments of national revival in your past, quite another to have to live through them. And I was glad then of the laughter at the pageant.  □

GRANTA

# TIM BINDING
## ASSAULT BY WATER

Standing on the huge, lettered rock, the clink of climbers' chains at the back of him, the breath of other untutored scramblers fading as they make their way back down the grassy, bee-infested footholds, he can see, lying in that open valley at the foot of Rumbles Moor, the town where he first learned the art of forgetting. To the north hangs the first rise of the wild hill country, stretching up to the Scottish border, where sheep strong enough to withstand the bitter winter chill still graze. To the south, further down the valley, the haze of the once vast industrial complex, shaped like a heart, which pumped day and night for the body of the nation—Leeds, with its mills and great engineering works; Bradford, head of the wool industry; and beyond, in a ragged clump, the other working towns and their forgotten products: Huddersfield for worsteds, Halifax for rugs, Barnsley's linen, Morley's tweeds; Yorkshire's woollen right ventricle to Lancashire's cotton left. Caught in the middle, between the hills and the haze, stands the town itself, with its wide streets and avenues of trees, its tumbling wooden-bridged public garden and its regiment of imposing houses that snake up the hillside to touch the moor. Down there, to the right, is the open green of the Ben Rhydding Sports Club, where that journey that he must now follow, and in which he recognizes he played no part, ended. Closer to the town on the other side, before the bend in the road where the railings stopped, shines the meridian blue of the lido, which has hardly changed since he last played at its edge more than forty years ago.

When he drove past earlier in the day and peeped through the fencing, though he could not be sure that the slide was still the same slide, there was no doubt that the pyramid fountain, with its concentric rings rising like a wedding cake out of the water into the air, layer on layer to the foaming, frothing top, was the same, the water cascading over the sides. It was as if he had never left, had never grown older, still six, the same water, the same laughter rising out of the splash.

The broad flat surface of the larger rock which is part of the entity known as the Cow and Calf is not smooth, marked only by the weather and clambering hands. It is festooned with names, the graffiti of a hundred years and more, a diary, a census, a record of those who have come and gone. Those of the previous century are more elaborately carved. Facing him as he pulled himself up was the mark of the hand of E. M. Lancaster of the XXIV Foot, 1882 (the same year that Sir Garnet Wolseley defeated Colonel Arabi Pasha at Tel-el-Kebir). There are messages from that time too, texts from scriptures chiselled out by zealous pilgrims in awe of the God who had created both them and this. Ranged in a half-moon, like the message above a doorway, he finds the inscription s WILL FIND YOU OUT. Tracing the lost word he understands swiftly that the s forms the last letter in the word 'sins'. SINS WILL FIND YOU OUT says the rock.

He walks back and forth, treading on their memory, speaking their names out loud. E. Douglas Hunsley, 1895. Near to it, on

the very lip of rock, the precariously named J. Clarke, balancing
his life out in 1814. Then

BASKET DB

RS SJ AJ

1976

and underneath

1990

PERCY

CHARLES

FRANKS

Having come here for a purpose, to trace the fault line of his
own history, he searches for the year that saw its inception. There
are a number from that decade. KL, FS, 1953; a C. Moss from
the United States in 1951; in 1952 J. W. Ray; in 1957 a bald
Fishbury. Yet he cannot find one for 1954. 1954 does not exist.
He is disappointed. He had hoped for a mark.

The story of Ilkley, of modern Ilkley, began with the growth of
the hydropathic establishments in the years between 1840 and
1870. Though the spirit of the Ilkley water was known beforehand,
and the White Wells bathhouse, perched between the town and the
moor, with its steep climb, its crude plunging bath, had already
gained a reputation as an effective, brutal cure, it was the coming
of hydropathy that advanced the town's prosperity and population
beyond anything which it might otherwise have hoped for.
Hydropathy made it respectable. Hydropathy gave it dignity.
Hydropathy for a brief time made it fashionable. Hydropathy,
invented by a Silesian farmer, Vinzenz Priessnitz, and brought to
Ilkley by a stuff merchant named Hamer Stanfield who had visited
Priessnitz's Hydrosumanian Temple in Gräfenberg and rushed
back to build his own, here in Ilkley—Ben Rhydding.

Later others grew in its shadow, but Ben Rhydding remained
the most glorious. Though Hamer Stanfield founded it, it was a
Scottish doctor, William Macleod, editor of *The Water Cure
Journal and Hygienic Magazine*, who had studied at Malvern
under the most famous of all the hydropathic doctors, Dr James
Manby Gully (among whose patients were listed George Eliot,

Dickens and Tennyson), who was to turn Ilkley's burgeoning hydropathic cure into an industry. Macleod started as an employee but by 1863 he had bought the premises outright, lavished money on them, extended them, turning rigour into splendour. Ben Rhydding, built in baronial style, accommodating eighty patients, with twelve private sitting rooms and bedrooms blessed with huge baths and unlimited water: below them a gymnasium, a bowling green, a library, a billiards room and above, thirty-five domestic servants freezing in the attic. Breakfast at eight in the *salle à manger*, and scriptures read in the drawing room immediately after; dinner at two; evening meal, seven. At ten p.m. all lights in the public rooms extinguished, with the main stopcock turned off at eleven p.m. sharp. No mustard in the cruet, no spices in the food, and no smoking in any part of the establishment. In the morning a strict regime of bathing and drinking water: wet sheets on stomachs filled with the ague, cold packs to drive out corrupt and foreign materials, cold plunges to dissipate morbidity, dripping sheets for nervous and excitable patients, wet-sheet envelopes for fever or inflammatory pain, dry packs for quinsy, rheumatism and influenza, head baths for the brain, footbaths for the heart, plunge baths and sitz-baths, and the all-powerful douche. In the afternoon, relaxation and long walks on the moor. The Ilkley Cure. Assault by water.

Other emporia opened: Wells House, Craiglands, Troutbeck, the Grove. But hydropathy's fortune fell as quickly as it had risen. Quicker. Macleod left in 1873 in bad health, sick from the one condition he knew hydropathy could not contain: heart disease. He died two years later. Quacks eager to ride the cold current of success initiated its decline: hypothermic deaths abounded. A year after Dr Macleod's death came the murder that was to destroy its credibility completely: the poisoning of Charles Bravo, handsome young barrister and sexually insistent drunk whose wife, Florence, it was revealed, had once taken the famed Dr Gully as her lover. Ilkley was luckier. The disdain that stilled the waters might have silenced the town too, but by that time the railways had been built. Now Ilkley was connected with Leeds and Bradford and the men who owned those clanking mills. Ilkley became a rich man's town, and though, in the long years between money's settlement and his own childhood, matters had evened out, there was still at that time a scattering of wealth, lying, like a factory's sweepings, on Ilkley's valley floor.

When he was taken on his tricycle (a red one with a boot that opened and shut) to the main shopping streets on a Saturday morning, he was always struck by how much room there seemed to be, not simply the width of the streets and pavements themselves, but the space to be found upon them; so few people to avoid, space to race up and down, space to bang and bash. He banged and bashed so frequently that his mother had been told by the greengrocer that he had never seen a tricycle in such a state—though what could a greengrocer know of such things? It was so easy, head down, charging about, oblivious to what might lie ahead. He did not know then that the reason for this space, this emptiness, was not that Ilkley was a small town, or that its population was mean or had turned suddenly belly-up, but simply that while he banged and crashed below, residential streets above were swarming with vans, green and blue and that deepening shade of shoe-polish brown which gave at once a sense of both independence and subservience; vans with their owners' names hand-painted on the sides; vans driven by men in aprons and caps, wielding baskets and order books and stubby pencils behind the ear; vans with back doors which swung open to reveal trays of bread and cake, a marble slab loaded with wet fish, a slatted wooden floor stained with the blood of its hung meat and parcels of wrapped sausage. Boys there were too, boys on bikes, great cast-iron jobs with no gears for the steep roads, only a loaded wicker basket up front and a slice of metal from handlebar to saddle bearing their proprietor's name, a name that had told the boy to mind his manners and no dawdling on the way back. Up and down they travelled all, to the houses where the matrons lived, waiting for their Saturday-morning side-entrance knock. Those who lived in Ilkley had their goods delivered.

There must have been small houses in Ilkley, but in truth he cannot remember any. Even the ground-floor flat in which his family lived was part of a large semi-detached building, one of a long row following the flow of the river. All he can recall are large houses that sat deep in dark and hidden gardens, or if not protected thus, then guarded by a bleak set of steep steps after which one stood, an intruder, in a porch of almost feudal dimensions, with a sluice of a letter box out of which poured words of harsh dismissal. There had been something uncertain about these houses, every man jack of them now converted into residential hotels for the old and sick or centres for bizarre-sounding organizations such as the World Mohair Centre. For in his childhood, though it was reputed that ordinary families lived in most of them, an ungodly number contained the residue of a past age—crazed old men made mad with money, hiding somewhere between the front door and the neglected garden that ran riot behind their treacherously spiked walls. Somewhere up the hill lurked the man who had brought a grand piano back from Leeds and, having enough grand pianos in his mansion already, placed it under a chestnut tree, thumping out its warped notes whenever the fancy took him. Down the road, in another gloomy monstrosity, sat the blind widow who every year gave a fireworks party of fabulous dimensions to which the only close witnesses would be her terrified Pekingese and her profoundly deaf gardener. Money seemed to cascade out of these overflowing pockets, pointlessly and endlessly, exactly like the water at the wedding-cake fountain he so favoured at the lido. The Ilkley Cure. Drowning in money.

Looking down to the long stretch of the town he can see it all, or rather nearly all. One thing is hidden from his view, and yet he knows it is there. It is the thing that he is seeking out; his eye can trace the line that he knows it takes, following the clues of the bridges and the roads and the line of trees that mark its path. For it is not the inscribed rocks of the Cow and Calf that dominate the town; it is that other thing—that wet tumbling thing, the thing that never ceases, that is always on the move, even when frozen, expanding, contracting, flowing ever forward—the river, the Wharfe, rising at its source some two-and-a-half miles above Outershaw, falling six hundred feet to its junction with the Skirfere and then through hills of rock to Burnsall, the woods of Barden, the old Abbey and its graveyard and then Ilkley, Otley, Wetherby, Tadcaster and the Ouse.

In summer there are boats to hire, and for the price of a beer you can push out from the overhanging branches, dip your hand and glide along the Wharfe's brown water, see the park, the sports club, the tennis club, the town at play. Boys and girls still leave their satchels and shoes in the bridge footings halfway across and wade about in the water. Near his old garden gate lies the sandbank where families gather to bathe, with an overhanging branch from which the braver souls can drop in. Swimming, splashing, even a little dam-building. But in the winter and spring, in the flood months, when the snows have melted, and the moors let slip their icy cover, the river becomes a rage, charging head down, furious, impatient, twisting and turning, thundering through the town, the colour no longer the clear brown of soaked peat, no longer something which one might want to drink, but dirty yellow and sludgy white, like a rabid dog foaming with flecked spittle, snapping at the town's heels, making those who approach it wary, fearful lest it strike out in its all-too-predictable wrath. This too is the water of Ilkley. It is the same stuff after all. But try a dip now. And what of the little dams you made? Here comes a great snagging branch and a dead sheep. Here comes the foam, here comes the thunder. Here comes Michael Airey on his tricycle, with his nanny and his brother, Jonathan, and sister, Nicola, in tow. It is Tuesday afternoon, 30 March 1954. Here comes the Ilkley Cure.

He is staying at Moorfields Hotel on the Skipton Road, built by Joseph Smith, adventurer, explorer, a very strange place indeed, not because of its decor or proprietors, far from it, they could not be kinder, but for the fact that it is identical in shape and structure to the house four doors down in which he himself grew up. When he takes his breakfast, it is in his parents' bedroom that he cuts his bacon and slices his egg; when he steps into the high-ceilinged drawing room, it is his parents' front room in which he is standing; and when he knocks timidly on the back-room door to ask a wholly unnecessary question, it is the bedroom he shared with his elder brother into which he peers: the long bay window at the back overlooking the lawn, the little forest and the dip where the swing stood, hanging on its rigid arms of steel which permitted him to perform a 360-degree turn, up and over the crossbar, plunging head down, oblivious, and beyond that the nettles, the little gate, the towpath . . . and the river.

It is stranger yet, for sitting in his room, preparing to go out and roam the town, he has discovered in the hotel's promotional pamphlet that it was in this very house where the event that he imagined had brought him here reached its dramatic climax, for up this very garden stumbled the stabbed boy, bleeding from the knife wound in the neck, banging on this back door, banging not simply from blind hope but because he knew that the doctor lived here. 'A man has stabbed me,' the boy had said. 'Am I going to die?'

This was the story he had come for, this stabbing of a schoolboy on his way to the playing fields of Ghyll Royd School; this stabbing at the bottom of his own garden, with the police cutting down the nettles in search of the discarded knife; this stabbing by the ragged man who had sat on the bench waiting, a man from the dark town of Leeds, a man who lived an odd life with another odd man in an odd lodging, an intruder who had found Ilkley out and come to punish it for its sins—its wealth and privilege (had he read the rock's scriptures?)—who had gone out that day filled with an uncontainable rage, who found its echo bubbling alongside him on that winter path. He had written a note to his lodging companion, beginning in a curiously scriptured tone, one of dignity and composure, and ending in a throwaway fatalism that stretched far beyond his time:

'I write this with deep regret. This morning I smashed my bike up. I was trying to fix the rear light but I could not make it work, and it seemed to get the devil in me. I could not help myself. I don't know what I am going to do and I don't care.'

So Peter Lawrence Hudson of Victoria Road, Hyde Park, Leeds, possessed himself of a dagger-type knife known as a William Rogers and came to Ilkley by train.

'I'd made up my mind to kill someone and I sat down on a seat for two or three minutes, and two lads came past me on bicycles. I walked slowly along the river bank and heard something behind me. I saw a lone boy on a

85

bicycle. I waited until he approached. When he saw me he stopped. I stabbed him. He dropped to the floor, and I ran away, ran away to the Skipton Road, hid the knife and walked about Ilkley.'

Later Hudson sent a postcard from Blackpool to the police wishing them well in their investigations, informing them that if they looked hard enough they might find the knife one mile south of the river (hidden, in fact, under a laurel bush in a small plantation in Queen's Road). 'I may give myself up, but don't bank on it. Signed Potential Killer. PS I have got a new knife.'

They caught him within a week.

Peter Lawrence Hudson showed no remorse for what he had done.

This was the tale he had gone to retrace, as a witness to times that had not changed, but when he presented himself at the offices of the *Ilkley Gazette* to find the record of this event, it was not this story which drew him close. It was the other, the one that taught him the art of forgetting, how to erase all foolish memory that might otherwise keep him awake, ticking in his head. He had been leafing through the years '52, '53, '54, unable to remember in which the stabbing took place, half expecting to see a photograph of himself in the infant percussion band, or perhaps his brother's name. Didn't he win some sort of writing competition then? Whatever, he could not find what he was looking for, though he learned more and more of the nature of the town itself, mesmerized by the grainy pictures unfolding before him. First the wedding-cake fountain, a photograph of men cleaning it in preparation for the summer months to come, and though he did not immediately appreciate the significance of this, as he turned the pages slowly, photograph complementing photograph, ordinary photographs not of weddings or rotary clubs, but everyday pictures of the town's innocent, steadfast heart, townsfolk skating on the winter tarn, mending the wooden bridge in Herbers Ghyll Garden, he began to feel the warmth from the quiet municipal pride that such towns as Ilkley generate steal over him. But he could not find the story. The woman at the newspaper's office, eager to help, rang the retired editor. 'Look for the picture,' he advised, 'not the story.' Moments after she put down the phone, he turned another long page, and there at the bottom was the photograph he had not expected, not the towpath and his garden gate and a policeman standing on the slippery bank, but another, of an empty road and a line of trees and an unexplained end to a wooden fence. Above he read:

Considerable sympathy has been aroused in Ilkley this week by a tragedy which resulted in the drowning of Michael John, the six-year-old son of Mr and Mrs W. E. Airey, of Beckfoot House, Middleton, Ilkley.

It was the first time he had seen the name in print even though he has carried the sound of it with him for more than forty years. Michael Airey, six years old, who lived in the white house halfway up the hill on the other side of the valley, opposite where he now stands. Michael Airey who helped him push the nursery-school summer house round on its circular rail, in imitation of the great marshalling device, the railway turntable. Michael Airey. His best friend. The boy had been out with his nurse, his sister and his brother, out for a walk along the Denton Road. It was Tuesday afternoon, and he was riding his tricycle, given to him, like his very own, at Christmas. Jonathan was walking beside his nanny; Nicola was in her pushchair; Michael rode ahead. As they reached the spot known as Nell Bank, Johnny cried suddenly, 'Michael! Michael!' but though the nanny ran to the end of the fencing she could see nothing. The Wharfe was very close, very fast, swollen with the might of the moor. She ran for help.

He devoured the story, fingering the letters, tracing the words, speaking the name out loud. At first he was paralysed by the potency of the page, unable to move. It seemed to him that there was nothing, apart from the arbitrary date, to suggest that this event had not taken place that very week. Like the river forever passing, it seemed that Michael Airey was still here, still drowning, had never stopped drowning, still riding that last cold journey down to Ben Rhydding and the sports club and the stretching arm of Police Constable Smithson, the water cascading over him . . . turning, turning, turning. The Ilkley Cure.

He left with a photocopy of the story under his arm. He has been walking about the town ever since, first along the other side

of the river, past the sewage works, making his way out towards
the little island that lies opposite the spot, standing at the water's
edge, looking down the slow bend where the branches hang and
the water sings, thinking of all the quiet things of life this bend
must have seen. Later he crosses the suspension bridge and walks
back to the place itself, a place that seems hardly changed, though
the river is a good deal lower than it would have been that late
March afternoon. Now he is standing on the Cow and Calf.
Halfway up on the opposite side stands the white of Beckfoot
House, Michael Airey's home, suddenly glinting in the sun. He
sees the slope of the garden and the expanse of french window
directed south towards Leeds and the little road that leads down
to the town. He sees it all so clearly from the vantage point of this
rock. Here comes Michael Airey now, with his nanny, with
Jonathan holding the kite, a toy thing on a simple string, and his
sister in the pushchair. It is mid-afternoon. They have left the
house no doubt after *Listen with Mother*, sung the nursery rhyme
and heard Daphne Oxenford tell the story. There is a slight wind
in the air, and they are wrapped up well. Michael pedals down the
slope, the others follow. When they reach the Denton Road and
the wide stretch of grass by the bank, the nanny unfurls the kite,
and together they watch it flutter over the raging water. The river
thunders and roars but a few feet away, almost next to them. It is
both terrifying and wonderful, and they are worried that the kite
might snag a branch or dip too far and into the water. They move
on, a walk to the lido perhaps and then back to the house for tea.
Michael Airey climbs back on his tricycle and pedals ahead.
Suddenly his brother calls; the nanny does not know why, but all
of a sudden there is an empty space, no Michael, no tricycle, no
cry, nothing. Michael Airey has gone, one moment gleeful and
purposeful and pedalling like crazy; the next moment, gone,
under, choking, cold, frightened, gasping, gulping, fading, dead.
Now he has passed his nanny and his brother, Jonathan, and his
sister, Nicola; now he has left his tricycle, more battered than his
friend's will ever be, the boot is waterlogged, and the bell cannot
ring; now Michael Airey has released his grip, he is turning and
twisting, floundering under the toll bridge, past the man now
running alongside, trying to keep pace with him—he saw

something floating down the river which looked like the back of a head, face downwards and absolutely limp—his nanny's calling voice fading, the water roaring. Who passes that spot now and thinks of him? Who remembers Michael Airey and what he might have been—Jonathan, Nicola and the nanny who had flown the kite? What became of her? Did she marry, have children of her own? What colour tricycles did they receive on their sixth birthdays, and by what rivers did she let them ride? And when she peered round her children's bedroom door and looked at their sleeping heads, did she think of Michael Airey—so much Michael Airey one moment and then Michael Airey no more?

He has not forgotten the name, and looking out upon the scene, from Beckfoot House to the ground-floor flat on the Skipton Road, he is trying to understand why he has carried the name within himself for so long; why, when he was younger, he had claimed to have been present at the drowning and why, in private moments of insomniac turmoil, he used to imagine that he had pushed Michael Airey in? What has driven him this close to the drowned boy? There is a part of him that believes that without Michael Airey's death, he would not be himself; that Michael Airey made him, made him think of the mystery of Michael, of what he was and what he might have been, save for the simple trick of—what? A bump in the road? A flick of the eye? A look back to Nanny?

Now, standing on the Cow and Calf, he wants Michael Airey to be always here, for people to read his name and perhaps wonder. He wants to carve out Michael Airey's name and hold it fast on this slab of rock, but he carries no hammer or knife and he knows that a smudge of stone on stone would be washed away before the winter is out. He searches in his pockets for something sharp. A paper clip? A clinking sound distracts his attention. Below a young man is teaching his girlfriend the art of seeking handholds, standing underneath her, holding her body more than his tuition demands. Next to them a boy is adjusting the saddle on his mountain bike. On the ground between them, beside a set of ropes and pulleys, there lies a small efficient hammer. He calls down to the couple and asks them if he might not borrow it for a moment. The man looks warily at him, as if he fears he might snatch it up and hit them about the head with it, so he tells them what he wants it for. The man, looking disdainfully at his incompetent footwear, tells him that he is not sure, that he doesn't hold with that sort of thing, writing on the rock. He shrugs his shoulders and begins to search for a stone. It is better than nothing. The boy with the mountain bike calls up, 'You could try this,' and throws up a small spanner. He has never been very good at catching, and as it travels through the air, he worries that it will hit his hand and bounce away down some impossible crevice. But it homes into his palm like a falcon coming to the glove. He walks over to where he can see the white of Beckfoot House and the path and the tricycle pedalling down. He starts scraping out the letters. It is harder work than he imagined, and he cannot fashion the letters as neatly as he would have liked. But he is still Michael Airey's best friend, the only best friend he ever had, the only best friend he ever will have. Perhaps Michael Airey is his best friend as well, his constant companion, keeping his counsel all these years.

It is done. He smoothes the rock over, brushing the chipped dust free. The name is clean and fresh:

MICHAEL AIREY

ILKLEY

1954

□

GRANTA

# NORMAN LEWIS
## GOD BLESS THE SQUIRE

Forty Hill was once the northernmost place from which people might commute to London. It was on the borders of Enfield Chase, a landscape covered with ancient oaks, many of them hollow, cleared, in the far past, of human habitation by terrible kings, and designed for hunting stags. The land and its hamlets were owned and ruled by Colonel Sir Henry Ferryman Bowles, a sporadically benevolent tyrant who would not have been out of place in Tsarist Russia. Further sharers in this rural emptiness were the Meux brewery dynasty and Field Marshal French, commander of the British expeditionary force during the First World War. He retired here in advance of the great slaughter on the Somme, having publicly admitted that this was a war he did not understand, and that could only be won by trebling the number of cavalry engaged up to that date.

From the age of five I attended Forty Hill Church School. Studies began every day with half an hour's catechism. 'Braithwaite,' the headmaster, Mr Eastaugh, would bark at a boy, 'what is it our daily duty to perform?' And Braithwaite would rattle out the first of a succession of dispirited responses: 'Sir, we must do our duty in that station of life into which it has pleased God to call us.'

It was here that many of us confronted the class issue for the first time when the Eastaughs' nephew began school, and pupils were instructed by Mrs Eastaugh that he was to be referred to not as plain Thomas but Master Thomas. The same distinction was conferred upon a young member of the Bowles family, the feudal landlords of the area. A dubious state of health prevented him being sent over to the selective prep school, and he was delivered to us in Sir Henry Ferryman Bowles's Lanchester, a prestigious car of the day that appeared to have neither bonnet nor engine, and was driven by a chauffeur in a green uniform. Master William, from the day he was settled smilingly at his desk in a small space respectfully cleared in the classroom, was evidently not quite right in the head. We took to him, for it was clear that he shared the democracy of the insane. Idiocy had released him from normal tensions. He made happy inarticulate noises, giggled endlessly and splashed ink on the walls. Mr Eastaugh was lavish in the use of the cane, especially in the case of young girls; Master William,

93

however, was not only above corporal punishment, but strenuously objected to others being subjected to it. Thus all of us benefited from his presence and were sad when he finally left us.

Isolation in relatively empty country, crossed with byroads going nowhere in particular, had never quite released the village from the previous century. An early photograph of it could have been of Russia in about 1913, with small houses of all shapes scattered about a ragged little prairie remaining deep in mud or dust according to the season. Livings in Forty Hill, too, had always been scraped, and this, added to its cut-off location, made the place a sort of museum of outworn social attitudes that could only be remedied by more freedom of movement and more cash in pockets.

Sir Henry owned everything down to the last rut in the road and the last tiny cabin perched over the cesspit at the bottom of narrow village gardens. The exception to odd hutments and bedraggled terrace houses were a few better dwellings inspired by a grand tour Sir Henry had undertaken which had included the Italian Riviera. He had liked the architectural style of San Remo and had several houses built to remind him of it. The result disappointed him as the development was in an area where a number of deep gravel pits had been dug. All the new houses had been given glamorous Italian names. 'What does *Buonavista* mean?' Sir Henry asked to be reminded. But the promised view was of the eroded slopes of a chasm with a stagnant pond at its bottom, and the new buildings were sold off cheaply to anyone indifferent to their surroundings.

The village possessed a few small shops giving tick to impoverished customers, a bookmaker, an alcoholic doctor, and two pubs in which sorrows were drowned in sourish ale at fourpence a pint. It had an immense fake-Gothic church and a canon of St Paul's with a voice like Pavarotti's for a vicar, who with his glowing pink cheeks and magnificent beard looked like an embittered Father Christmas. On Sunday mornings he preached powerful sermons to a congregation of county folk gathered in the three rows of pews behind the front row occupied by Sir Henry, his family and house guests. Attendance otherwise was slight. For the evening service the normal congregation was five elderly ladies. The villagers had lost their faith.

Three-quarters of the inhabitants of Forty Hill were members of the working class which itself contained subdivisions of the most complex kind. Most able-bodied men of the previous generation had worked for the squire or his relations; there had been some advantages and many drawbacks in this. Six social divisions existed among the estate workers. Those at the top carried out delicate manoeuvrings with plants in greenhouses, kept themselves clean in doing so and demonstrated more acquired skills than muscular power. Sheer strength was ill-rewarded, and at the bottom of the social pyramid were those who went out, whatever the weather, to plough Sir Henry's furrows.

Now, with the building of factories in the Lea Valley, half Sir Henry's labour force had deserted him, got on their bicycles and pedalled away down to Brimsdown where the implacable machines awaited them. They worked for 'good' money, among the voiceless chatter of machinery from which there was no escape until the end of the day. Sir Henry's esteem for his employees could never have compared with his affection for a well-trained working dog; nevertheless esteem was conveyed in a word, a glance, a nod—even occasional stuttered syllables of praise, and Brimsdown offered none of these rewards. Moreover estate workers passing through a door in an enormously high wall on their way home at the end of the day carried with them a trace of the atmosphere of protection and privilege in which they had worked.

Sir Henry paid little but showed no signs of shedding the courtesies of the past, never failing to ask after a grandmother's health, or remember the name of a child. Brimsdown was unconcerned with such things.

One native of Forty Hill stood apart from the rest. This was Jessop, butler at Myddelton House, home of Sir Henry's brother, the famous botanist A. E. Bowles. Jessop, a bachelor with a house in the caste-ridden Goat Lane, had completed a course at a training school for domestic staff, where he had been urged to limit his utterances to five words appropriate to the subject, and to refrain from smiling in public. Although he had little to say and was rarely to be seen, his influence was great. People who came to him for advice were given five words that always proved useful, after which he turned away with a brief 'good day'. It was believed that both Sir Henry and his brother took his advice on village matters. Only Jessop, armed with respect, had triumphed over the class system in Forty Hill.

In the case of my own family, class divisions remained an enigma never fully understood. My parents, both from South Wales, now found themselves among people they could only study and seek to emulate with, at best, partial success. The social complexities of Forty Hill were wholly foreign to rural Wales. Carmarthen divided its citizenry into three classes based upon wealth, language and the forms of religious observance. At the bottom of Welsh society the country people, mostly smallholders, spoke and sometimes only understood Welsh, and worshipped in Welsh Baptist chapels where not a word of English was heard. Above them came the townspeople of modest means, usually English Baptists who had ceased to speak Welsh but belonged to chapels where sermons preached passionately in English were acclaimed by loud cries of assent. The third category was made up of rich and successful members of the Church of England who were calmer in their approach to the Almighty—most of them could have passed for the real English across the border some sixty miles to the east. At this level of Carmarthen society it was demeaning to be heard uttering a word of Welsh, and some parents, such as my grandfather, even urged teachers to punish children overheard speaking the old language among themselves in school.

A problem in Carmarthen was the extremely limited choice of surnames. There were Morgans, Reeces, Davises, Thomases and Joneses galore, and for this reason the acquisition of double-barrelled names was an intelligent solution. Thus, something was done about a town with a population of ten thousand of which four hundred were Thomases, and I often wondered whether this useful device had been invented in Carmarthen and then spread to the rest of the country.

My grandfather appeared on his birth certificate as plain David Lewis, but having made a killing on the salvaged cargo of tea from a ship sunk in Swansea harbour, became thereafter David Warren Lewis, and all the members of our extended family, except my father, gladly followed him in this bold change of style.

My father having started promisingly enough in London as an analytical chemist had then taken employment with a drug company where he found himself involved in the production of Beecham's Pills. Later he moved into a ramshackle shop in Enfield Town, where, having come to believe that all medicines were poisons, he devoted himself to the sale of homeopathic remedies that depended almost entirely upon faith for their effect. He decided to settle in Forty Hill because houses in these dishevelled surroundings were cheaper than elsewhere. Our home was semi-detached with no more than a partial view of a pit. The name originally given it by Sir Henry was *Isola Bella*. This, although there were no other numbered houses in the vicinity, my father hastily changed to number three.

R elations between Sir Henry and the village were going through a bad patch at this time. Although it was three years since the end of the First World War field sports had not fully recovered, to some extent through the loss of gamekeepers and the time taken to train new recruits. As a result the pheasants left in peace for so many years had become so plentiful that they were to be seen everywhere, not only at the roadside but in the gardens. Cases were reported to Sir Henry of his tenants making meals of these errant birds, and his fury was said to have been terrible to behold. 'My God,' he screamed, 'they couldn't even shoot them decently. They actually used traps.' So stung was he by their ingratitude that he was reported to have threatened offenders with eviction.

These incidents coincided with charges in the popular press that despite the sacrifices of their elders the new generation were lacking in ideals. An example of this was reported in the *Enfield Gazette and Observer*, deploring the conduct of a number of teenagers in the local cinema, the Queen's Hall. This was a run-down fleapit charging a minuscule admission for a programme of outdated and often damaged films. The cinema had been urged to foil its patrons' habit of making a dash for the exit immediately before the ending of the last film to avoid having to stand to attention for the National Anthem. This was to be done by locking the exit door five minutes before the show ended. The cinema complied, but having heard that they were locked in the audience joined in a vocal accompaniment of the pianist with a ribald version of the anthem inspired, it was said, by the public image of Edward VII:

*God save our old tom-cat,*
*Feed him on bread and fat,*
*Long live our cat.*

My only encounter with Sir Henry had happened at an earlier period, at the age of about eleven. His reputation for accessibility encouraged me to trudge up the long drive to his mansion at the top of the hill in the hope of gaining his consent through any intermediary who would talk to me to go bird-nesting on the estate.

I banged on the door, which was opened by his butler, but behind him, to my surprise, came Sir Henry himself who waved the butler away and took over. Before this I had only seen him at a distance, and now at close quarters I realized he was small and unimpressive compared with, for example, the imposing Jessop, who by my standards put all other local males in the shade. He asked me what I wanted; I told him, and he began his reply, stopped suddenly then broke into a stammer, blinked, then after a silence the words poured out. Where Jessop would have dealt with me in five words Sir Henry needed fifty. Behind him the room sparkled like an Aladdin's cave, a tall, willowy girl twirled as if in the arms of a partner to the music of a gramophone, there were flowers everywhere, and for the first time I drew into my nostrils the spiced aroma of wealth.

What surprised me most was that this man who ruled our lives should appear to be pleased to see me. In between the stammer he smiled affably. Bird-nesting was permitted and not only that, he said, but he would like to have come with me to show me the best places for nests, but unhappily he had to address a meeting of the Primrose League that afternoon. 'Never mind,' he said. 'Come back and see me next week but make it the morning when there's less going on.'

When I got back home, my mother asked me if I'd seen any of his lady friends, and I told her about the girl dancing by herself. 'That's the one who reads poetry to him,' she said.

In later years I heard more about these 'relations', as the females who surrounded him were known. They came and went. There was the poetry reader, a games mistress who kept him fit, a young nurse who told somebody in a pub that all she did was inspect his urine. He kept several aristocratic ladies living in cottages on the estate with nothing whatever to do with their time but 'visit'. They were the bugbear of Goat Lane where the women had too many children and too many household tasks to have time to entertain these uninvited guests with empty chatter. But these visits were a matter of routine, and every house in the village would be visited several times a week; there was no way of escaping these intrusions.

The harassed wives and mothers of Goat Lane had little left to defend but their pride. Callers at the house for any purpose were expected to knock at the front door once or twice, and if there were no response to go away. Sir Henry's relations avoided this protocol by going straight through the tiny garden, usually littered with rubbish, to the back entrance. A soft tapping on the kitchen window would draw reluctant attention to the smiling face, and the woman of the house would realize that her poverty was on display. Unavoidably the kitchen door would be opened upon washtub smells, a grubby overall, soap-sodden hands, tired eyes and straggling hair. The visitor would be seated resentfully and offered weak, milky tea, while her victim settled with what grace she could muster to inane chit-chat, punctuated with the yowlings of her children.

It was an election that furnished the only instance of open opposition to Sir Henry's reign. As Conservative candidate he would normally be returned unopposed, but once, and to everyone's surprise, a most unlikely challenger came on the scene—a Liberal who happened also to be a pleasant young woman. Next a Liberal poster appeared in a Goat Lane window, put up by an old nightwatchman in one of the factories, thought of as weak in the head. At the weekend Sir Henry's steward called on him to drop a hint that as in the case of the pheasant-trappers, his tenancy of a tied cottage might be at risk. Any estate worker would have caved in on the spot, but with this the first glimmerings of proletarian solidarity were evident, for although no more Liberal posters went up, several Conservative ones were taken down. For all that, Sir Henry won in a landslide.

Life in the country had undergone much dislocation during the war and had continued to suffer from shortages of every kind for so long after its end, but was beginning to pick up again. Agricultural produce, still in short supply, fetched satisfactory prices. Farmers admitted to not doing so badly after all and could afford small increases in wages. The big houses were taking on staff, and girls brought up in the poverty-stricken democracy of the Lane now became domestics dressed in fashionably old-style uniforms, working fourteen-hour days and learning from butlers such as Jessop how to return short toneless utterances to orders received, 'Will that be all, madam? Shall I clear away now?' A better class of car was back on the roads with the appearance of a beribboned Bentley from Brimsdown snuffling softly through the dust of the Lane on its way to a wedding.

At this time of recovery and renewal the first shoot on a pre-war scale took place over Sir Henry's land. It was organized in a precisely planned fashion by Sir Henry and landowning friends, all of them military men and accustomed to dealing with bodies of men in warlike situations. First came the long front line of beaters followed by twenty-four guns on a half-mile front. Birds with no experience of such a disturbance scuffled aimlessly through the trees and fell an easy prey to the lady pickers-up with their dogs and the small steel hammers known as priests with which remnants of life would be deftly extinguished.

So successful was this pheasant holocaust that it was judged to have been almost worth waiting for. Champagne kept for such an event flowed in abundance, and the euphoria generated gave birth to the idea that an equivalent event—a fair of some sort—should be organized for the village. It was a project enthusiastically backed by Sir Henry himself, who despite his tyrannical outbursts remained a boy at heart and was noted for a passion for fairs. Until precluded by the disciplines of war, these had been held in his grounds on every possible excuse.

It was the brilliant idea of Canon Carr-Smith that Empire Day—24 May—should be chosen for this popular occasion in which a good time for all could be linked to pride in the possession of an empire which, leaving out the emptiness of the seas, now covered one-sixth of the globe. By this time I was in my last term at Enfield Grammar School, where the art mistress had produced a huge map in which these overseas territories stood out in brilliant scarlet among the extremely dull colours of those left in the possession of foreigners. This formed the background to the assembly-hall stage from which local dignitaries addressed us on imperial topics on the eve of the great day.

The fair held at Forty Hill was to outclass all previous entertainments of the kind. On the night before the village had been full of the iron noises of tractor engines crashing through the potholes, and by mid-morning on the twenty-fourth a great, garish encampment, so alien in this rustic setting, covered the summit of the hill and spread aggressively through the grey-green monochrome of hedgerows and fields. It was peopled by gypsies with fierce, handsome faces, flashing eyes and shrieking voices from whom the locals drew nervously away. At the entrance each child was presented with a Union Jack, but after a few perfunctory waves, these were tossed into the bushes.

Blocking access to swings, roundabouts, coconut shies, hoopla stalls, fortune-tellers and gypsy boxers who could defeat local challengers with ease, was a large tent bearing over its entrance the sign PEOPLES OF THE EMPIRE. Into this the villagers were firmly directed and here they were faced by a row of dark-complexioned men lined up on a platform, all in colourful—sometimes astonishing—garments, most baring their teeth in efforts to smile. Placards at their feet denoted their place of origin. Some of them had feathers stuck to bare chests, others wore tasselled loincloths, turbans or coolie straw hats, and carried clubs and spears. (In fact they were Lascars recruited from Bombay and shipped over to work on the London Docks where they had been tracked down by Sir Henry's agent and fitted out by a theatrical costumier to play their part.) The children giggled nervously at the sight, and a few of the younger ones showed signs of alarm. We were told to clap and we did, and the 'people of the Empire' bowed gracefully or waved.

Beyond this bottleneck the fair was in vigorous action, and those who finally escaped joined others who had bypassed imperialistic propaganda by better knowledge of the geography of the grounds. Life in Goat Lane was a matter of leaden repetition, and the whole village apart from the bedridden and a sprinkling of misanthropists were here for that tiny taste of excess that would encourage them to tackle survival with a new burst of energy.

The fair organs ground out their music, and the steam engines blew their exultant whistles. Despite the blatant cheating that went on, some of the cleverer villagers, whooping their triumph, won on the games. At first inexplicably, the latest in roundabouts brought specially from its place of manufacture was not in use, with access to its grinning, wide-eyed horses debarred by a rope. A dozen of the elderly estate workers wearing ceremonial collars and ties lingered in its vicinity, and shortly the lights came on, a preliminary gurgling started in the organ pipes, a woman's face appeared in the window of the little ticket office, the rope was removed, and it was clear that action was about to begin. Two men approached carrying an armchair which they placed with its back to the roundabout, and with that Sir Henry came on the scene and took his seat in the chair. He was wearing his decorations and a grey bowler with a strong curve in its brim. By this time the old men had formed a line and now they moved forward one at a time to take Sir Henry's right hand in a gentle squeeze and mutter a greeting suited to the moment. Sir Henry smiled and stuttered his thanks, then turned away to climb the steps of the roundabout, hoist himself up on a horse and begin his solitary ride. The crowd applauded, Sir Henry raised his hat, the roundabout began its rotation, while the organ wheezed into 'Alexander's Ragtime Band', still the anthem of moments such as this.

Such entertainments had to be paid for, although prices, subsidized by Sir Henry, were low. No charge was made for teas, and there was a bun fight for the children, also free. This could have been the last survivor anywhere of a traditional revel providing for the young a joyful escape from plain food and much amusement for those who looked on.

The bun fight at Forty Hill was held in the stable yard where three trestle-tables had been lined up for children momentarily released from disciplines that would imprison them again at the end of the day. Bun fight was an accurate description of what was to happen. The buns brought up from the bakery in large wicker baskets were tipped out on the table tops, and the children scrambled and pretended to fight for them. Sir Henry and several landowning friends invited to be present found these scuffles picturesque and were ready with their cameras. I remembered a previous occasion when the then prime minister, Stanley Baldwin, who had been at Harrow with Sir Henry, had turned up to applaud the maintenance of a custom so deeply rooted in our history. This year the feeling among the organizers was that due to the dispirited quality of the times the thing was calming down. The children fought each other on the table tops as tradition demanded, and cheeks were scratched and hair pulled, but it was a tame affair, and no blood flowed.

The women of the Primrose League who had inspired such antipathy among the housewives of Goat Lane were present. They made neat piles of the remnants of demolished buns before clearing them away and smilingly righted mugs that had been knocked over, refilling them with lemonade made from crystals of citric acid.

Jesus said of the poor 'they are always with you'. In Forty Hill it was the rich who were rarely out of sight. □

GRANTA

# JONATHAN MEADES
## UNCLES

*Father, Uncle Hank, Auntie Kitty, Uncle Wangle, Grandmother and Auntie Ann*

M y uncles were Uncle Hank and Uncle Wangle.
There was also Uncle Eric, but Uncle Eric wasn't blood,
merely marriage.

And then there were uncles who were not even uncles by that
familial fluke, whose title was honorific in accordance with lower-
middle-class practice of the Fifties, uncles whom I'd never have
considered addressing without that title: Uncle Donald the boffin,
Uncle Cecil the pharmacist, Uncle Edgar the optician and Uncle
Edgar the boho restaurateur/potter/antiques dealer/welsher on debts
whose raggedy truant children, my elders by at least a decade, I
envied for their licence to call my parents by their Christian names.
Uncle Os lived far away and owned a pub surrounded by orchards.
Uncle Ken had a daughter with a limp, a capacity for ire which
made subcutaneous ropes grow in his forehead, a reputation as an
endlessly passed-over RAF officer and subsequent career as a golf-
club secretary. Uncle Gerry had been among the first British
infantry officers into Belsen; he had no wife, so I had no auntie; he
drank; he killed himself with sleepers and Scotch when I was eleven.

# Uncle Eric

Uncle Eric might not have been blood, might not have been officer
class—he had no rank to prefix his name with in Civvy Street in the
days when such devices were supposed to prompt respect. He did
have a metal leg, the replacement of the original that he'd lost in
the defence of his country, a loss that caused him to postpone his
marriage by more than a year. He had an entire set of Giles
annuals, his own garage business, a subscription to *Glass's Guide to
Secondhand Car Prices*, a season ticket to watch Third Division
Southampton at the Dell where the sheer numbers excited me, and
the ancient cantilevered stands frightened me—I had read in
Charles Buchan's *Football Monthly* that such a stand had once
collapsed at Bradford or Stoke or somewhere, and regarded my
presence in Southampton's as a defiance of death, as an exhilarating
rite to be suffered in the process towards teenage, which had just
been invented and which was entirely associable with crowds,
groups, mobs and the crush of cities. The crush I necessarily

knew, for Uncle Eric was slow, gimping up the stairs to our seats whence he'd bark barrack-room calumnies: shirker, NBG, fairy.

Until I was nine, Uncle Eric, his wife, my Auntie Mary, my only cousin, Wendy, and their corgi dog, Jinx, lived with my maternal grandparents in Shakespeare Avenue, in Portswood, a suburb of Southampton, on the south coast. It was the house my mother had grown up in. There were two storeys at the front, four at the back: this part of Southampton swoops precipitously. It was, thus, a house of steep stairs, unsuited to Jinx's tiny legs. The placid, massively overfed dog developed a stentorian wheeze and adapted himself to a family of chronic hawkers and career wheezers. My grandmother did three packs of Kensitas per day and could really cough—Kensitas was not merely a brand of fag, it was an efficacious expectorant. Uncle Eric, no mean smoker himself but a Player's man, used to confide to me in no one else's hearing that she needed them for the coupons.

It was also a house of brute tables, of industrially incised wood, of lardy antimacassars and fussy beading, of oleographs and stevengraphs of Bridge of Allan, Stirling, stags and the Wallace Monument, of which my grandmother's grandfather had been the first keeper, i.e. janitor.

My grandparents' natal names were Baird (hers) and Hogg (his). Their families had moved south, stopping for a generation at this port or that: Glasgow, Liverpool, Southampton. There was always a city attached to the port. There was always a catheter attached to my grandfather after my grandmother died of lung cancer. He lived on five years, Pop did, treating me to *frites* and ice creams in St Malo where he had old friends from his lifetime with Southern Railways which ran the cross-Channel ferries, old friends who had stashes of wine from before the fall of France, from cellars that had been hidden from the Germans, so it was said. We got cheap fares and trophy wines. Pop gave me pre-war Sauternes from a tooth mug in a room we shared in the Hôtel du Louvre, St Malo, just eight weeks into his widowhood, the day after he'd bought me the Swiss Army knife I still own. The wine was a colour I got to know well, the colour of the contents of the catheter that I'd pour away in the morning.

My grandfather sold the house in Shakespeare Avenue, and

moved a mile away to Uncle Eric's and Auntie Mary's new house. He moved in without souvenirs. What happened to that furniture, to the souvenir biscuit tins and the souvenir biscuit-tin catalogues? It occurred to me many years later that these were the items that my father, a biscuit-company rep, had given his future in-laws to butter them up, to let them consent to a life with their elder daughter who would bear me after she'd given up wearing the coat of white aborted lambs' fleeces in a photo in the *Southern Evening Echo* a few days before they met, in collision, on Southampton ice rink. When the house on Shakespeare Avenue was taken from me, so was the thrilling walk from the alley behind it by way of further popular poets—Chaucer, Milton, Tennyson—back to the front door. This was a treeless labyrinth, all industrial brick and terracotta of 1910–11. They were the first tenants. I suspect a Baird held a shotgun to a Hogg head. My mother was born seven months after they married. They bought the house using a windfall as a deposit between the wars. But they never changed the way it looked. It was forever 1911.

I lived only twenty miles away, but in a different world, in the Church and Army city of Salisbury. In Southampton there were the red and black funnels of the great liners, there were the predatory cranes, there were the vast hangars on the Itchen where boats were built and where flying boats landed in furrows of silver spume. The river was crossed by the 'floating bridge', a chain ferry which landed you in Woolston where there were streets with names like Vespasian and more houses. Southampton was a city of relentless houses. They were built of yellow, of red brick, faced in stucco with bulbous bays in a coarse pastiche of Brighton. There were houses with gables, houses with diapering, houses with overblown capitals and crudely cast mouldings. There were houses where Lascars lodged—that epithet which signified Indian and Malayan seamen was still used then. There were the houses where Ken Russell and Benny Hill had grown up. There wasn't a house in Southampton that didn't rock with bawdy laughter. Fat bottoms, distended bosoms, big jobs, the barmaid's knickers, all the nice girls love a candle, all the nice girls love a wick. I didn't know whether to block her passage or toss meself off . . . This city lacked decorum; its police lacked decorum—at a public lavatory on the Common officers, curled in foetal discomfiture, spied from the eaves on sailors perpetuating the mores of sailors. Every house I knew had about it the whiff of the public house, of a particular public house, one whose guv'nor was Archie Rice, whose punters' tipple was Navy Gin. There was indeed a pub by the old town walls that was licensed to distil its own. The Juniper Bush, it was called, of course.

Uncle Eric kept a boat moored on the Netley shore of the estuary. It was a Royal Navy cast-off, a lifeboat. Uses of: drinking bottled beer and gin on Sundays, navigating under the influence. Apart from on holidays which occasioned postcards saying 'The beach is lovely, not steep at all. Eric can take off his leg and slide down into the water,' and rare trips to see relations in Manchester, Eric seldom ventured further than his boat. He didn't see much point in the country though he was happy enough provided he didn't have to get out of the car. Like all my mother's family, he belonged to the city, the smoke, the bevelled-glass gin palace rather than the mellow country inn.

Uncle Hank and Uncle Wangle never met Uncle Eric. They were country. Or so they deluded themselves. And they never made much effort to dissemble their contemptuous bemusement that their brother, my father, should have married a city girl. They wouldn't have thought much of Uncle Eric. I was apprised from an early age of the footling snobbery they subscribed to, of the hierarchy of places they believed in, of their explicit conviction that an affinity with England's grebe and pheasant was aesthetically and—more importantly—morally superior to a fondness, a weakness, for the fleshpots of the city. Some fleshpot, Southampton: the Port Said of the Solent. A poor whore has only to sit in a window in Derby Road, and a major police operation will be launched, all the filth who've been on Cottage Patrol squeeze out from beneath the rafters to race a mile east.

# Uncle Wangle

Uncle Wangle, né Reginald in Evesham, Worcestershire, in 1913, lived, when I first remember him, in a flat overlooking the sea in Southbourne, at the eastern extremity of Bournemouth, with his

*Uncle Wangle, c.1950*

frail, freckled, valetudinarian wife Auntie Ann, who was to be pitied because she was an orphan rather than because she was married to Uncle Wangle. Her maiden name was Pope, but that is all I know of her life pre-Wangle. It surely cannot have been as hermetic, frugal and loopy as that which she led during the twenty

or so years of her marriage (she was a war bride). Wangle had
enjoyed aborted careers as a mechanical engineer, a policeman, a
conscientious objector, an ambulance driver; now he wrote
technical manuals for the De Havilland Aircraft Company. A
mere view of the sea was evidently not enough for him—or indeed
frail, freckled, valetudinarian Auntie Ann whose health, he
decided, would improve if she were subjected to closer marine
contact. So they moved to a caravan at Mudeford. There were a
few other caravans, there were pines, there were dunes. Theirs was
no ordinary caravan. It was on the seashore. The waves broke
over it, they battered the sheet metal walls of the pioneering home,
they made tympanic mayhem, they promised natural disaster, their
potency was amplified so that a squall seemed like a gale, and a
gale like a typhoon. Auntie Ann's health did not improve. Uncle
Wangle remained convinced nonetheless that congress with the
elements was still best achieved in a caravan, albeit one in a less
exposed position—close by a railway line, for instance. They
moved three miles inland to Walkford Woods. The Bournemouth
Belle and the Southern Region's Merchant Navy-class locomotives
used to race past. I was forced to spend part of every summer
holiday with them and their Elsan and their neighbour's girl
Shirley, whose favourite record was 'Close the Door, They're
Coming in the Window', which I believed had something to do
with a plague of locusts. It terrified me. I prissily told Shirley that
my favourite record was Handel's *Water Music*.

Uncle Wangle's favourite record was anything gloomy by a
dead Scandinavian. When Auntie Ann's health once again failed to
improve they moved to a house, a lodge with an octagonal sitting
room whose floor was marked with Ls of white sticky tape. These
indicated where precisely to position a chair for maximum auditory
efficacy when listening to the new hi-fi which played Grieg, Grieg,
Grieg and occasionally Sibelius. Cruder music, the music which
excited me, was not welcome. My taste for Elvis Presley (I had
grown out of Handel) was incredulously mocked. I bought 'All
Shook Up' and got bollocked for it. I put on a pullover one chill
September evening and was told how soft I was, the implication
being that I was a mummy's boy who had inherited his mummy's
sissy city ways. When I admitted to having gone into Christchurch

to see a film called *Light Up the Sky*, a feeble ack-ack comedy with Benny Hill, Uncle Wangle rolled his eyes. He abhorred the cinema, never owned a television, listened only to the Home Service and the Third Programme, and read the *Manchester Guardian* (a day late; it took that long to arrive). He didn't eat meat. He ate a cereal called Grape Nuts, brown bread, brown sugar. Auntie Ann made nut roasts. All clothes had to be brown or brownish. Auntie Ann wore oatmeal hopsack and had a diarrhoea-colour pea jacket for best: she was oblivious to fashion. Uncle Wangle wore Aertex the whole year through, a hairy tweed jacket, a knitted tie, khaki drill trousers, sandals or canvas sailing shoes. It goes without saying that his house was virtually unheated, that his Morris Minor was a convertible, that Auntie Ann wore no make-up, that he was indifferent to the grandest house in the locality, the now ruined Highcliffe Castle, which he reckoned bogus and ugly—this would, of course, have been the characteristic reaction of most of his coevals to nineteenth-century medievalism. It was not the retrospection that Uncle Wangle deplored, but the theatricality of its expression, and the pomp. The stratum of old England he sentimentally connected with was yeoman rather than noble: stout, not flash; worthy, not chivalric.

There was probably some element of blood and soil in Uncle Wangle's and Uncle Hank's idealization of England. This ultimately pernicious hodgepodge of a doctrine was not, incidentally, a Nazi creation. It was merely hijacked by that regime. The identification of a particular people with a particular place and a particular past was a parochial goal whose paradox is that it was commonplace all over Europe in the years when Uncle Wangle and Uncle Hank grew up. Nazism was an extreme manifestation of it. In England the Arts and Crafts movement, organizations such as the Scouts and a few land colonies were about as far as it got. Not that Uncle Wangle ever went back to the land: he was merely a fellow traveller of bucolicism who was keen on camping. He revelled in the discomfort. He was a man who loved a Primus stove and who insisted in defiance of all evidence to the contrary that a half-raw potato half-baked in the embers of a campfire was a peerless treat. When I was thirteen I put my foot down and told my parents that I was no longer

113

*Jonathan Meades by Uncle Wangle and Auntie Ann's caravan, Walkford Woods, 1955*

willing to be farmed out to Uncle Wangle and Auntie Ann during holidays. I'd had enough of being sent to kennels.

Two years later Auntie Ann's health was failing. Her frailty was more apparent than ever. Her freckled skin was papery, yellow. But it wasn't her liver that was the problem; it was her heart. She had open-heart surgery, a procedure that was then in its infancy. The operation was performed at the Royal South Hants Hospital in October. It was, apparently, successful. She lay down a lot when she got home, and her face was drawn, but she was in good spirits. And as soon as he judged her fit, Uncle Wangle took her away to convalesce. He took her camping two weeks after she got out of hospital—in the Cairngorms, in November. Auntie Ann died soon after of complications resulting from pneumonia.

The next summer I was sent to stay with him, to keep him company, to cheer him up. I failed. After a couple of days of listening to his programme of deferred self-justification, oblique exculpation and sly self-pity, I packed my grip and went to crash with some friends who had rented a caravan only thirty yards from the one he'd first lived in. One night he turned up on the pretext of checking I was OK. There were girls from another van with us, and pop music and bottles of beer and cigarettes. I don't think I'd ever seen an adult look so woundedly bewildered. Outside his own milieu, which was halved by Auntie Ann's death, he was at a loss. He was the loneliest man in the world. His wife was dead. His arty-crafty but entirely artless friends Heather and Berty had returned to Canada. In his widowhood he was virtually friendless. His obstinacy and pride and self-delusion were such that he very likely never admitted to himself that it was his determination to adhere to his code of faith or whatever it was that had ruptured his world. When he died six years later, at the age of fifty-five, it was not so much from a broken heart as from an unconquerable isolation, from incomprehension of the world that her death had forced him to frequent if not quite inhabit. He was displaced. He was also temporally adrift: for my twenty-first birthday, a few months before he died, he gave me a model railway engine—a Hornby 00 shunter. It wasn't a joke either.

# Uncle Hank

Uncle Hank, né Harry in Evesham in 1907, also wore Aertex, hairy tweed and khaki drill trousers. He smelt of tobacco and of a sandalwood cologne and of coal-tar soap. He never married. Uncle Hank had been engaged before the war to a woman called Vera, who eventually married someone else.

Uncle Hank lived in digs. He lived in digs while at Birmingham University and he lived in digs when he went to work in that city's town clerk's office upon graduating. In 1934 he moved to Burton on Trent as deputy town clerk. Twenty-three years later he was appointed town clerk of Burton. All those years in Burton and for another fifteen till he retired in 1972 he lived in digs with two spinster sisters. There was a hectic week in 1949 when they moved from one suburb of Burton to another, and he moved with them. They addressed each other as mister and miss. At weekends and for holidays he drove home to Evesham. Evesham was always home for him. He'd never really escaped from his mother—my grandmother—nor from his spinster sister—my maiden, perhaps literally maiden, Aunt Kitty. And when he retired

115

he of course returned to that house to live with Auntie Kitty. It is a life out of Larkin—the carefully delineated confines, the eschewal of the exotic, the Midlands topographies, the walk through the foggy streets back to the digs. But we know now that Larkin's life was not quite Larkinesque. Both my mother, who was only too happy to entertain such ideas, and the woman with whom I lived throughout the Seventies used to wonder at the precise nature of the sibling relationship between Uncle Hank and Auntie Kitty. Whatever it was, they, like Wangle, were childless. Uncle Os, who had owned a pub surrounded by orchards and who became the owner of a string of hotels, once said of the three of them that 'they lived life in fear of life'.

Uncle Hank had a molar extracted when it was poisoned by a strand of pipe tobacco that was caught between it and the gum. That might suggest a cavalier attitude to personal hygiene, but Uncle Hank was a keen washer even in the days when the house had no bathroom, and a tin tub was filled in the kitchen. He was a wet shaver, a cold showerer. When he was eleven he swallowed a watch-chain and never knowingly passed it. It was presumably still there, lurking in his duodenum, when his corpse entered the fire at Cheltenham crematorium on a fine brisk day in February 1978. Auntie Kitty cried more than sisters are wont to cry.

Evesham is where two landscapes conjoin in collision rather than elision, the Cotswolds and the Vale. The Cotswolds and their satellite Bredon Hill are all oolitic limestone. Their buildings are geologically determined, now golden, now silver, now grey—but despite chromatic variation they are essentially homogeneous. All quarried stone. All out of the immediately proximate ground, supra-local. From Stow on the Wold, the road to Evesham descends the Cotswold escarpment through Broadway, the show village of all England, the perfect place—immemorial cottages, weathered stone mottled with lichen, greenswards ancient as time itself. But as you leave Broadway you pass beneath the bridge of a former railway, and the dream of olde Englande is ruptured, harshly and suddenly. The landscape of drystone walls and limestone cottages is of course atypical of England—but it is so persistently photographed, so persistently held to represent some

*Uncle Hank, c.1940*

sort of ideal that it becomes familiar, a norm. Now, on the Evesham side of that bridge is a landscape that is, so to speak, habitually swept beneath the carpet. Best place for it, too, was Uncle Hank's conviction. This is a landscape of fruitholdings, smallholdings, blinding greenhouses, roadside sheds selling pears and asparagus according to season, a landscape bright with the red industrial brick houses of market gardeners and with the caravans of itinerant pickers. Uncle Hank's despisal of it was prompted by its scrappiness, by the ugliness of the structures. Many of the market gardeners were Italians. They had no sentimental bond with the land. They had rendered the Vale of Evesham an industrial site. The earth was, for them, merely a resource. It was unholy, commercial, material. If you grow greengages or cauliflowers for a living you are very likely disinclined to seek spiritual succour from the earth—unless you have been instructed in such practices by an animistic townie. Uncle Hank wanted everywhere to be like the Malverns or Bredon Hill, places that were sacred to him, places of which he had taken solipsistic possession, places that spoke to him, places that were repositories of mysteries, places that had been invested with morbid magic by the poet A. E. Housman who came from the outer Birmingham suburb of Bromsgrove. Uncle Hank's conception of these places was a sort of religiose affliction.

117

Piety demands that we respect other people's faith, but what is there to respect in the delusion that a transcendental bond exists between people and place. Awe in the face of geological phenomena or overwhelming natural beauty is one thing. It is quite another to grant landscape powers other than affective ones. It is soft to conceive of the inanimate as though it possesses feelings or thoughts or human capabilities. It is daft enough to attribute these qualities to animals, but to hills and dales . . .

In Evesham, the exotic was represented by a singular trophy which captivated me when I was tiny, a Gothic arch formed by a whale's jawbone, brought back to the town by some lad who'd signed up as a whaler in the 1870s. Uncle Hank never went whaling. So far as I know he never left England in his seventy-one years. To have done so might have cracked the shell built of layers of habit which protected him from, say, the Brummie blue-collars who used to picnic in the park where the whale's jawbone stands, who used to ride in pedalos on the Avon. He enjoyed eavesdropping on them and mimicking their twanging inanities, a task he prosecuted with unmistakable contempt for the subjects of these parodic monologues. He had no fondness for them whatsoever. City dwellers were targets; townies were targets (he excused himself); towns themselves were targets, especially towns that had been built after the advent of canals and railways and which were not thus reliant on local materials for their buildings, e.g. Burton on Trent. Under his stewardship Burton destroyed itself. The mega-brewers, whom Uncle Hank sucked up to and who plied him with cases of limited-edition beers each Christmas, were men whose all-too-English mores he admired. They were given carte blanche to demolish the great brick warehouses that defined Burton, the brewery of the empire. The oast houses, the maltings, the cooperages—they all went. They were expendable (and Victorian). Cities are temporary things. Only the country, the specially sanctioned parts of the country, are eternal.

Uncle Hank's and Uncle Wangle's bucolicism may have been a state of mind—they were not, after all, farriers or farmers or hedgers—but they certainly practised the sort of thrift associable with the rural indigent. Uncle Wangle, who much preferred to be called Reg, owed his name to a supposedly charming childhood capacity to persuade people to give him things. Uncle Scrounger would not have had the same ring to it but would better have summoned his oblivious, unembarrassed tendency to 'borrow' and never to return. He was happy to abandon his vegetarianism if someone else had bought the meat. Uncle Hank was even more costive. My father, who earned less than him and had a family to support, was serially swindled by him over family wills—small sums certainly, but that's not the point. My father once found a 1932 Aston Martin for sale in a breaker's yard, put in a trunk call to Burton on Trent in the knowledge that this, of all cars, was the one Uncle Hank had always yearned for, and—against my mother's wish—paid a deposit of £100 (about £2,500 today). He never recovered it. Uncle Hank persistently tried to touch him on behalf of Auntie Kitty, who had never worked except during the war. And when Uncle Wangle, who was six feet tall, died, Uncle Hank, who was barely five foot eight, had all of Wangle's meagre wardrobe shortened to fit him so that had my father, also six foot, been inclined to claim a share in it, it would have been no use.

Meanwhile in Southampton, there were peals of dirty laughter and sweet sherry and sweet Marsala, and a room heated to eighty degrees, and fish and chips for a dozen in an enamel bowl, and gossip and ribbing and silly stories, and gaspers, and will someone let the dog out, else he's going to wee on the couch, and big wheezing and the feeling that you might be alive. ☐

# Three of the best from Minerva

## WILD MEAT AND THE BULLY BURGERS
Lois-Ann Yamanaka

'Fortunate reader. Here is a rare book ...
Yamanaka is brilliant'
E. ANNIE PROULX

## MIND READINGS
Writers' Journeys Through Mental States
edited by Sara Dunn, Blake Morrison and
Michèle Roberts
Inspiration, drugs, therapy, grief, disorder,
identity, depression, dementia and dreams.
Over fifty mind-readings to celebrate
the fiftieth anniversary of MIND

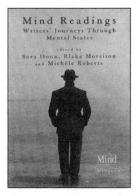

## THE WHITE BOY SHUFFLE
Paul Beatty

'What a wicked, wicked book. I laughed so
hard, I hurt. I hurt so hard, I laughed. He's
like a '90s Richard Pryor peaking ecstatically
on acid'
Jessica Hagedorn

Orders to: Reed Book Services Ltd  Tel: 01933-414400  Fax: 01933-414368
Registered Office: Michelin House, 81 Fulham Road, London SW3 6RB  Registered in England

# GRANTA

# HILARY MANTEL
## NADINE AT FORTY

Thomas arrived unexpectedly, jolting up the hill in the dust-covered taxi. She paid the fare, and he stayed for the summer. They chose to make love in that hushed grey hour which, in hot climates, can be taken for dawn or dusk. They slept till noon, and then, perfunctorily washed, yawned on to the small side terrace, where they were screened from human eyes. They took their bread and coffee here, overlooking the hillside that tumbled down to the sea. When Dea brought the tray she averted her eyes from the sun-flushed triangle at the neck of his robe, and turned away even more pointedly from the sight of her employer's body, slack and naked under silk.

After the first few days a new routine began. Dea would anticipate them, hurrying the tray to the table the second she heard the click of the latch of their bedroom door. Their breakfast would be waiting for them, as if placed by invisible hands. Sometimes they missed the maid so narrowly that the click of her sandals on the tiles was still fading when he reached out to take an orange from the basket, or her hungry fingers tore into crust and crumb.

The sea moved far below, a purplish blue.

When he left, in the autumn, she discovered that he had tampered with all the clocks. She hurried from room to room, incredulous. Some were running slow. Some had stopped altogether. She had to pack them in straw and take them to the town, where the man in the shop looked at her as if he judged her insane. 'All of these?' he asked in careful English. 'Each one of these requires to be mended?'

'Each one,' she said. 'You can see they all show different times.'

As she left the shop, the man said something to his wife, who was dusting shelves very slowly in the shadows at the back. It was something satirical that she didn't quite catch. His attitude is ridiculous, she thought. Surely he could understand that there must be one consistent time in every room of a house?

Ah, she thought: an Anglo-Saxon attitude.

All the clocks were restored, except her grandmother's tiny drawing-room clock, the clock that had tinkled so gently for

123

tea during years of Kensington twilights, at the hour when the sky had seemed to lower itself and rest tentatively on the treetops of Cornwall Gardens. It was a clock with a china case, roses of china strewn at its base, gilt fingers now indicating seven-thirty. She knew, by this, at what hour he had done the deed. But in the morning, or the evening?

Neither seemed possible. At seven in the morning Dea was already in the kitchen, or sweeping the long terrace with a monotonous whisper of brush strokes that broke into her sleep, transforming itself to the sound of steam trains, of waterfalls. At seven in the evening she herself would be walking from room to room, glass in hand, laughing, her silly skirts flouncing over the polished floors. But perhaps it was at some earlier hour—four o'clock?—that he had picked and probed at the tiny balances and springs . . . so that then the hands would falter, hesitate, move feebly for an hour or two, with less and less conviction, until finally, with a delicate shudder, they came to rest. Pre-dawn, then; he worked while she slept, his rather broad, coarse feet padding the tiles, and the moon a curving hoof, a lively bone, hooking at an open shutter for a chink to gain admission.

She missed the clock's silvery chime, and the loss made her peevish. Anyway it was time to go. The mornings were misty; the fires smoked, and Dea sulked at having to lay them. She packed her bags and closed the house till spring.

In June, unexpectedly, Thomas was back again. You could not say he had changed, except that there was a tension at the outer corner of each eye and the outer corner of each lip. She noticed this tension and saw how, in a year or two, his expression would harden. Age does not creep up, she thought, like a cat burglar—age fells you suddenly. She remembered when she had learned this, the shock it had delivered.

She was seventeen then. On a spree with her schoolgirl's allowance, in the curtained changing room of a London store; out-striding the black-clad women who would have helped her, making clear with a pout and a toss of her head that she would rather be alone with herself, a Narcissa, staring into the triple silver pool of the long mirrors. She recalled the minute click as she dropped on to a gilt hook the hangers of the experimental clothes. A swish of satin; her own frock dropped on to a chair. She saw the turn of her shoulder, ivory polished; her back's long curve.

As she raised her chin to admire herself, an overhead bulb, its rays like a ghost's baton, struck a glancing blow across her face. Gaping, she spun around; her future, in triplicate, bounced at her from the walls. It was a second, a fraction of a second, that Nadine was lost and gone—then her youth slipped back into her, attentive, poised, graceful like a dancer in a line.

But what she had seen, she could not unsee. There was a deep shadow under her chin. There were cavities gouged in the flesh, running from nose to mouth. There were marks under her eyes, as if a fist had made them.

Good morning, the face had said: I am Nadine at forty.

She had left the cubicle in a rush, hastily buttoning her pulled-on frock with one hand, while with the other she thrust into the salesgirl's arms a bundle of gaping bodices and fighting sleeves, of trailing belts and seams indecently turned out. Well, she said, scrutinizing herself now, I have passed forty, and it is not so bad; it is not so bad as all that.

There was a house party that year. Thomas sulked, scrambling each morning down to the crescent of shingle to kick at stones. If she had known he was coming, she would not have invited anyone else; both of them knew this.

'Be kind to my friends,' she said. 'You are too old to sulk.'

'You are just too old,' he said.

Etienne was one of her guests. She especially wished she had not asked him; or that he had come alone, for a short visit which would have been in the nature of a rest-cure. In the war, Etienne had been in a camp. He had been at Drancy, and then he was moved east. Sometimes he talked about his arrest and about an unknown person who had betrayed him, but he never talked about what came after that.

Etienne was not a bitter man. But he was aloof and dry. The shadow of what he left unsaid hovered always about his jaw and darkened it, like a nomad bruise, a cloud. His eyes, too, seemed

125

drained of colour, and he kept his hair clipped short, shaved almost, as if in obedience to some harsh regime that might one day march its soldiers south. He ate little, even after dark when it was cool. Something was wrong: he had suffered a digestive disorder, an ulcer of some kind, or perhaps it was typhoid. 'I keep best on bread and milk,' he said, 'the bread not too fresh.' He smiled a little. Dea started to keep rolls for him, yesterday's baking, which once she would have taken home to her children.

Thomas said, turning over in bed, 'That man I hate. He casts a pall of gloom.'

'A long time ago, Etienne's family and my family were friends,' she said.

He said, 'He might at least shave properly.'

She said, 'Why did you stop the clocks?'

He said, 'You know why.'

Her orgasms were regular, each night an efficient fleshly replica of the night before. She wondered about this and decided that, strangely, Thomas was more adept at dealing with the female body than with a clockwork mechanism. There should be more such men, she said, smiling to herself in the glass, pretending to share a crude joke with a female friend.

'One day,' Etienne said, 'sometime in the next century, we will all die, all of us survivors.'

She looked at him for a moment without speaking because she didn't understand what he meant. How can survivors die?

'And there will be no more of our convocations,' he said. 'No more assemblies of the walking dead. No more waking in the night. No more of this weeping and praying. We will be extinguished. We will be forgotten.'

'But you can't be forgotten,' she said. 'They have written books, made films. They have interviewed everyone and recorded what they say. They have opened the camps as museums. You can go to see them. There is a whole room full of shoes. I have seen pictures of it.'

'But I want us to be forgotten,' he said. 'It is a great error to believe the Nazis lost the war. For us, you see, they won it, and they win it each day. Each day we re-enact, on ourselves, what was done to us. They are the masters of our hours, and we are their obedient servants. Our ageing is a war, a long war, and each successive death will be a small victory. Each death will go to the wiping out of their triumph.'

'If you thought that . . . '

'Yes, Nadine?'

'The logical way—'

'Yes, of course. So many do. It is put down as falls on staircases. Sometimes as automobile accidents.'

Stifling August. Thomas said, 'I really want this to last for ever.' Sheets bunched under his body. Her sweat drying. Four in the afternoon; the garden silent. A tap running somewhere, Dea's tuneless hum from below, and the scent of falling lilies heavy as spice.

He said, 'You are no company, this summer, Nadine.'

'No.' She frowned. 'Perhaps not.'

'You are absent. Self-absorbed. Gone down the hill to play on the shingle.'

'Well . . . ' She frowned. 'There are things to think about.'

'So suddenly! And so little practice as you've had.'

'You must not—'

Not totally humiliate me, she had been going to say. He cut in on her. 'You have fallen in love with Etienne.'

'No.' He confused her: was this an accusation or a joke? 'I have some choices, but that is not one. Etienne has no future.'

'And you have one?' He was laughing. 'Oh, Nadine—and I stopped your clocks to preserve your past. How ungrateful you are!'

The days shortened. The guests went away. Birdsong grew shriller, sharpened, and the air seemed used. This time Thomas left without touching the clocks. Each hour was in its proper place. No arrangements had been made for next year. Finding herself alone, she stared into the mirror, trying to conjure out the woman behind it, the woman she had seen so briefly in the changing room—trying to will her into life. Nadine at sixty, she said to herself. □

# Take the plunge

## Subscribe.

You'll **SAVE** up to £28
on the bookshop price and get
*Granta* delivered to your home.

See overleaf for details.

'How much more fun it is to open
fat *Granta* than one of those thin,
starved magazines.' *Guardian*

'*Granta*'s heart is where it has
always been: good writing and,
more importantly, a fantastic range
of good writing is given a worthy
showcase.' *Daily Telegraph*

**GRANTA**

**YES** I would like to subscribe:

❑ 1 year (4 issues) at £24.95 *(saving 22%)*
❑ 2 years (8 issues) at £46.50 *(saving 27%)*
❑ 3 years (12 issues) at £67.00 *(saving 30%)*

(*Granta* sells for £7.99 in bookshops.)

**Subscribe for yourself**

Please start my subscription with issue no:_____

NAME & ADDRESS *(please complete even if ordering a gift subscription)*

_____

_____

_____

_____ POSTCODE _____

96L5B56B

Total* £_____

❑ Cheque (to 'Granta') ❑ Visa, Mastercard/Access, AmEx
Card no:

/__/__/__/__/ /__/__/__/__/ /__/__/__/__/ /__/__/__/__/

Expire date:/__/__/__/__/ Signature:_____

* POSTAGE: PRICES INCLUDE UK POSTAGE. FOR THE REST OF EUROPE (& REP IRELAND) PLEASE ADD £8 PER YEAR. FOR OVERSEAS SUBSCRIPTIONS, PLEASE ADD £15 PER YEAR.

❑ Please tick this box if you would prefer *not* to receive promotional offers from compatible organizations.

**or for a friend.**

I would like to give a subscription to the following. My name, address and payment details are above.

NAME AND ADDRESS: Mr/Mrs/Ms/Miss

_____

_____

_____

Return, free of charge if posted in the UK, to:
Granta, Freepost,
2-3 Hanover Yard, Noel
Road, London N1 8BR

Postcode _____

NAME AND ADDRESS: Mr/Mrs/Ms/Miss

☎ Or use our
CREDIT CARD LINES:
UK (free phone and fax):
FreeCall 0500 004 033
OUTSIDE THE UK:
Tel: 44 171 704 0470
Fax: 44 171 704 0474

_____

_____

Postcode _____

# DUNCAN McLEAN
# A GOOD MAN IS HARD TO FIND

*The Texan musical legend Floyd Tillman*

# Shanty Town

What was so special about Wichita Falls that all of its 1,154 hotel beds were occupied?

I tried the last name on my list of cheapo accommodation, the Trade Winds Motel on Broad Street. Full up. The clerk said I could always try the Sheraton. It sounded expensive, but I was getting desperate. Night had fallen. In the time it had taken for me to stroll in and out of the Trade Winds' lobby, the blazing sun had disappeared, and black night had swept in across the parking lot. And still I had nowhere to lay my head.

The Sheraton's reception area was bigger than my entire house back in Scotland. A few minutes' trek over the marble and shag, and I reached the desk.

Hello, I said, I was wondering if you had . . .

Sorry, we're full, said the clerk.

Oh shit, I muttered.

You could always try . . .

It's no use, I've tried them all.

I'm sorry. Let me check. She looked at her computer screen. Oh, yes!

Yes?

We have vacancies for tomorrow night.

*Tomorrow?*

Yes, sir.

Well . . . if I did book a room for tomorrow, how early could I check in?

How early were you thinking of, sir?

About twenty-four hours early.

She frowned. Like, *now*? I'm afraid that wouldn't work.

I sighed, was about to turn away and head off in search of a shady lay-by when I thought I'd have one more try. Spreading my list of hotels out on the counter in front of her, I said, Maybe you can give me some information. Is there really nowhere else but these places in the whole city?

She glanced down at the list, then away again, shifting uneasily. I'm not really supposed to help John Does, she said.

Unless they're guests. In which case they're not John Does.

How can I be a guest? I cried. You're full up!

She shrugged.

All right, all right, I said. What if I were to say I'd like to book a room, right now, for tomorrow night?

She looked at me. *Are* you saying that?

I sighed. Yes, I am saying that.

Very good, sir! Would you like smoking or non-smoking? North or south facing? How would you like to pay? Breakfast is not included, but a full choice is available from . . .

Listen, I said. We'll do that in a minute. But let's sort something out for tonight first, eh?

Certainly, sir! I'd be delighted! Let me see your list. She frowned over it, then shook her head. I'm afraid if they're all full, you'll have to go up to Lawton.

Lawton, where's that?

Oklahoma. About seventy-five miles north of here.

But listen, it's pitch dark out there, everybody's driving like maniacs, I'm likely to end up at the bottom of the Grand Canyon if I get into that traffic!

No, sir. That's in Arizona, not Oklahoma.

Plus, I'm meant to be heading south. I can't drive seventy-five miles back the way I've come when I've got five hundred miles to go forwards. It's mad. Old San Antone's where I'm headed, not Muskogee!

She was frowning. Well, there is . . . *no.*

What? Where?

Oh, nothing.

You were going to say something there, a name, a place I could stay.

I don't think you'd like it.

As long as it's got a bed, I'll like it fine!

Well, she said, then hesitated, a pained look crossing her face.

Well?

There is the River Oaks Motel. She whipped her head round to see if either of the other clerks had heard her suggestion and were coming after her with pitchforks. They weren't, so she looked back at me, leaned forward on the counter. I wouldn't recommend it, she whispered. In fact I'm absolutely not recommending it. But you might get a room there.

Great! I said. Can I phone from here? Have you the number? No, better still, you phone for me.

Ehm, all right. If you're sure.

I nodded, and she stepped to one side, spoke into a phone for twenty seconds, holding the receiver between thumb and first finger, as if it were contaminated. Then she hung up and turned back towards me. A smile of sorts across her face.

There was some kind of argument going on in the lobby of the River Oaks Motel. The fat, stubble-faced man behind the desk didn't want to give a room to the thick-necked skinhead and the young girl in party clothes.

I don't want none of that trouble like we had last night, the clerk shouted.

I wasn't here last night, the youth shouted back.

Fighting in the courtyard! Cops all over the place! How d'you like that?

Come *on*, Rocky, said the girl.

Sir, said the youth, I am with the US Air Force—I am not interested in violence.

The girl laughed.

The clerk glared at her, then wiped the back of his hand across his mouth. Cash, he said.

After they'd cleared off I stepped up to the desk. The fat clerk glanced over from the war film he'd turned back to. We're full, he said loudly. He had to speak loudly, because the telly was turned up high, and he was six inches away from it.

I booked, I said.

No you didn't.

Well, somebody booked for me. From the, eh, Sheraton. He looked me up and down. On the phone, five minutes ago.

He heaved himself up from his chair, came over to the counter. Twenty-six bucks, he said.

I gave him my credit card, he ran it through his machine and punched a few numbers in. The machine beeped. He frowned. Well, well, well . . .

133

What is it?

Rejected. Over your limit, boy.

It can't be!

He tossed the card across the counter at me. Got another one you'd like to try?

No. But, eh, I should have some money . . .

You better have, boy.

I emptied my pockets and came up with enough crumpled notes and chicken-shit coins to pay him. He fished a key out from under the counter, slammed it down. Have a nice night, he said, heading back to John Wayne versus the Japs.

The motel was a two-storey prefab arranged round a car park. I drove in, swerving to avoid a couple of speeding pick-ups racing out, and found my room on the ground floor near the end of the block nearest the interstate. I lugged my bag inside and looked around.

Everything in the room was *thin*. The carpet was threadbare; the bed had one sheet on it and one blanket no thicker than the sheet; the only furniture was a metal-legged kitchen chair and a television; the curtains were gauzy and orange, and the courtyard security lights glared through them. Worst of all, the walls and the door were like matchwood. From the room next door came television noises, a man talking in a low, urgent voice and a woman protesting shrilly; I couldn't tell if the argument was on the telly or actually going on in there. From outside came the roar of a car over-revving, somebody laughing, a snatch of deafening heavy rock; the sounds echoed around the court, booming and screeching.

I unpacked my bag and took my toothbrush through to the shower room. There was a strange smell in there, a burnt, meaty smell, as if somebody had been barbecuing road kills in the sink. The towel was made of a thin, bandage-like material that seemed to have been treated with some kind of water-repellent that made it quite impossible to dry my dripping hands after I'd washed them.

Back in the bedroom, I lay across the bed and tried to write a few notes on the day's drive. I found myself scribbling derogatory things about towns I hadn't even stopped in. How could I possibly say that Paris was an ugly, depressing place when all I'd done was drive on a loop road through its industrial outskirts? Terrible. But if I didn't write that then what the hell could I write about it?

> Dear Reader, As I was unable to settle in Paris, Texas, and live there for a couple of years—getting to know its quiet backstreets, its hidden charms, its friendly inhabitants, its cultural highspots, its lively nightlife—I feel I have no right to say anything about it whatsoever. Goodnight.

Jesus, I was getting myself in knots. It was hard to concentrate, there was that much noise going on. Outside tyres were skirling, engines throbbing, brakes screeching. Upstairs somebody was pacing the floor in cowboy boots. Doors were banging, hard enough to make the walls shake. The argument in the next room reached a crescendo; then there was a sudden silence, a slammed door, and almost immediately a gurgling roar: the pick-up parked next to my car speeding off.

I thought I heard the woman next door crying, but I might've been wrong; it might've been the telly.

I gave up on writing and picked up the phone. I called the free number on my credit card to try and find out why I hadn't been allowed to draw a measly twenty-six dollars. The line clicked and fizzed, then contact was made. I gave all the details and asked if there was some problem with my account.

No, said the voice.

So why was I not allowed twenty-six dollars on it?

I have no record of such a transaction being denied, she said.

But it was only ten minutes ago.

Ah . . . We did have a call from a River Oaks outlet in, eh, Wichita Fall. In TX. But that was a request for $20,358. And that's above your credit limit.

Too right!

So that was that. I lay back on the bed, wondering if the fat clerk had made a mistake, if his fingers had been too thick or something to hit the right keys, or if he'd deliberately tried to charge me 783 times the proper rate for the room. The worrying thing was, he could have charged seven or even eighty-three times the proper amount, and I'd probably never have known. Until I tried to buy some fuel or food next day and found myself busted: washed up in Wichita Falls.

I looked at my watch. Only nine o'clock. I switched on the telly. *Are You Being Served?* Jesus Christ. I switched it off again and rummaged in my bag. Mixed in with the clothes was my Walkman and a couple of cassettes. I stuck the headphones on and listened to the blood thudding in my lugs for half a minute till I found the tape I wanted: the Falls's finest, the Miller Brothers Orchestra.

First up was 'Marcheta', a Spanish-tinged love song set to a wonderful swaying swingbeat, with *mariachi* horns backing the singer and breaking out in brassy solos between verses. Next came 'Miller's Boogie', a driving twelve-bar instrumental, with a riff-based arrangement featuring sophisticated sax and piano interplay. Count Basie might have come up with something very similar and seen that it was good. Were the Miller Brothers influenced by Basie? I could guess so—after all, what swinging band of the Forties or Fifties wasn't?—but in truth I just don't know. In fact, I don't know much about them at all, despite the fact that, in 1955, *Cashbox* magazine rated them the third most successful western group in the United States. I know that the core of the band really was a bunch of brothers, but that their name was not Miller, but Gibbs. I know they started up shortly after the war and disbanded in the mid-Sixties. (But even this last statement is muddied by the fact that the band didn't actually split up as such. They just sold their name—to a fiddler called Bobby Rhodes from San Jon, New Mexico. I have no idea what he did with it.) I know that they owned a nightclub called the M. B. Corral, and played there regularly, as well as broadcasting six days a week in classic Texas-territory band style. When they were away on tour, other big-name acts would be booked in to play their nightclub; from this grew a booking agency, Sam Gibbs's Orchestra Service, and, ultimately, Sam's managership of Bob Wills and his Texas Playboys.

Bob Wills was the reason I'd come to Texas. About ten years ago, in an Edinburgh junk shop, I came across a record by him and his strangely named band. In fact, it was the daftness of the

*The Miller Brothers, 1959*                         COUNTRY MUSIC FOUNDATION INC

name that prompted me to buy the record. When I got home to my hi-fi, I found that the Playboys didn't make daft music, but the most exciting, eclectic, joyful stuff I'd ever heard. It was called western swing: a mix of jazz, blues, fiddle breakdowns, big-band dance music, Mexican *mariachi* and *conjunto* . . . you name it. I swiftly developed a strong interest in Wills's music; it had great songs and tunes, a swinging beat, wild and brilliant jazz solos from a collection of terrific musicians, and a crazy guy yelping and laughing and hollering over the top of the music—the great Bob himself! Interest led to passion, passion to obsession. And obsession led me to drive around Texas for a month trying to track down places and people associated with Bob Wills and the other western-swing greats I'd come to love.

Like the Miller Brothers, who recorded a handful of great swinging songs for Delta Records in 1947 and then went on to back vocalist Tommy Duncan in the studio after he left the Texas Playboys. In the late Fifties they laid down about fifty songs for 4-Star Records, though I've never heard any of them. My favourite of the early sessions is 'Shanty Town', a jazzed-up version of the old Tin Pan Alley hit, 'A Shanty in Old Shanty

Town'. Its hep lyrics had gained a whole new depth since I'd been wrestling with the band's home town, and I decided I should try and get them all down on paper. I got my notebook and pen, and played the song over and over on the Walkman.

*It's only a shanty on a little plot of ground*
*With the green grass growing all around, all around*
Something *old roofs are bending way down*
*On most of the shacks they are touching the ground*

*Just a little old shack and it's built way back*
*About twenty-five feet from the railroad track*
Something something *and my old black flivver*
*I'll head right back to the Mississippi River*

*If I were as sassy as Haile Selassie*
*And I were a king, it wouldn't mean a thing*
*But the boots in the hall read the writing on the wall*
*Now it don't mean a thing, not a doggone thing*

*There's a queen waiting there in a rocking chair*
*Just blowing her top on gators beer*
*Looking all around and trucking on down*
*Now I gotta get back to my shanty town*

Even through the music, noises kept seeping in from outside, and the state I was in they were making me nervous. I kept thinking I heard thumping on the door, or somebody scratching at the window. But when I whipped the headphones off there was nothing there. Well, there was plenty there, but it was nothing personal.

I switched off the light and lay back, trying to recall images from the Miller Brothers' final grab at glory—and their only appearance on film. It is 1972, and the band has been resurrected to play for a dance in a high-school gym. The movie is Robert Altman's *The Last Picture Show*.

# Dis Ja Liebe Spim

Driving south through Fort Stockton I stopped to take a photo of Paisano Pete, the world's largest roadrunner, a twenty-foot statue frozen in mid-scoot on a traffic island at a busy intersection. If I'd been mayor of the next town I'd have set up a thirty-foot Wile E. Coyote immediately, and given the Fort Stockton folk a real lesson in stupid tourist attractions.

At the Hill o' Beans restaurant, I ate green chilli *relanos* with a fried egg on top, then used the payphone to call ahead. To cold call ahead. To cold call one of the genuine legends of western swing, Adolph Hofner, and be greeted, not with the hesitation or reluctance I'd expected, but genuine enthusiasm and an invitation, in a strong Bela Lugosi accent, to visit and talk as soon as I arrived in San Antonio.

That could be tomorrow, if I make good time, I said.

That's fine, said Adolph. Come quick! I'm getting older every day: don't know how long I'll last!

Adolph Hofner was born in 1916, first recorded in October 1936 and was leading a band that gigged regularly well into the Nineties. In terms of sheer longevity, he has outdistanced them all, even Bob Wills. But it's not for the sixty-year career that he's so notable; it's for the unique sound he produced both on stage and on record. For Adolph was born in Moulton, one of Texas's many Czech communities; he had Czech as his first language and recorded dozens of Czech songs—'Dis Ja Liebe Spim', 'Strashidlo', 'Star Kovarna'—alongside the more standard western-swing fare of blues, fiddle tunes, rags and pop.

Western swing has always defined itself not on the basis of any spurious notions of musical purity, but rather on its all-inclusiveness, its willingness to accept anything and everything that its many practitioners wanted to throw into the melting pot. As long as the pot was heated to hottering, and people could two-step, it didn't matter whether you were singing in English, Spanish or Czech.

Hofner's popularity spanned across Texas into California, but was greatest in the south-eastern part of the Lone Star State

139

where many communities of Bohemian and Moravian immigrants
and closely related German ones are located. As well as the songs
actually sung in Czech, his band (they had various names: the
Texans, the San Antonians, the Pearl Wranglers—after their
sponsors, Pearl Beer) had a wide repertoire of waltzes and polkas
that appealed to the tastes of first- or second-generation settlers
from Middle Europe. Ironically, though, Adolph's greatest hit
came in 1941 with a traditional fiddle melody, 'Cotton Eyed Joe'.
This is a tune still played by just about every band south of the
Mason–Dixon Line, and quite a few north of it.

I'd been told that Adolph—now in his eightieth year—had
been ill recently and rarely performed in public, so it was unlikely
I'd get to see him on the bandstand. But to visit him at home
would still be a thrill.

I drove east—through Sheffield, Ozona, Sonora, Junction—
singing along to a tape of Adolph's greatest records, crooning and
yelping my way clean across the south Texas desert.

# Born to lose

The Gunter Hotel in San Antonio had a bakery in its lobby. I
bought a cinnamon croissant and two espressos for breakfast and
carried them up to my room. Sitting on the edge of the king-size
bed, I spread wide my street map of the city and traced out the
best route to Adolph Hofner's house. Then I phoned to fix exactly
when I should come round.

Hello. Is that Adolph?

Yeah. Hi. Who's this?

My name's McLean. We talked yesterday, remember . . .

Eh . . .

You said I could come round and talk—about your music.
I'm a big fan, you know.

Hey, you're the guy from Scotland!

That's me!

I got you. I got you.

Great! So, I was wondering: could I come round this
morning? Does that suit?

Oh dear me.

Well, this afternoon then?

Oh. Oh dear.

Well, any time. You name it, Adolph, and I'll come round. I've been waiting ten years to come to Texas, so a few more hours won't hurt.

There was a silence.

Are you OK? I said eventually.

Yes, yes, it's just—I'm sorry.

Why's that?

I said we could visit today, didn't I?

Yup. But I mean, tomorrow would be OK too, I suppose. I could stay another night.

Where are you?

The Gunter Hotel.

The Gunter? Very nice! I used to broadcast a radio show from there, back in the Forties I guess. Go to the first floor and look in the ballroom there. The Crystal Ballroom, that's where we used to do our shows.

I've got a tape of a great wee radio show from the Fifties on CD. It sounds like real fun, everybody goofing about. But the music's great too! That's what I wanted to talk to you about, really. Was that enjoyment real, or was the whole thing just a job for you? Were the live dances the same mix of stuff as that radio show? The same fun? How consciously did you set out to produce a new sound by adding Bohemian flavours to the western-swing hotpot? Or was it not a conscious choice at all, but just what audiences demanded? Did you see the other big bands—like Bob Wills's or Hank Thompson's—as rivals, or as friends and inspirations? What do you listen to now for pleasure? Still Milton Brown and Bing Crosby? How about the Mexican influence? For your '41 sessions in Dallas, did you copy 'Jessie Polka' from the Orquesta del Norte's 'Jesusita en Chihuahua' or from Cliff Bruner's version 'Jessie'? Or somewhere else completely? And when I say copy, I don't mean that in a bad way, I just mean . . . eh . . .

Hey, I know what you mean. He chuckled. That's a whole pile of questions you have there, and I sure would like to answer them.

Great!

But I don't think I can right now.

Oh yeah, you can't really talk over the phone. Like I said, I'll come round. Any time.

The thing is, I'm going away for the weekend.

That's OK. This is only Tuesday.

It's a long weekend.

Eh . . . how long?

It lasts seven days.

And when does it start?

In about ten minutes. I'm just waiting for my daughter to come round, then we're heading for the hills in the RV. When I talked with you yesterday, I clean forgot about the trip. Sorry.

Oh, I said. That's a . . . that's a shame.

There was a pause.

Could you come next week? Adolph said.

I'm sorry, I said. I can't. I've got to be up in Turkey this weekend, in the panhandle, for the Bob Wills memorial.

Too bad. Well . . .

Listen, I said. How about your brother Bash? Is he going off to the hills with you?

Bash? No, no.

Ah-ha! Maybe I could meet him instead. Do you think he'd mind?

The thing is, Bash is pretty sick—he's just had both his legs cut off.

An accident?

No, an operation.

Terrible. Will he be able to play again?

It's going to be hard playing lap steel with no legs. (Was that meant to be a joke? To be on the safe side, I didn't laugh.)

Anyway, Adolph went on. I don't think he's well enough to talk yet. In a couple of months maybe . . .

There were noises in the background at his end. I heard a female voice in the distance and Adolph shouting—in an even denser accent than the one he'd been talking to me in—that he was just coming.

That's Darlene, he said. I've got to go. Well, it's been real nice visiting with you. I sure do appreciate your interest. Any time you want to talk, just give me a call . . .

Closely linked with Adolph Hofner, and a Texas musical legend in his own right, was Floyd Tillman, who now lived near Marble Falls, out in the Hill Country. Born in 1914, he had started his professional career in 1933, playing take-off guitar with the Hofner brothers at their regular gig in Gus's Palm Gardens, San Antonio. He must've been hot even then, because the brothers took a twenty-five per cent cut in their dollar-a-night pay in order to hire him. By 1936, Floyd was one of the first generation of electric guitarists, exploring the possibilities of the instrument in Houston's Blue Ridge Playboys a good two years before Eddie

143

Durham—widely acknowledged as the pioneer of electric guitar—first recorded the instrument with the Kansas City Five.

The Playboys were a seminal group, featuring among others Moon Mullican on piano, Leon 'Pappy' Selph on fiddle and Ted Daffan on steel—all considerable musicians. Daffan went on to write such classic coronachs to love and loss as 'Worried Mind' (a hit for Bob Wills), 'Born To Lose' (one of the most recorded songs of all time) and 'Truck Drivers' Blues' (the first ever trucking song, from 1939—it's white-line fever all the way from there to 'Teddy Bear'). Tillman was a distinctive, drawling vocalist, as well as a fine guitarist, but he too made his biggest mark as a songwriter, penning dozens of hits, both for himself and many other artists at the honky-tonk end of country: 'They Took the Stars Out of Heaven', 'I Love You So Much It Hurts', 'Slippin' Around'. This last song provoked great controversy when it hit the charts in 1949, for its explicit depiction of adultery. It's not a celebration of slippin' and sleepin' around, you understand—the singer appears to be in a state of torment—but apparently the moral watchdogs of the music biz thought that even the mention of such behaviour was a bad thing. Nevertheless, he became established as a writer of laconic yet powerful songs that were covered by many major stars: Gene Autry and Bing Crosby both had a hit with 'It Makes No Difference Now', for instance, though the best version was recorded by Cliff Bruner's Texas Wanderers.

Since the early Fifties, Tillman had recorded only rarely and performed live even less, preferring to stay out of the limelight and live off the royalties of his old hits while trying to write new ones. A noble ambition. I'd never met anyone who'd met him, but I'd heard third-hand that he had a great fund of stories about his long career. I especially wanted to hear about his Houston years, the late Thirties and early Forties, when western swing got electrified, got laid-back, and started to mutate into honky-tonk—and he was right at the forefront of all the developments. I dialled his number. Fifteen rings.

Hello? It was a woman's voice.

Is this the Tillman household?

Who wants to know?

I explained who I was and why I wanted to talk to Mr

Tillman. She seemed extremely suspicious of my motives, but eventually, reluctantly, she said I might visit with her husband for a minute or two. She put the phone down. Floyd, Floyd! I heard her shouting. There's a man from Scotland wants to talk to you. There was thumping and muttering, then a new voice—a slow distinctive drawl—said: Hello, this is Floyd Tillman.

Hello, I said. It's great to talk to you.

Pardon? said Floyd.

I'm a great fan of your music.

What's that?

I love your music: 'This Cold War With You', 'Drivin' Nails In My Coffin', 'Why Do I Drink?' . . .

I wrote all of them, you know.

Eh, yes. I'm a fan, Mr Tillman. I'm especially interested in your days in Houston with the Blue Ridge Playboys—you made some great records then.

Pardon?

'Swing Baby Swing' from 1936—that's a great track.

What's that?

I said 'Swing Baby Swing'—you recorded it with Pappy Selph in 1936—it's great!

Oh no, I fluffed it.

Do you think?

Pardon?

I cleared my throat, made the effort to speak more slowly. I still think it's good, I said. At that time Bob Wills was still playing New Orleans two-beat stuff—I love that too—but you were already tuned in to what was coming next, the honky-tonk style.

I'm getting a bit deaf, said Floyd. You'll have to speak a bit slower.

Sorry, I said. OK. I cleared my throat again. I was hoping we could meet. I'm writing a book, you see, *Lone Star Swing* . . .

What's that?

*Lone Star Swing.*

*Lone Star Swig*—is it about beer?

No, no—*Swing*. It's about music. And you're a really important figure, if you don't mind me saying so. I'd really like to meet and talk to you about the way things were back then.

145

When's that?

Well, back in the late Thirties and early Forties, the golden age . . .

No, when do you want to meet?

Oh. Well. I'm in San Antonio right now.

Not where, when?

When, when. Right. Well, it'd take me a couple of hours to drive up to Marble Falls, I suppose, so . . .

You mean you're in Texas now? I thought you were calling from Scotland.

No, I come from Scotland, but I'm here travelling about, talking to folk: Roy Lee Brown, Cliff Kendrick, Adolph Hofner. I'm going up to Turkey . . .

Listen, he said. If you're planning to talk to all those people you've got a real busy schedule. You don't want to talk to me.

I do, I do!

Anyway, it's a real small house we have here. You don't want to see it.

You're right, I don't care about the house. It's you I want to . . .

A lot of people think, just because you've had a few hit records you live in a big old mansion with a swimming pool shaped like a guitar. No, sir, not me. It's just a small little house, that's all. Nothing special.

I'd just like to talk.

Pardon?

I'd like to TALK TO YOU.

It's not even real tidy right now. We've been doing some work, see, and it's a little mussed up.

There was a shriek in the background. Excuse me . . . Tillman covered the mouthpiece with his hand and spoke to his wife for a couple of minutes. Then he talked to me again. Well, sorry, it's not mussed up, it's clean as a pin. But it's just not convenient for you to come out here today: the house is too small.

I rolled my eyes to the Gunter's ceiling. That's too bad, I said. It would've been great to meet you. Maybe I could talk to you a little now though?

What's that?

Can we TALK NOW?

Now? Well, yeah, sure. But hold on, Frances is saying . . . get your address in Scotland. Yeah, we never thought nobody listened to us over there! Ha! You sure don't buy our records!

Well, I do, but . . .

Anyways, we'll take your address and . . . maybe write or something.

Great, I said. Ready? It's twenty-seven Alfred Street, Stromness, Orkney. OK so far?

I think I should get a pen, said Floyd. I'll never remember all that. Frances, a pen! And paper! He put his hand over the mouthpiece again, words were exchanged, then he was back. OK, he said, all set. Shoot.

Twenty-seven Alfred Street.

Frances, thirty-seven Alpha Street.

No, twenty-seven.

I'm sorry. Frances, score that out. Twenty-seven Alpha Street.

Actually, that's Alfred Street.

I'm sorry?

Alfred, as in King Alfred.

Ah, King Alfred Street.

Got it.

Thirty-seven King Alfred Street.

No, twenty-seven.

Twenty-seven?

Eh . . .

Yep, sorry, we did have that, I just read it wrong.

No problem.

So, twenty-seven King Alfred Street . . .

But cross out the King.

You want me to cross out the King?

Yeah, there's no King.

You said King! You got your own address wrong! Haw haw!

Twenty-seven King Alfred Street, said Frances in the background.

Is that it?

That'll do, I said. Great. Now. Next is the town: Stromness.

A pause.
Pardon? said Floyd.
Strom-ness.
Another pause.
Could you spell that?
S.
F?
No, S.
Pardon?
S for 'Slippin' Around', I said.
Oh, S!
Yes, S. Then T.
P.
No, T.
T?
Yeah, T. T.
Two Ts?
Sorry. I sighed. Just the one.
OK.
OK. R.
R?
Yes!
S?
No, just—yes, yes—you got the R?
I got it. Sure. So. F-T-R . . .
No, S-T-R.
I'm sorry, S-T-R.
That's it.
That's the name?
No, that's it so far, there's more. There's O, then M.
O, then N.
M.
M. OK.
Then N.
Another M.
No, N this time.
N. You getting all this, Frances?
Background mumbles.

What's that? More mumbles. She says could you hurry up. We've got to go shopping.

Yeah, sorry, I said. I've not much time left on my phonecard either. So where was I?

Where was he, Frances? What? You were at the second M.

The second? Oh yeah. Well put an N next.

Another one? Three of them in a row?

No, *N*, N for . . . for . . . Numptie.

Numptie, OK.

Then E.

E.

Then S.

N-S.

No, E-S.

So two Es then S?

No, sorry, one E then two Ss.

Two Ss. Then?

That's the end!

Another N?

No! END!

Oh, right. That's the end, Frances.

Hold on, I said, there's the next line of the . . .

The robot operator's voice fizzed in my lug. You have thirty seconds left on this charge card, it said.

I sighed.

What's next? said Frances, in the background.

What's next? said Floyd.

Just put Scotland after that.

Scotland? That it?

Listen, I said. About your music . . .

There was a click, and the line went dead; my phonecard was done.                                              □

# New Titles from *Yale*

## Shakespeare's Edward III

*An Early Play Restored to the Canon*
**Edited by Eric Sams**

*Edward III* was first published, anonymously, in 1596. Though most scholars now discern Shakespeare's hand in the play, academic uncertainties over "collaboration", "plagiarism" and "memorial reconstruction" have kept it firmly outside the canon. Now Eric Sams offers a fastidious new edition that authenticates *Edward III* as Shakespeare's own, unaided work. Exactly four hundred years after its first appearance, *Edward III* is at last restored to the stage, the literary world and to Shakespeare himself.

**256pp. £18.50**

## Voyage to the Sonorous Land, or The Art of Asking *and* The Hour We Knew Nothing of Each Other

**Peter Handke**
**Translated by Gitta Honegger**

In these two plays, here translated into English for the first time, Peter Handke, renowned Austrian writer and author of screenplays (*Wings of Desire*) and prose works (most recently, *His Jukebox and Other Essays on Storytelling*), inquires into the boundaries and life-affirming qualities of language. At a time when language no longer seems to serve the purpose of a genuine human community, Handke asks, is such a community possible?

**160pp. £18.50**

## The Sound of Virtue

*Philip Sidney's Arcadia and Elizabethan Politics*
**Blair Worden**

Written around 1580, Philip Sidney's Arcadia is a romance, a love story, a work of wit and enchantment set in an ancient and mythical land. But, as Blair Worden now startlingly reveals, it is also a grave and urgent commentary on Elizabethan politics. Under the protective guise of pastoral fiction, Sidney produced a searching reflection on the misgovernment of Elizabeth I and on the failings of monarchy as a system of government.

**432pp. Illus. £40.00**

## Visionary Fictions

*Apocalyptic Writing from Blake to the Modern Age*
**Edward J. Ahearn**

"Visionary" writers, says Edward Ahearn in this original book, seek a personal way to explode the normal experience of the "real", using prophetic visions, fantastic tales, insane rantings, surrealist dreams and drug- or sex-induced dislocations in their work. Beginning with the appearance of visionary writing in the work of William Blake, Ahearn traces the development of the form in texts by widely scattered authors writing in French, German and English. He includes Novalis, Lautréamont, Breton, William Burroughs and contemporary feminists Monique Wittig and Jamaica Kincaid, among others. Quoting liberally from these authors, Ahearn summarises the works and places them in context.

**224pp. Illus. £20.00**

## Yale University Press • 23 Pond Street • London NW3 2PN

# GRANTA

# PHILIP HENSHER
# TRYING TO UNDERSTAND

Philip Hensher

I was avoiding Quentin.
I could see him approaching across the crowded concourse at Heathrow. An unmistakable figure, tall and loping, he moved between the late holidaymakers and the unserious flocks of unicoloured stewardesses like the only man in the terminal with somewhere to go and something to do on this October Sunday evening. He hadn't seen me yet; it was important that he should not see me just yet.

'There's Quentin,' Richard said.

'I know,' I said from behind my newspaper. 'Don't let him see you.'

'Why not?' Richard said. 'Shouldn't you be telling them all where to go?'

'Yes,' I said. 'Quentin's going to have to get himself through security. I can't speak to him until then.'

Richard—whose first select committee trip this was, who, there to explain any technical points about financial policy and the European Union, could not reasonably be expected to take an interest in the finer points of select committee protocol—gave me an old-fashioned look. I didn't care. I was the one who had to get half a dozen Members of Parliament halfway across Europe and back without losing any.

'And, if it can be helped,' I said, 'it would be better if you didn't, either.'

'Too late,' he said. 'He's spotted us. Here he comes.'

I liked Quentin Davies; I liked his humourless intelligence, so redundant and so excessive in an MP. His braininess was, twice weekly, on display in Committee Room Six of the House of Commons, where it was also largely ignored because nobody else could ever quite tell whether he was raising matters of huge, though complex, import to British economic policy, or matters of complete abstruseness which shouldn't be delaying the committee's deliberations. It was common for Quentin to inflict his ruthless line of questioning about methods of measuring inflation, or whatever, on some hapless, clueless witness while the rest of the committee flung themselves around in merriment.

I liked him; I thought his forensic manner and periodic intense social charm went together in an unexpected, pleasing way.

152

But I suppose it could be understood why such an intelligent man had never made it to being a minister. He reminded me of a comment from Burton's diary on the famously dull seventeenth-century Member Serjeant Wylde that 'in the time of the Long Parliament, he was always left speaking, and members went to dinner, and found him speaking when they came in again'. His suspect origins as a Foreign Office official and his failure to understand that people in error do not always need to have their errors explained to them would have seen to that. And right now, unknown to him, he was being a complete pain in the arse.

About a week before the Treasury Committee left on its visit to Rome and Prague, I had a phone call from a contact in the House of Commons travel office. She confirmed all the flight details; I sat, ticking things off on the latest agenda for the visit.

'And Mr Davies is coming back from Rome two days early,' she finished.

'Not as far as I know,' I said.

'Hold on,' she said. 'Yes, that's right. We had a request to change his ticket, bring it forward by thirty-six hours.'

'Not from this office,' I said. 'Are you sure?'

'Yes,' she said. 'I've issued the ticket. Haven't you had it?'

'No,' I said. 'Did you issue it to us?'

'Oh, now I remember,' she said. 'He came in himself last week and asked us to change it and send it directly to him, so we did.'

'Well,' I said, 'you should have checked with us first. That's infuriating.'

'I can't very well refuse a Member,' she said.

'Well, you should have let us know,' I said.

'I am letting you know,' she said. 'I'm letting you know now.'

The problem was that it just couldn't be done. The rule was absolutely inflexible; I knew it perfectly well, but I looked it up anyway in the Red Book, the little manual of guidance for clerks of select committees. I knew the rule because I'd helped to write the Red Book a year or two before. I wished now I'd had the sense to cross out the sentence, but there it was. *Members must take part in the whole of a select committee visit.* No skiving off early; no late arrivals; no bunking off to visit mistresses in Trastevere (a possibility greatly enhanced when another rule, *Members' wives may not take part in a select committee visit,* had been introduced in the late 1980s). So Quentin's unilateral decision to come home two days early presented a problem.

'Oh, I don't know,' my boss said, panicking in her turquoise suit. 'What do you think we should do?'

'Tell him he can't do it,' I said.

'I suppose so. But we don't know about it.'

'Yes we do,' I said. 'The travel office told us.'

'But he hasn't told us.'

'Does that make a difference?'

My boss looked at me, helplessly. It could not be suggested that, in possession of this information, we should tell Quentin he couldn't go, or couldn't come home early. On the other hand, we could always forget anyone had told us anything. Which, in the House of Commons, was always a useful standby.

'The problem will be,' my boss went on, 'if he tells you that he's going to come home early before you set off. Then we couldn't really say that we didn't know. But if he doesn't tell you until you're on the plane, let's say, then it would really be too late to do anything about it, if anyone asks about it later.'

'So we cover our backs by pretending not to know anything about it until we've set off,' I said. 'Just one thing. At what point could the trip be reasonably said to have started? How early?'

'Well, when the plane's taken off?'

'Check-in?'

'Security check?'

'Done,' I said, the haggling between propriety and face-saving complete.

Unfortunately, all that, which seemed to solve the problem, would be quite technical if Quentin managed to ruin the whole plot by telling me he was coming home early before he had even checked in. Then, I couldn't see how I could avoid telling him that he couldn't go, and therefore precipitating a huge row. If, having been told this, however, I didn't tell him in return that he couldn't go, there would be a huge row with the big boys in the department when we got back to England. Neither seemed an appealing prospect. I had decided to avoid Quentin altogether until he had passed through the airport security, and then to acquiesce in the bad news, knowing that I could do nothing about it. It was this perfect scenario that was in danger of being wrecked by the fast-approaching figure coming through the check-in queues towards us.

'Just going off for a second,' I said to Richard, getting up and walking briskly in the direction of the Sock Shop.

As I stood among the racks of undesirable hosiery, I could see Quentin talking to Richard. He looked round and seemed to glimpse me. I smartly turned, left the Sock Shop and ducked into the next franchise, which happened to be a chemist; in case this was not enough, I walked to the back of the shop, left by a side entrance and went into the public lavatories.

Five minutes later, I emerged cautiously. There was no sign of Quentin; Richard was still there.

'Where's he gone?' I said.

'I told him you'd gone to change some money upstairs,' Richard said. 'What's all this about?'

'Nothing,' I said. 'Just can't face talking to Quentin right now. Let's go through.'

He looked at me sceptically. 'He said he's leaving early. I said he ought to mention it to you.'

'You didn't tell me that,' I said. 'Let's go through.'

'They haven't all arrived,' Richard said.

'They're all grown-up,' I said. 'They've been to an airport before. Let's go.'

Standing in the queue for the X-ray machine, I made myself only dimly aware of Quentin, ten places behind, gesturing in my direction; it wasn't until we were on the other side of the barrier, standing by the duty-free, that he caught up.

'Hello there,' he said. 'I don't know whether Richard said anything, but I'm going to have to leave early.'

'How early?' I asked, as if it made any difference.

'A day and a half,' he said.

'Well, it isn't really permitted,' I said. 'But I can't see what I can do to stop you. Of course, I can't rearrange your ticket, much as I would like to be helpful.'

Quentin beamed; it occurred to me that he, too, must have put himself in the position of wilful ignorance, of not making the formal gesture of being informed of what, from his days in the

Foreign Office, he already knew to be the rules. Now we had
completed the contract, and I wondered whether he, in fact,
understood the contractual agreement as well as I did; that he
would tell me when I could no longer prevent a breach of the
rules; that I would allow myself to be told when the rules could no
longer be invoked.

To sceptical strangers, it was not always easy to justify my job
or the purpose of the committee I worked for. I'd done the
job for about five years by this time. The House of Commons has
never been much good at looking at the detail of government, and
in particular it's always been hopeless at looking at how the
Government spends its money. In 1979, in the first flush of
excitement at being new in government, the Conservatives set up a
system of committees, one to each government department, of
Members of Parliament. The idea was that each committee would
look at its department's spending, administration and so on in
detail and at length; it would act as a collection of well-informed
Members, ferreting out and disseminating vital information to the
press and public and to the House at large.

That was the idea, and had it worked efficiently, the
Government might have had cause to regret it about once a week
ever since. Of course, though, it didn't work. My purpose was
general bag-carrier; I thought up questions which they might like to
ask, I sucked up the expertise of people who, unlike me, knew
something about the subject, and, in the end, I wrote reports which
sank like stones. As far as I could see the whole thing was driven by
personal obsessions, a strong desire to get into the headlines and the
desire to irritate or mollify the whips, according to taste. It was a
moderately entertaining job, and I had been far less jaded during
my first months in it. My partner was pleased I'd got a job at all.
But the idea of what a select committee might achieve baffled him.

'The thing I don't really understand is, what do select
committees do, exactly?' He looked genuinely puzzled. But they
didn't have select committees where he came from, and, though
I'd only been working for one for a month, I would do my best to
justify it.

'They scrutinize things.'

'What things?'

'Government spending, government administration, that sort of thing.'

'What do they do when they've scrutinized it?'

'Issue a report saying what the Government ought to do.'

'And then the Government has to do it?'

'No, but it probably would carry out the recommendations if that was what it was going to do anyway.'

'Can the committee insist that anything be done?'

'No.'

'Can it tell the Government to pass laws?'

'No.'

'So it just tells the Government to do things, and if the Government was going to do them anyway, then it does, and if it wasn't, then it doesn't?'

'That's about it.'

'So what's the point?'

'Well, it represents informed opinion in the House of Commons.'

'Meaning?'

'Gives people a chance to talk indefinitely about a pet obsession or two.'

'I see.'

I hadn't quite managed to put the point across, I felt, but he now seemed to have grasped what the committee did to his own satisfaction, if not mine.

In black moments, I thought that the real reason select committees were so popular was that they could say anything they liked in the sure knowledge that anything too mad would not be followed by any consequences, since the Government would simply ignore it. Fantasy government, I sometimes thought, watching a lot of unpromotable people saying 'If I ruled the world, if I ruled the world,' over and over again. Sugaring this futile situation were a number of small treats afforded committees by the Government. Select committees could talk to anyone they wanted, and some committees behaved like small boys, summoning all the glamorous and famous criminals and celebrities they'd always wanted to meet and chat with. They could guarantee a certain minimum audience for their opinions, and, if the opinions were really ridiculous, or strongly opposed to the opinions of the Government, a good audience. Among the journalists who have to cover the work of Parliament, at least.

Not the smallest of the treats afforded committees by the Government was the ability to travel abroad. If they could justify a trip, a committee could go wherever it liked. The carnival air which always surrounded a visit produced its own recklessness, and frequently a series of fairly predictable disasters and embarrassments. Select committee trips abroad—in fact, any kind of trip abroad—produced two kinds of record among the parliamentary officials, the Clerks of the House of Commons, of which I was one. In the first place, there was the series of official records of what was done; where was visited; which eminences were seen; what expenditure was incurred. From the initial proposal, set down in two or three lines in the minutes of proceedings of the select committee—*That the Committee do visit Martinique in February*—to the ambitious agenda, drawn up, fought over in committee—'I think we ought to have lunch with the governor of the Bundesbank'—and finally reduced to more modest ambitions, sketchy notes made in overheated or overcooled rooms, over lunch, over dinner, over, sometimes, even breakfast, and finally to the polished and absurd summary of what the committee discovered on its jaunt to be printed in some unreadable report, the committee presented the acceptable face of its travels, in writing, to the outside world.

But, apart from the written record, the clerks preserved an oral tradition of catastrophic or spectacular happenings when a select committee travelled abroad, or when they, free for a week of their hopeless charges, travelled to Strasbourg to work, for vast and tax-free sums of money, for the Council of Europe. This wasn't supposed to happen; part of the ethos of the clerks' department is that, however badly members of the department behave when overseas, something informally referred to as 'Strasbourg rules' meant that it wouldn't be chattered about when back in Westminster, and, however fascinating the story of some Member or clerk insulting a distinguished foreigner, getting drunk or arrested, might be, it was not quite the thing to discuss it.

Like all such rules, it never worked, as I discovered when, on a trip to Paris, I picked up a boy in a bar in front of ten distinguished colleagues. Somehow, though such disgraceful misbehaviour shouldn't be gossiped about back home, each individual story was just too good not to retell in some form, and, like most of my more drunken colleagues, I found the narrative—in my case, how I ended up at eight in the morning at Charles de Gaulle airport, without the faintest idea of how to get back to my hotel, back into a pinstripe suit, and back down to the Western European Union to start minuting its proceedings by nine—passing effortlessly into the rich oral tradition of anecdotes about Members and clerks. Any clerk coming back from abroad would be expected, over the cold meat pie and tinned potato salad in the Tea Room, to produce some spectacularly salacious story about his own, his colleagues', his Members', or the whole committee's misbehaviour. It was part of the genuine, as opposed to the written ethos of the Palace of Westminster; the only unbroken rule was that none of these stories ever be written down.

Instead they formed a tapestry of anecdotes, told and retold, looked forward to eagerly: the epic of the Member who lost his shoes in Paris, or the Member who was robbed by a prostitute in Rio, or the simple, colossal tale of a committee's two-week trip to the Bahamas to look at nothing in particular, at the delicious height of the season.

I'd added in a small way to this tradition with my only previous select committee visit. The committee, concerned with energy policy, could only rarely justify a trip abroad, and then, only to very unexciting places. The Agriculture Committee could always go to a Caribbean island to watch bananas grow; the Trade and Industry Committee could go, if they had insufficient shame, to Brazil on no better excuse than that they wanted to think about British trade with Brazil. But, whatever the Energy Committee decided they wanted to look at, they always seemed to end up going to Düsseldorf to look at some power station, and it was hard to see how it could be managed otherwise.

The trip I went on was a characteristically unexciting one—burning rubbish to generate electricity in Germany, Sweden and Denmark over five days—but was greatly enlivened by a fine source of tea-room anecdotes, the late Geoffrey Dickens. Dickens was a Member much admired by those who didn't know him, who found him an amusing fellow, full of blunt speaking and common sense. Most people who had to work with him thought him a buffoon who never said a sensible thing in his life. Most of those anecdotes came from him directly—I forget the number of times I heard, in the five days, the story of how he came to write 'To my dear horse face' on a photograph of himself and send it to a lady admirer. The only intelligent or perceptive thing I ever heard him say was his account of how he canvassed any given old-people's home in the minimum time possible.

'The first old dear who says to me, "I bet you can't guess how old I am," I always say, "You must be at least a hundred and fifty, you old witch." The thing is, any old lady who says that to a visitor, she's always going to be the one they all hate. So you lose one vote but you gain twenty-five. Saves a lot of time.'

Dickens was regarded, in the House and by the clerks, with opinions ranging from amused tolerance to unamused contempt. How he ended up on a committee passing judgement on energy policy was a matter of some mystery. His most impressive moment came in Germany. There is a certain sort of Englishman to whom Germany is not the country of Goethe, Beethoven and Caspar David Friedrich; nor indeed, a country which perpetrated and was torn apart by a series of terrible historical tragedies, the Kaiser Friedrich, the Great War, the Holocaust and partition; but to whom it means only a joke about goose-stepping, don't-mention-the-war and a nation whose defining characteristic is its lack of a sense of humour. Dickens was very strongly one of these people; it had been apparent, even from his conversation on the aeroplane, that he would need to be watched carefully and, if necessary, apologized for.

A day or so passed without incident. On the second day, the committee visited a major power plant where some innovation or other was being put into effect. It had been impressed on us by the embassy that the man whom we were to meet was exceptionally distinguished, of almost inconceivable importance and greatness; that we had been very lucky to find such a terrific fellow free to talk to us at the very short notice of six weeks. The terrific fellow came in and smiled benignly while one of his underlings explained, with the help of a yard-high perspex model, the workings of the power plant. By the side of the plant, there had been placed, by the thoughtful model-makers, two human figures in orange plastic, one waving at the other, to show the scale of the thing. The explanation went off without hitch; the committee, after lunch, was rather subdued, and the meeting dissolved into coffee with Dickens looking rather pensive. I felt an unexplained danger signal when I saw him heading straight for the grand panjandrum, and followed in his wake.

'You know what I thought,' I heard him saying, 'when I first saw your model and those two little chaps. You know, I thought, that one on the left, with his arm raised, I thought, is he supposed to be giving the Hitler salute or something?'

I shut my eyes. The man from the British embassy, standing alongside, seemed momentarily beyond speech or, indeed, movement. The big cheese, however, did not seem to be responding at all. It was clear that he didn't think this comment was intended to be funny; nor did he think it intended to be offensive; he simply failed to classify the comment as any kind of meaningful utterance at all, and continued to talk about new methods, ever more unlikely sources of generating electricity. Dickens, however, was delighted with his own brilliant sally, and three days later, in Denmark, was retailing to some very bewildered Danish civil servants the story of how he had successfully punctured the pomposity of the German nation with a well-directed shaft of wit.

None of that was going to happen on this trip. The Treasury Committee, my current posting, was famously argumentative, famously unsparing of the sensitivities of whomever its members might meet, but they weren't buffoons on that scale. On one famous occasion, a few years before, on a visit abroad, they had unforgivably engaged a tremendously grand ambassador in a row while they were eating his food, and still more unforgivably, insulted him by telling him that he was a traitor to British interests. The accusation of unpatriotism was bad enough, but might have been worn, if not exactly laughed off, if it hadn't been made in front of a lot of foreigners. The ensuing row was of such proportions—

telegrams to London, a formal meeting of the committee at eight in the morning in the chairman's hotel bedroom to discuss the bounder's misbehaviour—that it was judged wise not to return to the country in question until the ambassador had retired.

That was always a danger. It was still more acute, on this occasion, because the subject the committee was supposed to be inquiring into in the course of the trip was European monetary union, a subject guaranteed to produce twelve separate opinions among any given eleven Members, and guaranteed to produce ample opportunities to insult anyone the committee happened to come across. I had decided that none of this was my problem, and that I shouldn't worry about it.

The chairman of the committee, always addressed as Chairman, and known behind his back as Tom, was invariably excellent at this sort of thing. He had been catapulted into a position of slight prominence by an unnecessary amount of horse-trading between those who couldn't stick the idea of Nigel Forman, a nice man crippled by his constant loyalty to the Government, as chairman and those who seriously thought Quentin might have ambitions to do it. Tom, an improbably rakish fellow who wore red socks and tasselled loafers with his sharp suit, said little, intervened little, and, I sometimes wondered, might very well have regretted letting himself in for two or three meetings a week of desperate dullness. Sparked off by a sudden sense of the absurdity of the whole thing, he was capable of strange spasms of laddishness which ensured fondness in anyone who worked for him; for the rest of the time, he seemed, like Nancy Mitford's Lady Alconleigh, to float in a cloud of boredom, only occasionally to descend with a comment of such sharpness as to make one wonder whether, after all, he wasn't the most attentive of the lot.

'Why are we going to Prague?' he said to me, once we were ensconced on the plane.

It was difficult to answer. Sitting around a couple of months earlier, the six staff of the committee had been thinking about where the Members might like to go to find out about the prospects for monetary union. Of course, the real answer to the question was that the committee shouldn't go anywhere; the

Members should stay at home and read some of the papers they had been sent. But that wouldn't do as a proposal, since that was what they were supposed to do anyway.

The lunchtime suggestion we came up with in a spirit of mild hilarity was that the committee should go on a grand tour of Europe, going not only to countries that were in the European Union, but to countries which weren't but perhaps hoped to be, and countries which might one day start to think about it. The lunacy of this idea, which culminated in a proposal for a tour of Europe and beyond—'Have we thought about Morocco?' someone said, only partly joking—unsurprisingly went down pretty well with the committee, but less well with the authority which granted money for select committees to travel. By the end of the bidding process, we were left with a trip to find out about the prospects for monetary union which would go to only Italy, Austria and the Czech Republic. Austria inconveniently had a general election, meaning that everyone we might see would be campaigning or unavailable.

The ambassador to the Czech Republic was civil, driving into Prague, but slightly bemused concerning the motives for a select committee to visit a country in these circumstances, where membership of the European Union was only a distant possibility. The Czechs, on the other hand, were delighted to see us.

'You are the functionary?' a man said at the tiny Parliament, a glittery toytown affair of brightly dressed guards and Ruritanian riotousness, where we were having lunch with the Czech finance committee.

'I am,' I said.

'I too,' he said. 'Look, your chairman is making a speech.'

'I know,' I said across the table. Lunch was just beginning, and the formal exchange of greetings and thanks just under way. It didn't occur to the Czech clerk not to talk, nor to most of the Czech politicians, and the lunch got under way in a cheerfully unstructured manner. A beer-drinking hearty joined in.

'I speak little English,' he began. 'Why do we as Czechs wish to join the Union? I do not know.'

It went on, the lunch, moving from clear soup with slightly gritty dumplings, to an elaborate dish of chicken with half a tinned peach on top and a slice of processed cheese. The beer was good, though.

'Czechs are a very proud people,' someone else added. 'No Czech would join the Union to take money out of it. We would only join if we could add to it.'

'Well, why join at all?' I said. 'Why not aim to be a sort of island, making money out of your freedom of action, outside the Union? Do you suppose Brussels would have your best interests at heart?'

'No,' he agreed. 'There is something true there.'

'No,' someone else said. 'It's not true. Like everyone else, you talk as if we were you. You talk as if we were an island, like you. You must remember: we are not an island. The options which you see for you are not always there for us. You must try and understand, you English, the point of view of the rest of us, the point of view of anyone apart from you.'

I was aware, somehow, that I had said something tactless.

'Why do we want to join, in the end? It is for political reasons, for reasons of security. We live at the edge of Europe— or, you think we do. And our neighbours have not always been very nice. And we worry about that, and we want to know how we can bind ourselves in.'

'So, politics again,' I said. A kind of weariness came over me. I had a sense that nobody wanted monetary union because it would work; everybody who wanted it, wanted it because they thought it would save them from themselves, from their neighbours, from politics.

'This man,' the Czech clerk said cheerily, 'he has his own point of view.'

The Ambassador gave a dinner for us that evening. The Czechs invited were almost entirely people who had lived outside Czechoslovakia for years, in Canada or America, returning when communism fell and Slovakia was so conveniently offloaded, to the chagrin of some Slovaks. I couldn't work out, and couldn't think of a way to ask, whether they had been invited because they were important or because they all spoke good English.

'We privatized everything,' one said. 'We gave it all away. We could have made money, and we didn't. We wanted a real popular capitalism, but we knew no one could afford to buy shares. So we just gave shares away—the same number for everyone—in whatever utility people wanted. And then people were free to sell them, and make a little money immediately, or hang on, or start to deal in them. And people have.'

'But you must have lost a lot of money.'

'We did.'

'So why do it? You must be in need of a lot of capital.'

'The great problem for us is that no one has felt that the state has anything to do with them. People here always felt helpless, that the way things were run wasn't their business, and that they were at the mercy of some distant figure behind a desk.'

I found it hard to imagine. Prague was so small that the institutions seemed unthreatening. Government buildings went semi-guarded, and we wandered in and out, bumping by chance, or so it seemed, into unretinued Ministers. It was hard to connect this informal place with the city of ten years ago.

'The important thing was to try and use the sale of the utilities for social reasons. For cohesion. Look at it another way. We lost—or we spent—a lot of money. But if your Government could buy social cohesion, don't you think they would?'

'And it worked?'

'It's working.'

I looked at his bright face, his thrilled excitement at the possibility of success, and I, too, felt excited at the idea of something which, this time, might just not go wrong.

The first morning in Rome went entirely to plan, both the official one and the one I had quietly envisaged, of blunt statement of opposition, or, at worst, a row. The issue at question, for the whole trip, was simply this. The Maastricht Treaty had set up four conditions, to do with the state of each national economy, which had to be met before a currency could be admitted to monetary union. If you applied these four conditions strictly—and the Treaty seemed to say that they should be applied strictly— then hardly any country now in the European Union would qualify. Britain probably, but it didn't look as if Britain would want to. France maybe (but we wouldn't talk about that). Germany pretty definitely. But, when it came to the crunch, without anything resembling a partner in monetary union, why on earth would Germany want to abandon the most successful currency in history, and one which was such a focus of national pride that patriotic discontent could easily arise?

Italy, by the rules of the Treaty, didn't seem to stand a chance. Their economy was shot to pieces, the much-vaunted *sorpasso*, or overtaking, of the 1980s seeming rather a quaint delusion by now. The situation shouldn't really have been complicated by the fact that they all wanted desperately to be in monetary union, almost as a demonstration of national pride; it shouldn't have had anything to do with the fact that almost every Italian one ever meets says, with varying degrees of honesty, that they'd rather be ruled from Brussels than from Rome. And yet it was. Talking to the Treasury, talking to the Bank, the constant sense was 'Brussels can't leave us out'. The committee was growing a little testy.

'What about the conditions in the Treaty?'

'The conditions in the Treaty are flexible.'

'They certainly are not flexible. That's the point of them.'

'We think they may prove to be flexible.'

'How flexible do they have to be?'

The man—tremendously elegant in an English blazer and cream trousers, oddly dressed, to an English eye, for the occupant of such a crucial position—smiled, faintly.

'We think they may be flexible enough. We think that if matters turn out to be improving, even if they have not reached the limits specified, the Treaty may allow us to join in any case. Imagine it from our point of view. It is an absurd situation; if the criteria are interpreted strictly, we may not join even though we wish to; you may join, but you do not wish to. In these circumstances, the idea of monetary union can only be described as a confrontation between the unwilling and the unable. That is why we think the criteria will, in the end, be interpreted flexibly.'

'But, but, but, but, but—'

One of the Members was almost purple, flicking through the Treaty in search of the crucial passage. Richard leapt up and showed him the passage. I wrote down *a confrontation between the unwilling and the unable.* A Jesuitical debate followed about the meaning of the crucial sentence, to nobody's satisfaction. Smoothly, the Italian moved on to something we were, officially, not interested in: political union. Things quickly degenerated.

'You see, our political institutions are very young. They are not ancient as yours are.'

'How old do political institutions need to be?' someone asked.

'And we need to learn,' he went on, 'from other traditions, intellectually richer institutions.'

This seemed to stun the committee into silence. I'd heard it all before, from my partner, an Italian economist. Like most Italians, he thought that the Roman political culture was corrupt and beyond reform; he viewed the prospect of abdicating responsibility for ruling a nation and handing it over to what seemed to me the barely less corrupt and patronage-ruled culture of Brussels and the European Commission with less alarm than the prospect of carrying on being ruled as before. Vain to suggest that people have a responsibility for themselves; vain to suggest that the reason given by Italians for giving up power, that it's the least bad option, is not and never will be a good enough reason. Perhaps it's all a matter of perspective. From Rome, Brussels looks like a model of good government; from London, it looks very much like a place where patronage is institutionalized. It reminded me that in India I had once seen an advertisement for a television, or perhaps a car, with the slogan 'Italian technology!' It would not work in Britain; but no Indian, looking at it from quite a different angle, could see why it struck an Englishman as being so funny.

Lunch was rather chilly—both metaphorically and literally, since the opening speeches of welcome and the responding speech went on so long that the waiters started openly rolling their eyes in despair at the plates of delicious pasta congealing in front of the gentlemen. Even Tom's graceful speech couldn't rescue the occasion, and the committee went off for its afternoon sight-seeing, clutching the favoured gift of Italian institutions, boastful expensive catalogues of the art collections of the Bank of Italy or whatever, with a vague sense of unfulfilment. I went for a walk with Richard, the committee's professional economist, in the general direction of the Piazza del Popolo.

'What are we doing here?' I said.
'You tell me,' he said. 'Fact-finding mission, I thought.'
He twinkled, slightly.
'Well, quite,' I said. 'I mean, what have we found out this morning?'
'I thought you were taking notes.'
'Yes, and I've got pages and pages about Quentin's opinion, and Sedgemore's opinion of Quentin's opinion, and some question that Malcolm asked which I hadn't heard before, and about three lines of that cynical twat's views on Europe, which mainly weren't what we're here to find out anyway. And we got a good phrase for the report about the unwilling confronting the unable.'
'Only three more days,' he said.

The Ambassador's house in Rome is a villa of astonishing beauty—it's one of those Roman buildings which have belonged to an almost comic sequence of grand names out of history. Pauline Borghese, Goebbels, those sort of people. There aren't many houses in Rome with an aqueduct in the garden.

The small talk at the dinner that night lasted about a minute. With the arrival of the *sformato*, Quentin, speaking horribly wonderful Italian, began straight away on the Maastricht criteria, to the slight puzzlement of his neighbour, the wife of a smart industrialist. The harangue continued; the table fell silent. Finally, one of the Italians from the Bank responded, and something resembling a conversation began. I concentrated on the meal, and acknowledged to myself that the dinner was going to follow the usual course of these things: delicious food, slightly too cold; not enough wine; and, worst of all, condemned to silence. It was a relief, as ever, when it came to an end.

As quickly as I could, I went out to the cloakroom to fetch some fags; a flunky would be out with all this on a silver tray in a moment, but I wanted an excuse not to listen to anyone setting out their opinion for a moment or two. Outside there were some men, having a sit-down and a smoke; they made a desultory gesture of standing up and putting their cigarettes out; I made an equally desultory gesture in their direction. There was no one minding the coats, but, as I began to rifle through them in search of mine, a boy about my age appeared. It wasn't clear whether he was the coat attendant or a waiter or, indeed, another guest.

'There it is,' he said, plucking out my coat. I was impressed.

'How did you know which mine was?' I asked.

'I noticed it when you were getting out of the car. Beautiful coat.'

I was delighted with this, getting praise for clothes from an Italian. I'd bought the coat a few weeks before in a fit of extravagance, and it was, it's true, a striking object; furred like a teddy bear, falling in three sheets of cloth unpunctuated by trappings plainly to the ground, it was almost the thing I loved best in the world just at that moment.

'Do you like my suit?' I said, daringly, knowing that Italian men talk readily about clothes and mean almost nothing by it. It was a green tweedy suit bought, like most of my suits, in a fit of irony, a sense of how comic the idea was that I might work for the House of Commons, and possess a tweed suit for Fridays, and which, finally, reached a charred and sorry end when, three months after this conversation, I leaned back on a window sill at a drunken dinner in Soho and learned, not from the sensation of heat, but from the smell of burning tweed, so like the smell of burning hair and flesh, that what I was leaning back on was a lit candle.

'Very nice,' he said, fingering my lapel. 'You speak Italian well. Unusual for an Englishman.'

'Not well,' I said truthfully, and observing how strikingly his very blue eyes set off his very black hair. 'I had an Italian lover.'

It was late; my spirits were high. I used a word the Italians would probably not use. In conversation, they said boy, or they said friend, and they did not fear to be misunderstood. I feared being misunderstood; I feared the slightest possibility that this boy would think I had used an inappropriate word, which meant only that I had a friend who was Italian. So I used a poetic, an over-emphatic word, wanting only to be understood.

He carried on looking at me in an amused way.

'*Anch'io*,' he said. 'Me too.'

'I'm staying in the Belvedere,' I said. 'We are here for three days.'

'*Lo so*,' he said. 'I know.'

169

And, not wanting, especially, to know what he had meant by *anch'io*, not wanting to know what he meant by *lo so*, I turned my back on him and went back into the ambassador's party, forgetting my cigarettes.

'So, what have we learned?' Tom said suddenly the day after next, on the plane.

I answered him, somehow, but I didn't know. What did we learn? I think we just went abroad, and told people what our views were, and were not listened to; and then they told us their views, and they were not listened to in return.

'What do you think we learned?'

'I think,' Tom said, 'we achieved a frank and informative exchange of views.'

He twinkled, very slightly. The oldest and absurdest of the dreams of the Enlightenment died here, for me; the dream that one could understand the world by seeing it. We had seen the world, or a fragment of it, and we had only seen ourselves in it, only talked about our own views. We were both unwilling and unable; unwilling to listen to other people, unable to do so. But I could not see why we had travelled at all to fail to understand strangers; we could have stayed at home, and failed to understand each other there.

A few months later I lost my job for writing indiscreetly about it. It was very sudden, although I had been expecting something rather like it for a while, and I had no chance to say goodbye to the other clerks, let alone the committee. I'd never got round to writing up the trip to Prague and Rome, though the blank notebooks were not so much a reproach to my lack of industry as an honest account of my inability to understand what people meant when they talked to us.

A friend on the committee gave me a little summary of what happened when the subject of the abrupt loss of a clerk came up.

'I hope he wasn't dismissed for his sexual proclivities,' Quentin remarked.

'No,' Richard said. 'He was sacked because he was in blatant breach of his contract.'

There was a little muttering. Nigel Forman seemed to rouse himself from a conversation with his neighbour.

'Sorry,' he said. 'What did he look like? Did he have a beard?'

Someone set Forman right, and the discussion came to an end. Well, what then? What do they do? I suppose they begin to divide up the questions someone else has written for them, and begin to make a few notes about points they would like to make to whomever that day's witness is. I suppose they tease each other, and then ask a member of the committee staff to go out and fetch the witness; I imagine the witness, a grey-faced, bald man, perhaps nodding and smiling at the committee as he sits and begins to sort his papers, hoping that this time it won't be too bad, knowing that it probably will be. I imagine the committee facing the man's bravado, seeing how little it means; I imagine the chairman nodding at the shorthand writers in a sign that they should start, and, as they begin to write, as ever, the committee begins to talk. □

**JEANETTE WINTERSON** | Gut Symmetries

**NIGEL WILLIAMS** | Stalking Fiona

**BLAKE MORRISON** | As If

**CHRISTOPHER JOHN FARLEY** | My Favourite War

## THE NEW GRANTA BOOKS • JANUARY 1997

**IAIN SINCLAIR** | Lights Out for the Territory

**LEILA BERG** | Flickerbook

**KIRSTY GUNN** | The Keepsake

**STEVEN HEIGHTON** | Flights Paths of the Emperor

**GRANTA BOOKS** 2/3 HANOVER YARD, NOEL ROAD, LONDON N1 8BE TEL: 0171 704 9776 FAX: 0171 354 3469

# JEREMY SEABROOK
## AN ENGLISH EXILE

It is a familiar fate that those who start life as radicals mellow with the years and finally become reconciled to the limits of the socially, as well as existentially, possible. A less common, more unsettling experience is to have begun life as a passive dissenter, only to be awakened and radicalized by time.

I was never a revolutionary, not really a Marxist. I couldn't reconcile the sulphurous prose of Marx with my gran, with her sweet smile, sitting under the plum tree in the little back garden of her terraced house, or with the laconic placidity of our boot-factory uncles, who carried with them a feral tang of leather and a pessimistic conviction that all politicians pissed in the same pot, and what couldn't be cured must be endured.

And I have never known want, thanks to the fierce protectiveness of a mother determined to preserve me and my brother from the poverty she had known as a child. If I ever expressed sympathy with the poor, she was swift to deny my right to any such social concern with the question: what do you know about it? I had evidently taken the wrong lesson from her admonitions: she wanted not that her poverty should be remembered, but that it should be forgotten.

We had the best of everything. Nothing was too good for me and my twin brother; even in wartime she miraculously produced the most nourishing food, as well as the consolations of otherwise unavailable sweets and exotic fruit, the best-quality clothes, including liberty bodices, the function of which was the opposite of their name but which protected our chests against winter fogs.

She anticipated the welfare state. Orange juice, rose-hip syrup and cod-liver oil left a chain of circular stains on the shiny 1930s sideboard. Later, I was clapped in irons as a cure for knock knees; I blinked at the world through National Health spectacles within a month of the system being in place. If those who foresaw the bankruptcy of Britain in consequence of the working class having its teeth ripped out in order to enjoy the amenity of dentures, and ruining its eyesight for the sake of glasses, had come to our house, their worst fears might have been confirmed.

Only later, we discovered to what degree this obsessive concern for our well-being was expiatory: my brother and I were illegitimate, not the offspring of our putative though syphilitic father, and when we were six weeks old, our mother decided to throw us from the bedroom window and then to follow us. Something restrained her; and we came to understand that her failure to carry out this plan was the greatest of her many sacrifices.

Other factors muted the radicalism I might have inherited from the dour, suspicious, levelling, shoemaking culture of our home place; the most significant of which was being clever. I spoke without the regional accent, in an idiom I had learned from the wireless. This seemed to suggest that my destiny lay elsewhere. Everything I did was achieved without effort. Schoolteachers took anticipatory credit for the spectacular career that they predicted for me. I came to accept the homage of adults as my due. If any of my relatives suggested what I most needed was a damn good hiding, I remained in ignorance of it.

The heights I was forecast to climb were, of course, social. At our grammar school we were told repeatedly that we were the top, not one per cent, but 0.1 per cent of the population. We passed exams as naturally as others passed water. Our future was without horizons. Nothing is more effective than flattery for blunting the spirit of self-criticism. We were shown an appealing version of aristocratic distinction and we could not wait to sample its *douceurs*. Poverty is quickly forgotten; even more swiftly, we accepted privilege as our due.

When I left Northampton for Cambridge in the late Fifties, it was a ceremonial departure. Even though the distance was less than fifty miles, socially it was incalculable. The old lady next door gave me a silver clock from part of the decaying wedding trousseau that had been locked in the little back bedroom since her fiancé was killed on the Somme. I felt like an ambassador to a foreign court. I was, my mother said, fulfilling all her dreams. I had been so penetrated by them, they eclipsed any I might have conceived of my own.

We, who had gone to grammar school and Cambridge, knew we were no longer destined to a life of labour and penury and we made the perhaps understandable error of believing that this had something to do with our merit. We did not see it as part of the epic social and economic changes of the time. No child of mine is going to work in a boot factory, our mothers had heroically cried, as though they had failed to observe that the factories were all closing down anyway.

We felt that we alone were moving on, leaving behind a working class that was static, our 'background', something enduring against which we would define and distinguish ourselves. We didn't know that the working class was itself on the threshold of the great transformation that was to change it beyond recognition. My twin, who did not accompany me on the heroic academic voyage, remained at home, cycling to work every day of his five-year apprenticeship in a joinery and accumulating a rancour he did not then express. This separation was to presage a more enduring break in later life. We haven't spoken for twenty years.

At that time, it seemed safe to leave the working class. It was in the secure protective hands of the welfare state. Disadvantage, exploitation, all social wrongs seemed to be simply residual problems. If poverty remained, this was because we had not yet created quite enough wealth to bring all our fellow citizens within the embrace of the better life to which we had been summoned. They would doubtless get there in due course. It was as easy and natural as our own progression had been. Unemployment was negligible. The health of the people had improved dramatically. It seemed the time of blood and ashes in Europe was past.

Because it was economic breakdown that had created the horrors of Nazism and the Holocaust, it seemed reasonable to conclude that economic growth was the surest guarantor of social peace and harmony in the world. Because poverty and insecurity had been the source of such violence, it was assumed that the protection of our liberties could best be safeguarded by affluence. Welfare would do what was no longer required of flesh and blood, and furnish people with security in sickness and old age. The dissolution of the 'classic' working class had begun.

But it was not to be so simple, either socially or personally. It wasn't just a question of discovering in Cambridge that I was less clever than I had thought, although that was also an element in my reassessment of the breathless upward trajectory. The discovery of forms of privilege to which I could certainly not aspire was equally significant. My own ascension had still not wafted me into the empyrean inhabited by those I was now meeting. Much work remained to be done for anyone who wished to complete the epic ascent of the north face of the social glacier. I observed others from the grammar schools lose their rough edges, assume the authoritative air of those born to rule and merge with them, on their terms, in their environment. The pose of working-class *enfant terrible* was transformed into a posture of deference. Northern accents yielded to a mimicry of the cadences of command.

I couldn't do this; a social and psychological defect, no doubt. But other things held me back. One was the tradition of the surly shoemaking culture from which I came: a refusal to do what was expected, a perverse delight in being awkward, a compulsion to dissent from prevailing orthodoxies—I had not been able to shed these cultural encumbrances.

There was something else too: the discovery, and the fearful shame, that I was queer (not in the sense in which the word has subsequently been reclaimed, but as stigma) inhibited me from imitating my betters and being absorbed into their society; although I well understood this attribute was, in theory, scarcely an obstacle. I had heard, repeatedly, from homophobic uncles, that homosexuality was a disease of the upper classes, and it seemed I had contracted it by my arrival in the ranks of modest privilege. God alone knew what perversions I might discover within myself if I were to become more closely associated with them.

At university I studied hard. I would force myself to be the last to turn out the light in the rooms overlooking the ugly nineteenth-century courtyard, even though by four in the morning the work I was doing was neither effective nor useful. But I knew all Dante's arguments about the proper areas of adjudication between pope and emperor and I could write beautiful essays on the polyvalent symbolism of the celestial rose in *Paradiso*.

We were perhaps the last generation to have been brought up in the aristocratic conviction that a liberal education prepared people for any career they might choose, and indeed, many of my contemporaries, wise in a way that I was not to these soon-to-be cancelled possibilities, finished up as cabinet ministers, industrialists, senior civil servants, artists, ambassadors and academics.

But at the end of it, I had acquired no skills, no accomplishments. I felt socially and intellectually inferior and as despondent then as I had been elated when I first went to Cambridge. I returned to Northampton on the bus and found work in the public library for seven pounds and ten shillings a week. My mother thought it was a damn poor do after everything she had done to make my life easier. If I was to do something so conspicuously below the ambition she had entertained for me, she wished I had gone to some more distant place, where the vanity of her efforts on my behalf would have been less obvious.

It was discovered I had a shadow on my lung. This gave me new hope: I could die before early promise was completely dashed. I sat under the pear tree in our back garden and cried over Werther and the sepulchral poets and watched the sun sink into the chimney pots of the houses behind. After three months I got better. Only I felt worse. My mother said, 'What are you going to do? I only want you to be happy.' She didn't see that like her, my supreme gift was for being miserable; I could not understand why she did not wish to let me practise it. All I heard were the words 'I want'.

At that time, to be possessed of a degree was still rather rare in our town, and it was considered a qualification for everything, including teaching. I taught at what later came to be called a 'sink school' on the poorest estate in town. The staff, hearing that I had graduated from Cambridge, posed the obvious question: what's wrong with him? They assumed either that I had had a nervous breakdown, or that I was a pederast, because they could conceive of no other reason for so strange a choice of career.

I made the error of thinking I would let the pupils know that I was their friend, that we had a shared background, that I knew all about the boot-and-shoe culture from which they too had emerged. But like me, they had already been fashioned by other values than those of a decaying industrial base; we appeared, puzzlingly, to have gone in different directions. They were not moved by the expression of my solidarity with them, but would have preferred me to beat them about the head, to lay the slipper with greater vigour across their arses, as was then the custom.

The other teachers, morose and cynical, came and peered into the room where I was teaching, from which an astonishing volume of noise was issuing. Haughtily, but uneasily, I explained this was

179

a drama lesson; most of it involved an improvised version of the previous night's television film, screened at what I then primly calculated to have been long past their bedtime, and in which Nazi and other atrocities played a disturbingly over-prominent role.

At that time, I spent much of my free time visiting the towns and cities of the Midlands which were then being redeveloped: the chocolate-painted terraces and courts that were falling to the bulldozers, mildewed tenements where the sun had not penetrated for a hundred years, the sour smell of earth turned for the first time since the 1850s fascinated me. I was drawn to the people whose skills, evolved in response to what had given the towns and cities their function, were now being extinguished. I watched as the old were carried out of blood-red buildings to newly built streets in the sky, where many of them soon died.

I returned always to the slum-clearance areas, the lodging houses where men had slept leaning on a string which was cut in the morning, so that they fell in a heap on the bare floorboards; the cinemas where the man from the board of guardians had sat in the balcony observing those who were squandering their parish money in the stalls; the ornate bathhouses erected by those who believed cleanliness would do more to elevate the poor than any increase in wages; and pubs that had echoed with the choruses of swaying women as they sang 'Vilia' or 'The Last Rose of Summer'.

Teaching taught me that schools were not places where the really significant social forces were at work. You had to go deeper. In any case, I could not hold the attention of the children long enough to impart to them my message of warm, sympathetic kinship. In other words, in the shaming indictment of the headmaster, I had no discipline.

All the teachers had repeated daily, 'It all starts in the home.' Clearly, the homes were the places to get into. Everybody knew that the only people who had more or less unimpeded passage into the private lives of the people were social workers. My next step was clearly indicated.

I went to the London School of Economics for a diploma in social administration, which also, at that time of easy access to the professions, conferred upon me the right to call myself a social worker. The Sixties were, for me, not a time of experimental hedonism with prohibited (or even permitted) substances, not trips to Kathmandu in an old bus or ambulance, not even Italian suits and doing the twist, but about commitment to the caring society—an extension to the house of welfare that Labour had built in the 1940s. This was the tangible pledge of the better world that was coming into existence, manifested in the great expansion of higher education, welfare services and social housing.

Such problems as persisted in the almost universal improvement would be attended to on an individual basis. This way, all the talents of the people would soon be released, and those incapable of taking part would be affectionately tended and borne up by the armies of professionals recruited by the caring society for its casualties.

At that time when you told people you were a social worker, they didn't spit in your face. They looked at you meltingly and said they thought it was wonderful, more of a calling than a job; wished they could do it but thought they were a bit too sensitive, and didn't you sometimes get depressed? Although not repudiating the heroic role others were prepared to concede, I would always say, deprecatingly, well somebody has to do it.

I found employment as a social worker in a school for educationally subnormal children, as they were then designated: this was already a euphemism for the earlier stigma, mental defective. Such categories have now been abolished, leaving them to fend for themselves, as the failures and no-hopers of society, filling the prisons or lighting fires on pieces of waste ground in the city centres.

It soon appeared that the high status then attributed to social workers was exaggerated. It proved impossible to live up to, and their future fall and scapegoating as causes of the persistent, no longer residual, social evils they were called upon to alleviate, would not be long delayed.

And social work was disturbing. In the high-rise, low-esteem renewal of the East End, it was the women who came to us crying 'I can't cope'—women, confronted by violence, hunger, insecurity and loss, who had for generations demonstrated their supreme capacity for coping. How many men, having ascertained that their child was backward, educationally handicapped, a wally, had blamed their wives and pissed off? It was clear by then that the social dislocations were not simply the problems of a few unhappy individuals beached by a rising tide of affluence, but were actually built into the structures of the consumer society—the very agent of our deliverance and hope.

It was a time of rapid change. Towns and cities were being transformed for the sake of mobility, both social and spatial. In Northampton, the house where I grew up was under threat from an expressway that would scythe through the town and demolish a thousand houses. The violence of 'development' was for the first time striking against the satisfied desires of the people.

A powerful community resistance to the demolitions had grown, even in Northampton, this passive, grudging, somnolent place. Their houses, people declared, were 'little palaces'; to own one was the achievement of a lifetime, an ambition consummated. They were, unknowingly, uttering the supreme blasphemy against the consumer society, namely that they were content with what they had.

In the years that followed I became, briefly, a Labour councillor, committed myself to gay liberation and helped to run a telephone advice service for people who were probably no more confused about their sexuality than I was. If I entertained fantasies of doing something prosaic and useful, like becoming a postman or working on a building site, I was not tempted to put them into practice. I became a writer because it seemed I'd used up all other options. My mother and her sisters had always displayed a somewhat exaggerated respect for writers; having been the victims of a largely thwarted education, they had been deeply influenced by the written word. In my mother's bookcase were all the romantic poets, George Eliot, Dickens, William Morris, Robert Blatchford, Shaw's *Intelligent Woman's Guides* to this and that. When she went into a nursing home at eighty-five, crippled by Parkinson's, she took her two favourite novels, *Bleak House* and *The Mill on the Floss*. These she left in a prominent place in the room so that the care assistants looked at her with wonder and respect; it was also a signal to them that they should not mess her about, infantilize her, or assume that she didn't know what was going on. It worked. She had, she always told us, revered her teachers—a response a million miles away from the indifference I felt to the functionaries who oversaw what passed for my education, and from the mild contempt I inspired in those who passed briefly under my tutelary care.

I had been contributing from the beginning to *New Society*, mostly versions of lectures I had given to the Workers' Educational Association, and another, even more exciting, form of labour opened up readily. I got commissions to write books, though there was no evidence that there was a market for them, as indeed, there rarely was.

I could not detach myself from what some saw as a morbid preoccupation with the disintegration of the old working class. I had always longed to escape from the regional sensibility of my own drab town, with its reserve, its undemonstrative pessimism, the self-righteous puritanism of the boot-and-shoe people, the censorious observation of neighbours and the rigid proprieties of a social life that was as structured and predictable as their work time; even their pleasures were punitive, playing darts, growing rhubarb on their allotments and dour philosophic discussions revolving around the conviction that life would get worse before it got better.

The staple occupation of our town, which was its reason for existence and its identity, disappeared. Shoes were no longer of good local leather but were increasingly throwaway plastic objects stamped with the place of origin: Italy, Portugal, later Brazil and Taiwan. The old shoemakers looked at them with disdain: was it for this that the factories were closing down, the red-brick workshops on the corner of almost every street being transformed into warehouses, shops, restaurants? They were particularly scornful of restaurants because they could not understand what was wrong with eating at home. My mother used to say that anyone out of doors after nine-thirty at night was either thieving or whore-hopping.

It was not easy to see the direction in which the changes were tending; we were still too close to the asperities and squalor of the early industrial era. And the material gains were highly visible. At the time, it did not occur to anyone that we might have been trading our liberties for the sake of material improvement; because material improvement was what people had most desperately needed, it seemed both churlish and insulting to ask on what terms this was being won. The assumption was that growing purchasing power was synonymous with growing freedom, and that it could go on for ever. Troubling possibilities that it might be otherwise did not disturb the serene consensus.

At that time, whenever anyone protested at the loss of neighbourhood, community and the social supports of kinship, he or she was derided as being in the grip of incurable nostalgia or mired in a hopeless romanticism about the joys of poverty. If you argued that there might be alternative routes out of poverty, other forms of wealth; if you said that there were other kinds of poverty than a measurable absence of cash; if you insisted that the voluntary poverty of some religious order was not joyless, you were likely to be dismissed as a crank. Significantly, in the Sixties, it was the Left that tolerated no dissent from the notion that more money was the principal object of all human endeavour.

Around 1970, I had co-written a television play based on a queer-bashing incident on Wimbledon Common. Granada TV expressed a keen interest, but there was a problem, which turned out to be ideological. The real-life victim of this assault died, and his attackers had come from the Roehampton Estate, showplace of working-class improvements, shining example of that better world in which we had housed our people. Would it not be more appropriate to set the play in the slums, rather than a place that had won prestigious awards for design? But this is where it happened, I said. That is not the point, they replied. We dutifully rewrote it, transposing the event into the backstreets of Birmingham, so as to free the Roehampton Estate from any taint of scandal. The play was, of course, never screened.

This kind of denial by the Left characterized the Sixties and Seventies. Around that time, I spoke to a Fabian Society meeting, where I mentioned the growing fear of crime on some of the new estates. This was vehemently denied by my audience, armed with the archaic perception that all you had to do to make people good was to alter their 'environment', which, at that time, still meant the construction of modern municipal housing, no matter how wanting in amenity, how skimpy, badly conceived and lacking in any consultation with the people compelled to make their home there.

That the economic goods came in necessary attendance with ugly and worsening social evils did not register on the instruments employed to measure economic development. It became increasingly exasperating to write about the relationship between these two areas of our common experience, and to be dismissed as 'wanting to go back to the past'.

It became harder to maintain faith in the revealed and progressive pathways out of the old evils of industrial society. Yet the doubts of many who had become teachers, social workers, crusading journalists, activists, were, to some extent, laid to rest by the not insignificant rewards for our work of improvement.

Was it illusory? Or was there an optimum moment when unemployment and poverty were at a minimum, when crime was still at a containable level, and family and neighbourhood were not in the state of advanced decay which we now see? Was there a point at which mitigable wrongs abated? Was there ever a balance between the freedom to make money and adequate provision for the poorest? And if there was, did we pass it, without perceiving it? And even if we had been aware, would it have been possible to institutionalize the moment, freeze it indefinitely; or would it have been swept away anyway, by the dynamic of a system become autonomous and unbiddable?

My departure from the working class now appears in a different light; it was merely one of many departures. Indeed, the discovery of an 'underclass' in the 1990s is like an exhumation of the remains of the working class, the skeleton left behind when all those who could leave have gone, abandoning those who might have been perceived as the undeserving and the helpless, but who were also sheltered within the old working class, enfolded by the values, the sometimes punishing charity and abrasive protectiveness of the majority. The poor and incompetent have not been held secure in a welfare net that replaced the embrace of living flesh and blood, but have been left to find their own salvation. In this sense, crime is indeed a consequence of the privatization of social hope, individual remedies against wrongs which are no longer collectively remediable.

By the mid-Seventies it seemed that as we ceased to be the makers of material things, the material world become the object of strange cults: a new caste of advertisers, sales people and publicists sang their hymns to material objects, artefacts and products that no longer spoke to us of the division of labour within Britain— shoes from Northampton, textiles from Lancashire, woollens from Yorkshire, pottery from Staffordshire, coal from the North and Wales, steel from Sheffield, ships from the Clyde, hosiery from Nottingham and Leicester, railways from York, engines from Coventry or Birmingham. Everything now came from afar, and could all the more readily become the focus of quasi-religious reverence. As the manufacturing districts vanished, shrines full of exotic merchandise were erected at their heart: the shopping centres, galleries and piazzas were consolations offered for our obliterated function and ruined sense of purpose.

At the same time, the streets where we lived were no longer full of neighbours, relatives, workmates, friends, but thugs, vandals, rapists, weirdos, alkies, druggies, nutcases, fiends, molesters, abusers, beasts, crooks, no-hopers, winos, thieves, muggers, villains, slags and bastards. The people we had called Auntie or Uncle were transformed, little by little, into strangers, and malevolent strangers at that. An extensive renaming of humanity took place. The lesson that people are not to be trusted, but that money and what it can buy will never fail you, tends to prise apart the most precious and tender of human bondings and associations, undermines ancient consolations of kindred and friendship. Is it by accident that we discover our aloneness in the healing presence of the inexhaustible plenitude of a buy-in culture?

The development of this dualistic culture—the perpetual improvement in material things and the growing moral decrepitude of humanity—has smothered the distinctive temper of our regions, obliterated our local culture, altered our sense of who we are. Cultural identity has been stripped away, so that we are pared down to the most irreducible characteristic of our being—black or white, young or old, female or male, gay or straight. We have been divested of everything else.

Market values, applied with relentless rigour to the outer circumstances of our lives, also invade and colonize the spaces within, so that even our most intimate relationships and profound involvements with others are now governed by emotional and psychic economics. We interrogate our human associations to discover whether or not they are profitable: what's in it for me? Will it pay dividends? What's the pay-off? What sort of emotional investment am I making? What return do I get? What's the bottom line? Is it worth while? I gave you everything, they say, the wounded rejects of consumed relationships, and what have I got out of it?

Those who have exultantly reaffirmed the imperatives of the market respond to their own creation with what it must be assumed is only feigned horror; for in the high morality of capitalism, good is having money and evil not having it. Those who have determined that all the multiple and diverse forms of wealth in the world should be melted down into a monoculture of money recoil from the consequences of an ideology they can no longer control.

During the Eighties, I wrote about unemployment and taught unemployed people in bleakly named unemployment centres. I listened incredulously to the thirty-eight-year-old who said 'I'm finished, I'm on the scrap heap.' I read the suicide note of the miner who apologized for the sense of futility that made him take his life. It was impossible not to hear the pain in the boastful machismo of the young, whose energies and abilities had been ignored, a generation with no contribution to make to the work of society. I had felt the sadness of the unemployed, the haunted faces wandering around the empty factory with its broken glass and mangled metal, willowherb growing on the spot where a workbench had been; but I did not think then that I would share their sense of brutal expulsion.

But now, like all those others evicted from a sense of function and purpose, I feel I have gone into exile, even though I have remained in the country where I was born.

The welfare state, the caring society, humanitarian values: all this represented only a rearranging of the decor of capitalism, a superficial and temporary strategy to conciliate a disaffected and potentially destructive working class. Those of us who had protested that the break-up of community, the fraying of the bonds of kinship, the weakening of social cohesion, were grievous

187

and irreparable losses, had been scorned as standing in the way of progress, of material improvement, of the well-being of the people.

Now the better tomorrow we were obstructing has arrived. In the graffiti on the walls is inscribed a culture of racism and hatred; the old, imprisoned on estates they call Sing-Sing or Alcatraz; the women who will not go out after dark for fear that the disordered sexual desire of strangers, kindled by anonymous, powerful others for profit, will work itself out upon them; the thwarted creativity of the young, hurling rocks and bottles half-filled with petrol across the streets at police shields in a choreography of destructiveness; the girls, some of them still children, displaying their legs in the glare of the sodium lights to kerb-crawlers who will pay them the cost of the next heroin fix. Those who complain of the mindless violence of this age might perhaps reflect on the other forms of mindlessness offered to the people: mindless work, mindless pleasure, mindless spending.

Was the making of useful and necessary things really more oppressive than the culture of guns, drugs, crime and fear which has replaced it? Or is this merely another stage on the sunny road to a golden future? Certainly, voices are no longer raised against its inevitable coming. And in the course of these benign changes, all those characteristics, the self-flattering myths with which Britain has consoled itself—our unique tolerance and good humour, our sympathy with the underdog, our fair-mindedness and sense of justice—have been violently disconfirmed. It is clear that we have become less tolerant, that we celebrate power and wealth with a fawning sycophancy that makes even archaic deference to birth and breeding appear modest and reasonable. Our love of fair play has turned into an admiration for nice work if you can get it. As for the underdogs, we regularly step over their bodies sprawled on the sidewalk. We are xenophobic, unjust and unkind; qualities no doubt appropriate in a people on whose behalf its leaders must now, and for the foreseeable future, manage economic and social decline.

If Britain is no longer Britain, then it is unreasonable to expect Northampton to be Northampton. Shoemaking, which employed a majority of the population half a century ago, is now a residual activity, and our town has become the kind of territory from which new products are test-launched into the inner spaces of consumer need, a suitable place for the sampling of opinions, those windblown ideas that lodge like thistledown in the minds of punters just long enough to be reproduced in surveys which prove that people obligingly reflect what the opinion-formers have already decided they will believe. The shoemakers of Northampton, like most workers of the early industrial era, wanted only security and sufficiency. These modest and readily attainable goals have been bypassed by the compulsion for *more*.

When I go back to Northampton now, if I search for traces of the culture that I could once not escape quickly enough, I am looking in the wrong place. The factories have been demolished or have fallen into ruin, and the fabric of the town is no longer half-town half-country, with its coaching inns and chapels, the green fields visible at the end of streets whose back gardens enclosed the plum trees and apple trees of ancient orchards. It is now the site of shopping precincts, motorways scribbled across fields of barley and buttercup meadows, and a metal sculpture dedicated to St Crispin, patron saint of shoemakers, who has also given his name to the extensive and busy psychiatric hospital on the edge of town.

The values borne by the shoemakers are not extinct. Their radical dissenting sensibility lives on within their scattered descendants—we who once could not wait to rid ourselves of their oppressive influence. Their world was narrow, but also deep. The clatter of boots on the pavement, the boneshaking bicycles, the ruby heart of allotment dahlias disgorging earwigs, the scuffed linoleum of their corridors and kitchens—the objects of our mockery did not touch the core of their defensive pride, their opposition to unfairness of all kinds, their contempt for snobbery and swank, their egalitarian humour and plain talk.

I am glad now that their influence was not so easily left behind. They have bequeathed us their sceptical, critical spirit, that flame of dissent which burns so low in these times of gaudy conformism; a dissent which is also more ancient and more rooted in our tradition than the noisy, showy culture of appearances, the doomed and alien cargo cult of consumerism to which the common wisdom has annulled all alternatives. □

## THE CURIOUS ENLIGHTENMENT OF PROFESSOR CARITAT
### STEVEN LUKES

'This book is a box of delights, often wonderfully funny and always deliciously clever, a contemporary political satire to set among the best.'
*New Statesman and Society*

'A delightfully edifying comedy.'
*Guardian*

PAPERBACK £9.00   1 85984 073 6

## LONDON REVIEW OF BOOKS
### AN ANTHOLOGY
*Foreword by* ALAN BENNETT

'The London Review of Books seems to me to be the liveliest, the most serious and also the most literary radical magazine we have.'
Alan Bennett

HARDBACK £40.00   1 85984 860 5
PAPERBACK £12.00   1 85984 121 X

## WALTER BENJAMIN A BIOGRAPHY
### MOMME BRODERSEN

'Momme Brodersen has produced a book which can be recommended for its vivid writing, pleasure in detail and wealth of knowledge.'
*Die Zeit*

HARDBACK £25.00 100 B/W PHOTOS   1 85984 967 9

V E R S O

GRANTA

# DONOVAN WYLIE
## OUT OF IT

Donovan Wylie

I started taking these photographs of Julie and her friends in 1994, after a colleague suggested I spend some time following a group of 'New Age Travellers'. They were then contentious and in the news; roaming bands of young people who were seen by their many critics and opponents as scruffy, noisy despoilers of rural England and the trespass laws.

I found a large site on a lay-by on a main road in Gloucestershire. About a hundred people were living there in old buses, trucks and caravans. The local council had provided water tanks and a couple of portable lavatories. Unreliable electricity came from temperamental generators. Stoves provided a little warmth. Food supplies were uncertain. These people were living a very minimal existence. They said that was what they wanted.

At first I befriended Julie, then in her late twenties, who had two sons, and then over several weeks got to know many of the rest. Every one of them had similar stories of pain and loss— broken families, parental neglect or abuse, failure at school, material disadvantage. This seemed to be the meeting place for some of Britain's most vulnerable young people. Their fragile personal histories rather than any philosophy seemed to explain why they had turned their backs on society, embraced each other, and collectively taken on so extreme an identity and way of life.

It seemed to work, then. There was a feeling of hope and signs of camaraderie and mutual affection. I remember Julie saying to me: 'Poverty? There's no poverty here. This is paradise.'

Two years passed. I next photographed Julie in London in 1996. New legislation had made rural sites more difficult to find. London offered a more permanent place to park which was also less conspicuously provocative—an abandoned bus station in the East End.

It was irredeemably sad. The group were much more dependent on drugs, begging and welfare payments. Vodka and heroin had invaded all their lives, and Julie had aged considerably. Her children had their heads shaved to prevent lice infestation. They could not read or write.

The sense of optimism and collective protection that I had caught in Gloucestershire had been brief. For this group, perhaps inevitably, it turned out to be a misplaced ideal. DONOVAN WYLIE

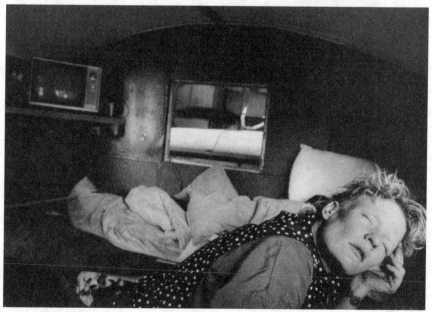

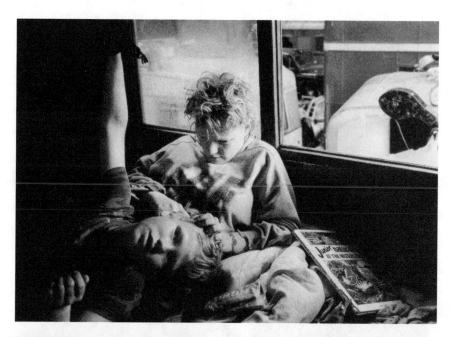

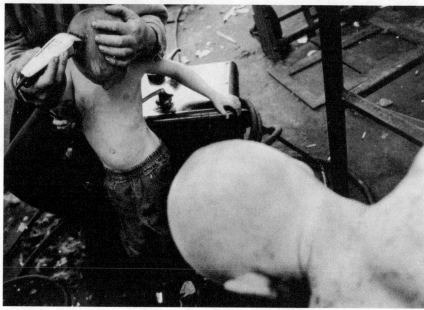

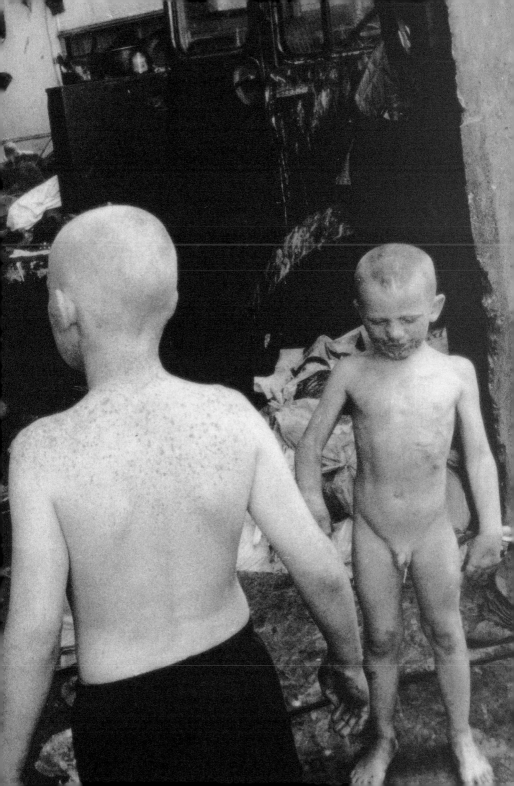

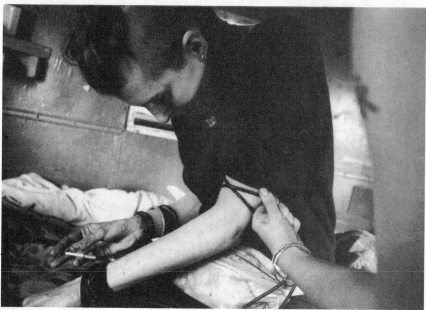

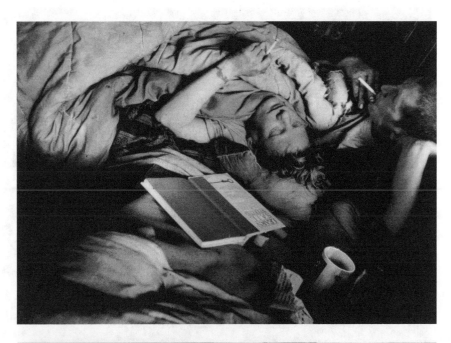

# William Maxwell
# SO LONG,
# SEE YOU TOMORROW

On a winter morning in the 1920s, a shot rings out on a
farm in rural Illinois. Lloyd Wilson is dead, and a tenuous
friendship between two lonely teenage boys is shattered.

"For writers of my generation, William Maxwell's *So Long, See
You Tomorrow* is *the* book that made us think we needed to
write a short novel...But my God, what a model to take on!
Easier to bottle the wind. It possesses that daunting quality
impossible to emulate: it makes greatness seem simple"

RICHARD FORD

"This is one of the great books of our age. It is the subtlest of
miniatures that contains our deepest sorrows and truths and love
- all caught in a clear, simple style in perfect brushstrokes"

MICHAEL ONDAATJE

"Maxwell's voice is one of the wisest in American fiction; it is,
as well, one of the kindest"

JOHN UPDIKE

PUBLISHED IN PAPERBACK BY THE HARVILL PRESS ON 16 JANUARY 1997
ISBN 1 86046 307 X    PRICE: £8.99

GRANTA

# HANIF KUREISHI
## IN A BLUE TIME

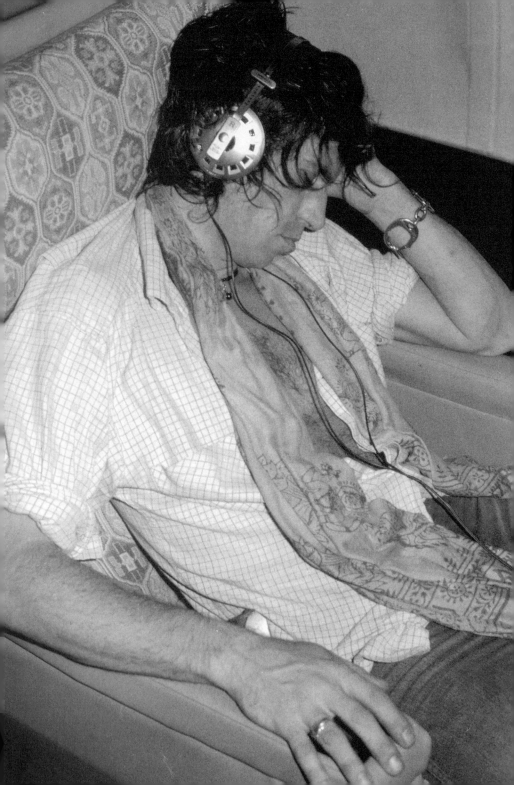

W hen the phone rings, who do you most want it to be? And who would you hate it to be? Who is the first person that comes into your mind, Roy liked to ask people, at that moment?

The phone rang, and Roy jumped. He had thought, during supper in their new house, with most of their clothes and books still in boxes they were too weary to unpack, that it might be pleasant to try their new bed early. He looked across the table at Clara and hoped she'd let the phone run on to the answering machine so he could tell who it was. He disliked talking to his friends in front of her; she seemed to scrutinize him. Somehow he had caused her to resent any life he might have outside her.

She picked up the phone, saying 'hello' suspiciously. Someone was speaking who didn't require or merit a reply. Roy mouthed at her, 'Is it Munday? Is it him?'

She shook her head.

At last she said, 'Oh God,' and waved the receiver at Roy.

Moments later he was putting on his jacket in the hall.

'Are you going to him?'

'He's in trouble.'

She said, 'We're in trouble, and what will you do about that?'

'Go inside. You'll get cold standing there.'

She clung to him. 'Will you be long?'

'I'll get back as soon as I can. I'm exhausted. You should go to bed.'

'Thank you. Aren't you going to kiss me?'

He put his mouth to hers, and she grunted. He said, 'I don't even want to go.'

'You'd rather be anywhere else.'

At the gate he called, 'If Munday rings, please take his number. Say that otherwise I'll go to his office first thing in the morning.'

Munday was a producer, and she knew this call was important to Roy, indeed to both of them. She nodded and then waved.

It wouldn't take him more than fifteen minutes to drive to the house in Chelsea where his old friend Jimmy had been staying the past few months. But Roy was tired and parked at the side of the road to think. To think! Apprehension and dread swept through him, though he had no idea why.

Roy had met Jimmy in the mid-Seventies in the back row of their university class on Wittgenstein. Being four years older than the other students, Jimmy appeared ironically knowing compared to Roy's first friends who had just left school. After a day of lectures Jimmy never merely retired to the library with a volume of Spinoza, or, as Roy did, went disappointedly home to study, while dreaming of the adventures he might have, if only he were less fearful. No; Jimmy did the college a favour by popping in for an hour or so after lunch. Then he'd hang out impressing some girls he was considering for his stage adaptation of *Remembrance of Things Past*.

After he'd auditioned them at length, and as the sky darkened over the river and the stream of commuters across Blackfriars Bridge thinned, Jimmy would saunter forth into the city's pleasures. He knew the happening cinemas, jazz clubs, parties. Or, since he ran his own magazine, *Blurred Edges*, he'd interview theatre directors, photographers, tattooists and performance artists who, to Roy's surprise, rarely refused. At that time students were still considered by some people to be of consequence, and Jimmy would light a joint, sit on the floor and let the recorder run. He would print only the trifling parts of the tape—the gossip and requests for drinks—satisfying his theory that what people were was more interesting than their opinions.

Tonight Jimmy had said he needed Roy more than he'd ever needed him. Or rather, Jimmy's companions had relayed that message. Jimmy himself hadn't made it to the phone or even to his feet. He was, nevertheless, audible in the background.

Roy hesitated on the doorstep. Next morning he had a critical breakfast meeting with Munday, about the movie he had written and was, after two years of preparation, going to direct. He was also, for the first time, living with Clara, who was pregnant. It had been a sort of choice, but its consequences—a child on the way—had somehow surprised them both.

He couldn't turn back. Jimmy's was the voice Roy most wanted to hear on the phone. Their friendship had survived even the mid-Eighties, that vital and churning period when everything had been forced forward with a remorseless velocity. Roy had cancelled his debts to anyone whose affection failed to yield interest. At that time, when Roy lived alone, Jimmy would turn up late at night, just to talk. This was welcome and unusual in Roy's world, and as they didn't work together, there was no question of loss or gain between them. Jimmy wasn't impressed by Roy's diligence. While Roy rushed between meetings, Jimmy was idling in bars. But though Jimmy disappeared for weeks—one time he was in prison—when Roy had a free day, Jimmy was the person he wanted to spend it with. The two of them would lurch from pub to pub, from lunchtime until midnight, laughing at everything. He had no other friend like this, because there are some conversations you can only have with certain people.

Roy pushed the door and cautiously made his way down the uncarpeted stairs, grasping the banister with feeble determination. Someone seemed to have been clawing at the wallpaper with fingernails. A freezing wind blew across the basement: a broken chair appeared to have travelled through a window.

There was Jimmy, with a broken bottle beside him on the floor. The only object intact was a yellowing photograph of Keith Richards pinned to the wall. He was lying on the floor like a child in the playground, with the foot of a bully on his chest. The foot belonged to Marco, the owner of the house, a wealthy junkie with a bloodstained white scarf tied around his throat. Another man, Jake, stood beside them.

'The cavalry's arrived,' said Marco, lifting his boot.

Jimmy's eyes were shut. His twenty-one-year-old girlfriend, Kara, the daughter of a notable bohemian family, ran and kissed Roy gratefully. She was accompanied by an equally young friend, wearing a leopard-skin hat and short skirt. If Roy regretted coming, he particularly regretted his black velvet jacket. Cut tight around the waist, it was long, flared out over the thighs and shone. The designer, a friend for whom Roy had shot a video, had said that ageing could only improve it. But wherever he wore it, Roy understood now, it sang of style and money and made him look as if he had a job.

Kara and the girl took Roy to one side and explained that Jimmy had been drinking. Kara had found him in Brompton Cemetery with a smack dealer, though he claimed to have given that up. This time she was definitely leaving him until he sorted himself out.

Jimmy cried, 'They stole my fucking booze and drank it, found my speed and took it, and stole my money and spent it. I'm not having these bastards in my basement, they're bastards.'

Jake said to Roy: 'Number one, he's evicted right now this minute. He went berserk. Tried to punch us around, and then tried to kill himself.'

Jimmy winked up at Roy. 'Did I interrupt your evening, man? Were you talking about film concepts?'

For years Roy had made music videos and commercials, and directed episodes of soap operas. Sometimes he taught at the film school. He had also made a sixty-minute film for the BBC, a story about a black girl singer. He had imagined that this would be the start of something considerable, but although the film received decent reviews, it had taken him no further. In the mid-Eighties he'd been considered for a couple of features, but like most films, they'd fallen through. He'd seen his contemporaries make films in Britain, move to LA and buy houses with pools. An acquaintance had been nominated for an Oscar.

Now, at last, Roy's own movie was in place—apart from a third of the money and therefore the essential signed contracts and final go-ahead, which was imminent. In the past week Munday had been to LA and New York; he said that with a project of this quality he wouldn't have trouble raising the money.

Kara said, 'I expect Roy was doing some hard work.' She turned to him. 'He's too much. Bye, bye Jimmy, I love you.'

While she bent down and kissed him, and he rubbed his hand between her legs, Roy looked at the picture of Keith Richards and considered how he'd longed for the uncontrolled life, seeking only pleasure and eschewing the ponderous difficulties of keeping everything together. He wondered if that was what he still wanted, or if he was capable of it.

When Kara had gone, Roy stood over Jimmy and asked, 'What d'you want me to do?'

'Quote the lyrics of "Tumblin' Dice".'

The girl in the hat touched Roy's arm. 'We're going clubbing. Aren't you taking Jimmy to your place tonight?'

'What? Is that the idea?'

'He tells everyone you're his best friend. He can't stay here.'

The girl went on. 'I'm Candy. Roy said you work with Munday.'
'That's right.'
'What are you doing with him, a promo?'
From the floor Jimmy threw up his protracted cackle. Roy
said, 'I'm going to direct a feature I've written.'
'Can I work on it with you?' she asked. 'I'll do anything.'
'You'd better ring me to discuss it,' he said.
Jimmy called, 'How's the pregnant wife?'
'Fine.'
'And that young girl who liked to sit on your face?'
Roy made a sign at Candy and led her into an unlit room
next door. He cut out some coke, turned to the waiting girl and
kissed her against the wall, smelling this stranger and running his
hands over her. She inhaled her line, but before he could dispose
of his and hold her again, she had gone.
Marco and Jake had carted Jimmy out, stashed him in Roy's
car and instructed him to fuck off for good.
Roy drove Jimmy along the King's Road. As always now,
Jimmy was dressed for outdoors, in sweaters, boots and heavy
coat; in contrast, Roy's colleagues dressed in light clothes and
would never inadvertently enter the open air: when they wanted
weather they would fly to the place that had the right kind. An
overripe gutter odour rose from Jimmy, and Roy noticed the
dusty imprint of Marco's foot on his chest. Jimmy pulled a pair of
black lace-trimmed panties from his pocket and sniffed at them
like a duchess mourning a relative.
It was the opportunity, Roy decided, to use on Jimmy some
of the honest directness he had been practising at work. It would
be instructive and improving, surely, for Jimmy to survive without
constant assistance. Besides, Roy couldn't be sucked into another
emotional maelstrom.
He said, 'Isn't there anywhere you can go?'
'What for?' said Jimmy.
'To rest. To sleep. At night.'
'To sleep? Oh I see. It's OK. Leave me on the corner.'
'I didn't mean that.'
'I've slept out before.'
'I meant you've usually got someone. Some girl.'

215

Hanif Kureishi

'Sometimes I stay with Candy.'
'Exactly. Who's she?'
'The girl in the hat.'
'Really?'
Jimmy said, 'You liked her, yeah? I'll try and arrange something. Did I tell you she likes to stand on her head with her legs open?'
'You should have mentioned it to Clara on the phone.'
'It's a very convenient position for cunnilingus—'
'Particularly at our age when unusual postures can be a strain,' added Roy.
Jimmy put his hand in Roy's hair. 'You're going grey, you know.'
'I know.'
'But I'm not. Isn't that strange?' Jimmy mused a few seconds. 'But I can't stay with her. Kara wouldn't like it.'
'What about your parents?'
'I'm over forty! They're dying, they make me take my shoes off! They weep when they see me! They—'
He was rummaging in his pockets where he kept his phone numbers on torn pieces of cigarette packet and ragged tube tickets, saying, 'You remember when I brought that girl round one afternoon?'
'The eighteen-year-old?'
'She wanted your advice on getting into the media. You fucked her on the table in front of me.'
'The media got into her.'
'Indeed. Can you remember what you wore, who you pretended to be and what you said?'
'What did I say?'
'It was your happiest moment.'
'It was a laugh.'
'One of our best.'
'One of many.'
They slapped hands.
Jimmy said, 'Except the next day she left me.'
'Sensible girl.'
'We'd exploited her. She had a soul which you were

216

disrespectful to.' Jimmy reached over and stroked Roy's face. 'I just wanted to say, I love you, man, even if you are a bastard.'

Jimmy started clapping to the music. He could revive as quickly as a child. Nevertheless Roy determined to beware of his friend's manipulations; this was how Jimmy had survived since leaving university without ever working. For years women had fallen at his feet; now he collapsed at theirs. Yet even as he descended, they liked him. Many were convinced of his lost genius, which had been perfectly preserved for years by procrastination. Jimmy got away with things; he didn't earn what he received. This was delicious but also a provocation, mocking justice.

Roy had pondered all this, not without incomprehension and envy, until he grasped how much Jimmy gave the women. Alcoholism, unhappiness, failure, ill health, he showered them with despair, and guiltlessly extracted as much concern as they might proffer. They admired, Roy guessed, his having made a darkness to inhabit. Not everyone was brave enough to fall so far out of the light. To Roy it also demonstrated how many women still saw sacrifice as their purpose.

Friendship was the recurring idea in Roy's mind. He recalled some remarks of Montaigne. 'If I am pressed to say why I loved him, I feel it can only be explained by replying: "Because it was he; because it was me."' Also, 'Friendship is enjoyed even as it is desired; it is bred, nourished and increased only by enjoyment, since it is a spiritual thing and the soul is purified by its practice.' However, Montaigne had said nothing about having the friend stay with you, as Jimmy seemed set on; or about dealing with someone who couldn't believe that, given the choice, anyone would rather be sober than drunk, and that once someone had started drinking they would stop voluntarily before passing out— the only way of going to sleep that Jimmy found natural.

Roy no longer had any idea what social or political obligations he had, nor much idea where such duties came from. At university he'd been a charged conscience, having acquired dozens of attitudes wholesale, which, over the years, he had let drop, rather as people stopped wearing certain clothes one by one and started wearing others, until they had unintentionally transformed themselves. Since then Roy hadn't settled in any of the worlds he'd inhabited but only passed through them like hotel rooms and in the process he had never considered what he might owe others. Tonight, what love did this lying, drunken, raggedy-arsed bastard demand?

'Hey.' Roy noticed that Jimmy's fingers were tightening around the handbrake.

'Stop.'

'Now?' Roy said.

'Yes!'

Jimmy was already clambering out of the car and making for an off-licence a few steps away. He wasn't sober but he knew where he was. Roy had no choice but to follow. Jimmy was asking for a bottle of vodka. Then, as Jimmy noticed Roy extracting a fifty-pound note—which was all, to his annoyance, he was carrying—he added a bottle of whisky to his order. When the assistant turned his back, Jimmy swiped four cans of beer and concealed them inside his jacket. He also collected Roy's change.

Outside, a beggar extended his cap and mumbled some words of a song. Jimmy squatted down at the man's level and stuffed the change from the fifty pounds into his cap.

'I've got nothing else,' Jimmy said. 'Literally fuck all. But take this. I'll be dead soon.'

The man held the notes up to the light. This was too much. Roy went to snatch them back. But the bum had disappeared with them and was repeating, 'On yer way, on yer way . . .'

Roy turned to Jimmy. 'It's my money.'

'It's nothing to you, is it?'

'That doesn't make it yours.'

'Who cares whose it is? He needs it more than us.'

' . . . On yer way . . .'

'He's not our responsibility.'

Jimmy looked at Roy curiously. 'What makes you say that? He's pitiful.'

Roy noticed another two derelicts shuffling forward. Further up the street others had gathered, anticipating generosity.

' . . . On yer way . . .'

Roy pulled Jimmy into the car and locked the doors from inside.

Along from Roy's house, lounging by a wall with up-to-something looks on their faces, were two white boys who occupied a nearby basement. The police were often outside, with their mother begging them to take the boys away; but the authorities could do nothing until the lads were older. Most mornings when Roy went out to get his *Independent* he walked across glass where the cars had been broken into. Several times he had greeted the boys. They nodded at him now; one day he would overcome his fear and speak to them properly. He didn't like to think there was anyone it was impossible to contact in some way, but he didn't know where to begin. Meanwhile he could hardly see out of his house for the bars and latticed grilles. Beside his bed he kept a knife and hammer, and he was mindful of not turning over too strenuously for fear of whacking the red alarm button adjacent to his pillow.

'This the new house? Looks comfortable,' said Jimmy. 'You didn't invite me to the house-warming, but Clara's gonna be delighted to see me now. Wish I owned a couple of suitcases so I could stand at the door and tell her I'm here for a while.'

'Don't make too much noise.'

Roy led Jimmy into the living room. Then he ran upstairs, opened the bedroom door and listened to Clara breathing in the darkness.

Before returning to Jimmy he went into the room next door. Clara had bought a changing table on which lay pairs of mittens, baby boots, little red hats, cardigans smaller than handkerchiefs. The curtains were printed with flying elephants; on the wall was a picture of a farmyard.

What had he done? She puzzled him still. Never had a woman pursued him with the passion of Clara over the past five years. Not a day had passed, at the beginning, when she didn't send him flowers and books, invite him to concerts and the cinema, or cook for him. Perhaps she had been attempting, by example, to kindle in him the romantic feeling she herself desired. Whatever, he had accepted it like a pasha. At other times he'd attempted to brush her away, or continued to see other women. He saw now what a jejune protest that was. Her love had been an onslaught. Set on him, she wanted a family. He, who liked to plan

219

everything, but had really only known what sort of work he sought, had complied in order to see what might occur. He had been easily overrun; the child was coming; it gave him vertigo.

He had been tugging at a mattress leaning against the wall. Jimmy would be cosy here, perhaps too cosy, reflected Roy, going downstairs without it.

Jimmy was lying with his feet on the sofa. Beside him he had arranged a beer, a glass and a bottle of Jack Daniels which Roy had already taken from the drinks cupboard. He was lighting a cigarette from the matches Roy had collected from the Royalton and the Odeon, smart New York restaurants, and kept to impress people.

There was no note from Clara about Munday and no message on the machine.

Roy said, 'All right, pal?' He decided he loved his friend, envied his easy complacency, and was glad to have him here.

Jimmy said, 'Got everything I need.'

'Take it easy with the Jack. What about the bottles we bought?'

'Don't start getting queenie. I didn't want to break into them straight away. So—here we are together again.' Jimmy presented his glass. 'What the fuck?'

'Yeah, what the fuck!'

'Fuck everything!'

'Fuck it!'

The rest of the Jack went, and they were halfway through the vodka the next time Roy looked at the clock. The records had come out, including Black Sabbath. A German porn film was playing with the sound turned off. The room became dense with marijuana smoke. They must have got hungry. After smashing into a tin of baked beans with a hammer, and spraying the walls, Roy climbed on Jimmy's shoulders to buff the mottled ceiling with a cushion cover and then stuffed it in Jimmy's mouth to calm him down. Roy didn't know what time the two of them stripped in order to demonstrate the Skinhead Moonstomp or whether he had imagined their neighbour hammering on the wall and then at the front door.

It seemed not long after that Roy hurried into Soho for buttered toast and coffee in Pâtisserie Valérie. In his business, getting up early had become so habitual that if, by mistake, he woke up after seven, he panicked, fearing life had left without him.

Before ten he was at Munday's office where teams of girls with home-counties accents, most of whom appeared to be wearing cocktail dresses, were striding across the vast spaces waving contracts. Roy's arrival surprised them; they had no idea whether Munday was in New York, Los Angeles or Paris, or when he'd be back. He was 'raising money'. Because it had been on his mind, Roy asked seven people if they could recall the name of Harry Lime's English friend in *The Third Man*. But only two of them had seen the film and neither could remember.

There was nothing to do. He had cleared a year of other work to make this film. The previous night had sapped him, but he felt only as if he'd taken a sweet narcotic. Today he should have few worries. Soon he'd be hearing from Munday.

He drifted around Covent Garden, where, since the mid-Eighties, he rarely ventured without buying. His parents had not been badly off, but their attitude to money had been, if you want something, think whether you really need it and whether you can do without it. Well, he could do without most things, if pushed. But at the height of the decade money had gushed through his account. If he drank champagne rather than beer, if he used cocaine and took taxis from one end of Soho to the other five times a day, it barely dented the balance. It had been a poetic multiplication; the more he made, the more he admired his own life.

He had loved that time. The manic entrepreneurialism, prancing individualism, self-indulgence and cynicism appealed to him. Pretence was discarded. Punk disorder and nihilism ruled. Knowledge, tradition, decency, and the lip-service paid to equality; socialist holiness, talk of 'principle', student clothes, feminist absurdities, and arguments defending regimes—'flawed experiments'—that his friends couldn't live in for five minutes: such pieties were trampled with a Nietzschean pitilessness. It was galvanizing.

He would see something absurdly expensive—suits, computers, cameras, cars, apartments—and dare himself to buy it, as if to discover what the consequences of such recklessness might

221

be. How much fun could you have before everything went mad? He loved returning from the shops and opening the designer carrier bags, removing the tissue paper, and trying on different combinations of clothes while playing the new CDs in their cute slim boxes. He adored the new restaurants, bars, clubs, shops, galleries, anything made of black metal, chrome or neon.

It had become like a party at the end of the world. But now he was sick of it, as one might tire of champagne or of kicking a dead body. It was over, and there was nothing. If there was to be anything it had to be made anew.

He had lived through an age when men and women with energy and ruthlessness but without much ability or persistence excelled. And even though most of them had gone under, their ignorance had confused Roy, making him wonder whether the things he had striven to learn, had thought of as 'culture', were irrelevant. Everything was supposed to be equal: commercials, Beethoven's late quartets, pop records, shopfronts, Freud, multi-coloured hair. Greatness, comparison, value, depth: gone, gone, gone. Anything could provide some pleasure; he saw that. But not everything produced the sustenance of a deeper understanding.

His work had gone stale months ago. Whether making commercials, music videos or training films, Roy had always done his best. But now he would go along with whatever the client wanted, provided he could leave early.

Around the time he had begun to write his film, he started checking the age of the director or author if he saw a good movie or read a good book. He felt increasingly ashamed of his still-active hope of being some sort of artist. The word itself sounded effete, and his wish seemed weakly adolescent, affected, awkward.

In a restaurant in Vienna, during a film festival, Roy saw that Fellini had come in with several friends. The maestro went to every table with his hands outstretched. Then the tall man with the head of an emperor sat down and ate in peace. And what peace it would be! Roy thought often of how a man might feel, had he made, for instance, *La Dolce Vita*, not to speak of *Eight and a Half*. What insulating spirit this would give him, during breakfast, or waiting to see his doctor about a worrying complaint, to endure the empty spaces that boundary life's occasional rousing events!

Bergman, Fellini, Ozu, Wilder, Cassavetes, Rosi, Renoir: the radiance! Often Roy would rise at five in the morning to suck the essential vitamin of poetry in front of the video. A few minutes of *Amarcord*, in which Fellini's whole life was present, could give him perspective all day. Certain sequences he examined scores of times, studying the writing, acting, lighting and camera movements. In commercials he was able to replicate certain shots or the tone of entire scenes. 'Bit more Bergman?' he'd say. 'Or do you fancy some Fellini here?'

In New York he went to see *Hearts of Darkness*, the documentary about Coppola making *Apocalypse Now*. He was becoming aware of what he wouldn't do now: parachute from a plane or fight in a war or revolution; travel across Indonesia with a backpack; go to bed with three women at once, or even two; learn Russian, or even French, properly; or be taught the principles of architecture. But for days he craved remarkable and noble schemes on which everything was risked.

What would they be? For most of his adult life he'd striven to keep up with the latest thing in cinema, music, literature and even the theatre, ensuring that no one mentioned an event without his having heard of it. But he had lost the thread and didn't mind. What he wanted was to extend himself. He tormented himself with his own mediocrity. And he saw that, apart from dreams, the most imaginative activity most people allowed themselves was sexual fantasy. To live what you did—somehow—was surely the point.

In his garden in the mornings he began to write, laying out the scenes on index cards on the grass, as if he were playing patience. The concentration was difficult. He was unused to such a sustained effort of dreaming, particularly when the outcome was distant, uncertain and not immediately convertible into a cheque or interest from colleagues. Why not begin next year?

After a few days' persistence his mind focused and began to run in unstrained motion. In these moments—reminded of himself even as he got lost in what he was doing—the questions he had asked about life, its meaning and direction, if any, how best to live, could receive only one reply. To be here now doing this.

That was done. He was in a hurry to begin shooting. Private satisfactions were immaterial. The film had to make money.

223

Compared with his contemporaries at school, he had prospered. When he was growing up, the media wasn't considered a bright boy's beat. Like pop, television was disparaged. But it had turned out to be the jackpot. Yet the way things were getting set up at home, he had to achieve until he expired. He and Clara would live well: nannies, private schools, holidays, dinner parties, clothes. After setting off in the grand style, how could you retreat to less without anguish?

All morning his mind had whirled. Finally he phoned Clara. She'd been sick and had come downstairs to discover Jimmy asleep on the floor amid the night's debris, wrapped in the tablecloth and the curtains, which had become detached from the rail. He had pissed in a pint glass and placed it on the table.

To his surprise she was amused. She had, it was true, always liked Jimmy, who flirted with her. But he couldn't imagine her wanting him in her house. She wasn't a cool or loose hippy. She taught at a university and could be formidable. Most things interested her, though, and she was able to make others see why she was interested. She was enthusiastic and took pleasure in being alive, always a boon in others, Roy felt. Like him, she adored gossip. The misfortunes and vanity of others gave them pleasure. But it was still a mostly cerebral and calculating intelligence that she had. She lacked Jimmy's preferred kind of sentimental self-observation. It had been her clarity that had attracted Roy, at a time when they were both concerned with advancement.

Cheered by her friendliness towards Jimmy, Roy wanted to be with him today. He hailed a taxi.

Jimmy came out of the bathroom wrapped in Roy's bathrobe and sat at the table with scrambled eggs, the newspaper, his cigarettes and *Let It Bleed* on loud. Roy was reminded of them at university, when, after a party, they would stay up all night and spend the next day sitting in a pub garden, or taking LSD and walking along the river to the bridge at Hammersmith, which Jimmy, afraid of heights, would have to run across with his eyes closed.

Roy read his paper while surreptitiously watching Jimmy eat, drink and move about the room as if he'd inhabited it for years. He was amazed by how slowly Jimmy did everything and what lengthy periods between minor tasks were spent staring into space, as if each action set off another train of memory, regret and speculation. Then Jimmy would search his pockets for phone numbers and shuffle them repeatedly. When, finally, he had licked his plate and given a satisfied burp, and when Roy had brushed the crumbs from the floor, he decided to give Jimmy a little start.

'What are you going to do today?'

'Do? In what sense?'

'In the sense of . . . doing something.' Jimmy laughed. Roy went on, 'Maybe you should think of looking for work. The structure might do you good.'

'Structure?'

Jimmy raised himself to talk. There was a beer can from the previous night beside the sofa which he swigged from and then spat out, remembering he'd used it as an ashtray. He fetched a beer from the fridge and resumed his position.

Jimmy said, 'What sort of work is it that you're talking about here?'

'Paid work. You must have heard of it. You do something all day—'

'Usually something you don't like—'

'Whatever. Though you might like it.' Jimmy snorted. 'And at the end of the week they give you money which you can spend on things, instead of having to scrounge them.'

This idea forced Jimmy back in his seat. 'You used to revere the Surrealists.'

'Shooting into a crowd! Yes, I adored it when—'

'D'you think they'd have done anything but kill themselves laughing at the idea of salaried work? You know it's serfdom.'

Roy lay down on the floor and giggled. Jimmy's views had become almost novel to Roy. Listening to him reminded him of the pleasures of failure, a satisfaction he considered unjustly unappreciated now he had time to think about it. In the republic of accumulation and accountancy there was no doubt Jimmy was a failure artist of ability. To enlarge a talent to disappoint, it was no good creeping into a corner and dying dismally. It was essential to raise—repeatedly—hope and expectation in both the gullible and the knowing, which would then be shattered. Jimmy was intelligent, alertly bright-eyed, convincing. With him there was always the possibility of things working out. It was an achievement therefore, after a calculated build-up, to bring off a resounding fuck-up. Fortunately Jimmy would always, on the big occasion, let you down: hopelessness, impotence, disaster, all manner of wretchedness—he could bring them on like a regular nightmare.

Not that it hadn't cost him. It took resolution, organization, and a measure of creativity to drink hard day and night; to insult friends and strangers; to go, uninvited, to parties and attempt to have sex with teenage girls; to borrow money and never pay it back; to lie, make feeble excuses, be evasive, shifty and selfish. He had had many advantages to overcome. But finally, after years of application, he had made a success, indeed a triumph, of failure.

Jimmy said, 'The rich love the poor to work, and the harder the better. It keeps them out of trouble while they're being ripped off. Everyone knows that.' He picked up a porn magazine, *Peaches*, and flipped through the pages. 'You don't think I'm going to fall for that shit, do you?'

Roy's eyes felt heavy. He was falling asleep in the morning! To wake himself up he paced the carpet and strained to recall the virtues of employment.

'Jimmy, there's something I don't understand about this.'

'What?'

'Don't you ever wake up possessed by a feeling of things not done? Of time and possibility lost, wasted? And failure . . . failure in most things—that could be overcome. Don't you?'

Jimmy said, 'That's different. Of mundane work you know nothing. The worst jobs are impossible to get. You've lived for years in the enclosed world of the privileged with no idea what it's like outside. But the real work you mention, I tell you, every damn morning I wake up and feel time rushing past me. And it's not even light. Loneliness . . . fear. My heart vibrates. I keep thinking this is a heart attack. I feel terrorized and have to get out and walk around town.'

'Yes! And don't you think, this is a new morning . . . maybe this day I can redeem the past? Today something real might be done.'

'Sometimes I do think that,' Jimmy said. 'But most of the

time . . . to tell you the truth, Roy, I know nothing will get done. Nothing. Because that time is past.'

When the beer was gone, they went out, putting their arms around one another. On the corner of Roy's street was a rough pub with benches outside, where many local men gathered between March and September, usually wearing just shorts. They'd clamber from their basements at ten-thirty and by eleven they'd be in place, chewing a piece of bread with their beer, smoking dope and shouting above the traffic. Their women, who passed by in groups, pushing prams laden with shopping, were both angrier and more vital.

One time Roy walked past and heard Springsteen's hypodermic cry 'Hungry Heart' blaring from inside. He'd lingered apprehensively: surely the song would rouse the men to some sudden recklessness, the desire to move or hunt down experience? But they merely mouthed the words.

He thought of the books which had spoken to him as a teenager and how concerned they were with young men fleeing home and domesticity, to hurl themselves at different boundaries. But where had it led but self-destruction and madness? And how could you do that kind of thing now? Where would you run?

Roy's preferred local was a low-ceilinged place with a semicircular oak bar. Beyond, it was long and deep, broken up by booths, corners and turns. Men sat alone, reading, staring, talking to themselves, as if modelling for a picture entitled *The Afternoon Drinkers*. There was a comfortable aimlessness; in here nothing had to happen.

Jimmy raised his glass. Roy saw that his hand was trembling, and that his skin looked bruised and discoloured, the knuckles raw, fingers bitten.

'By the way, how was Clara this morning?'

'That was her, right?' said Jimmy.

'Yeah.'

'She's big out front but looking great. A bit like Jean Shrimpton.'

'You told her that?'

Jimmy nodded.

Roy said, 'That's what did the trick. You'll be in with her for a couple of days now.'

'Still fuck her?'

'When I can't help myself,' said Roy. 'You'd think she'd appreciate the interest, but instead she says lying beside me is like sleeping next to a bag of rubbish that hasn't been collected for a fortnight.'

'She's lucky to have you,' said Jimmy.

'Me?'

'Oh yes. And she knows it too. Still, thank Christ there's plenty of pussy back on stream now the Aids frenzy has worn off.'

Roy said, 'All the same, it's easy to underestimate how casual and reassuring married love can be. You can talk about other things while you're doing it. It isn't athletic. You can drift. It's an amicable way of confirming that everything is all right.'

'I've never had that,' said Jimmy.

'You're not likely to, either.'

'Thanks.'

After a time Jimmy said, 'Did I mention there was a phone call this morning? Someone's office. Tuesday?'

'Tuesday?'

'Or was it Wednesday?'

'Munday!'

'Munday? Yeah, maybe it was . . . one of those early days.'

Roy grasped him by the back of the neck and vibrated him a little. 'Tell me what he said.'

Jimmy said, 'Gone. Everything vaporizes into eternity—all thoughts and conversations.'

'Not this one.'

Jimmy sniggered, 'The person said he's in the air. Or was. And he's popping round for a drink.'

'When?'

'I think it was . . . today.'

'Christ,' said Roy. 'Finish your pint.'

'A quick one, I think, to improve our temper.'

'Get up. This is the big one. It's my film, man.'

'Film? When's it on?'

'Couple of years.'

'What? Where's the hurry? How can you think in those kinda time distances?'

Roy held Jimmy's glass to his lips. 'Drink.'

Munday might, Roy knew, swing by for a few minutes and treat Roy as if he were a mere employee; or he might hang out for five hours, discussing politics, books, life.

Munday embodied his age, particularly in his puritanism, Roy thought. He was surrounded by girls; he was rich and in the film business; everywhere there were decadent opportunities. But work was his only vice, with the emphasis on negotiating contracts. His greatest pleasure was to roar, after concluding a deal: ''Course, if you'd persisted, or had a better agent, I'd have paid far more.'

He did like cocaine, but he didn't like to be offered it, for this might suggest he took it, which he didn't, since it was passé. He did, nevertheless, like to notice a few lines laid accidentally out on the table, into which he might dip his nose in passing.

Some coke would surely help things go better.

As Roy guided Jimmy back, he considered the problem. There was a man—Upton Turner—who was that rare thing, a fairly reliable dealer who made home visits and occasionally arrived on the stated day. Roy had been so grateful for this—and his need so urgent—that when Turner had visited in the past, Roy had enquired after his health and family, giving him, he was afraid, the misapprehension that he was a person as well as a vendor. He had become a nuisance, and the last time Roy phoned him, Turner had flung the phone to one side, screaming that the cops were at the door and he was 'looking at twenty years!' As Roy listened, Turner was dumping thousands of pounds' worth of powder down the toilet, only to discover that a neighbour had called to borrow a shovel.

Despite Turner's instability, Roy called him. Turner said he'd come round. At once, Munday's office then rang.

'He's coming to you,' a cool girl said. 'Don't go anywhere.'

'But when?' Roy whined.

'Expect him in the near future,' the voice replied, and added, with a giggle, 'this century, definitely.'

'Ha, ha.'

It gave them some time at least. While listening for Turner's car, Roy and Jimmy had a few more drinks. At last Roy called Jimmy over to the window.

'There.'

229

'No!' Jimmy seized the curtain to give him strength. 'It's a wind-up. That isn't Turner. Maybe it's Munday.'

'It is our man, without a doubt.'

They watched Turner trying to land the old black Rolls in a space, his pit bull sitting up front, and music booming from the windows. He couldn't get the car in anywhere, and finally left it double-parked in the road with the traffic backing up around it, and rushed into the house with the noisy dog. Turner was small, balding and middle-aged, in a white shirt and grey suit that clung to his backside and flared at the ankles. He saw Jimmy drinking at the table and came to an abrupt standstill.

'Roy, son, you're all fucking pissed. You should have said you were having a bit of a laugh, I'd have brought the party acid.'

'This is Jimmy.'

Turner sat down, parting his legs and sweeping back his jacket, thus exposing the outline of his genitals. Turner reached into his pocket and tossed on to the table a plastic bag containing fifty or sixty small envelopes. Jimmy was rubbing his hands together in anticipation.

Turner said, 'How many of these are you having? Eh?'

'Not sure yet.'

'Not sure? What d'you mean?'

'Just that.'

'All right,' Turner conceded. 'Try it, try it.'

Roy opened one of the envelopes.

'Never seen so many books an' videos as you've got in these boxes,' Turner said, pacing about loudly. He halted by a pile and said, 'Alphabetical. A mind well ordered. As a salesman I evaluate the people from the houses I perceive. Read 'em all?'

'It's surprising how many people ask that,' Roy said with relaxed enjoyment. 'It really is. Turner, d'you want a drink or something else?'

'You must know a lot then,' Turner insisted.

'Not necessarily,' Jimmy said. 'It doesn't follow.'

'I know what you mean.' Turner winked at Jimmy, and they laughed. 'But the boy must know something. I'm gonna offer credit where it's due. I'm generous like that.' He lit a cigarette and surveyed the kitchen. 'Nice place. You an' the wife getting the builders in?'

'Yeah.'

"Course. I bet you have a pretty nice life, all in all. Plays, travel, posh friends. The police aren't looking for you, are they?'

'Not like they are for you, Turner.'

'No. That's right.'

'Turner's looking at fifteen. Isn't that right, man?'

'Yeah,' said Turner. 'Sometimes twenty. I'm looking at—' He noticed Jimmy suppressing a giggle and turned to see Roy smirking. He said, 'I'm looking at a lot of shit. Now, Mr Roy, if you know so fucking much, I'll try and think if there's something I need to ask you while I'm here.'

Jimmy said to Roy, 'Are you ready for Mr Turner's question?'

Roy tapped his razor blade on the table and organized the powder into thick lines. He and Jimmy hunched over to inhale. Turner sat down at last and pointed at the envelopes.

'How many of them d'you want?'

'Three.'

'How many?'

'Three, I said.'

'Fuck.' Turner banged his fist on the table. 'Slags.'

Roy said, 'You want a piece of pie?'

'That I could go for.'

Roy cut him a piece of Clara's cherry pie and gave it to Turner, who ate it in two large bites and cut himself another piece. This time he leaned back in his chair, raised his arm and hurled it across the kitchen as if he were trying to smash it through the wall. The dog thrashed after it like a shoal of piranhas. It was an aged creature, and its eating was slobbery and breathless. The second it had finished, the dog ran back to Turner's feet and planted itself there waiting for more.

Turner said to Roy, 'Three, did you say?'

'Yeah.'

'So I have come some considerable miles at your instant command for fuck all. You know,' he said sarcastically, 'I'm looking at eighteen.'

'In that case four. All right. Four Gs. Might as well, eh Jimmy?'

Turner slapped the dog. 'You'll get another go in a minute,'

231

he told it. He looked at Jimmy. 'What about ten?'

'Go for it,' said Jimmy to Roy. 'We'll be all right tomorrow. Ten should see us through.'

'Smart,' said Turner. 'Planning ahead.'

'Ten?' Roy said. 'No way. I don't think you should hustle people.'

Turner's voice became shrill. 'You saying I hustle you?'

Roy hesitated. 'I mean by that . . . it's not a good business idea.'

Turner raised his voice. 'I'm doing this to pay off my brother's debts. My brother who was killed by scum. It's all for him.'

'Quite right,' murmured Jimmy.

'Hey, I've got a fucking question for you,' Turner said, 'little Roy.'

'Yes?'

'Do you know how to love life?'

Jimmy and Roy looked at one another.

Turner said, 'That's stumped you, right? I'm saying here, is it a skill? Or a talent? Who can acquire it?' He was settling into his rap. 'I deal to the stars, you know.'

'Most of them introduced to you by me,' Roy murmured.

'And they are the unhappiest people I've seen.'

'It's still a difficult question,' said Roy.

'But a good one,' said Jimmy.

'You're pleased with that one,' Roy said to Turner.

'Yeah, I am.' Turner looked at Jimmy. 'You're right. It's a difficult question.'

Roy put his hand in his pocket and dragged out a wad of twenty-pound notes.

'Hello,' Turner said.

'Jesus,' said Jimmy.

'What?' Roy said.

'I'll take a tenner off,' Turner said. 'As we're friends—if you buy six.'

'I told you, not six,' said Roy, recounting the money. There was plenty of it, but he thumbed through it rapidly.

Turner reached out to take the whole wad and held it in his

fist, looking down at the dog as his foot played in its stomach.

'Hey,' Roy said and turned to Jimmy, who was laughing.

'What?' said Turner, crumpling the money in his hand. Roy pulled the cherry pie towards himself and cut a slice. He had a drink; his hand was shaking now. 'You are in a state,' Turner said. He took the mobile phone out of his pocket and turned it off.

'Am I?' Roy said.

'What are you going to do with that money?' Turner got up and took a step towards Roy. 'Answer the fucking question!'

Roy put up his hands. 'But I can't.'

Turner pushed three small envelopes towards Jimmy, put all the money in his pocket, yanked away his drug bag and, pursued by the dog, charged to the door. Roy ran to the window and watched the Rolls take off down the street.

'You wanker,' he said to Jimmy. 'You fucking wanker.'

'Me?'

'Christ. We should have done something.'

'Like what?'

'Where's the knife! You should have stuck it in the bastard's fucking throat! That pig's run off with my money!'

'Thing is, you can't trust them proles, man. Sit down.'

'I can't!'

'Here's the knife. Go after him then.'

'Fuck, fuck!'

'This will calm you down,' said Jimmy.

They started into the stuff straight away and there was no going back. Roy attempted to put one gram aside for Munday, but Jimmy said, why worry, they could get more later. Roy didn't ask him where from.

Roy was glad to see Turner go. He'd be glad, too, to see the end of the chaos that Jimmy had brought with him.

'What are your plans?' he asked. 'I mean, what are you going to be doing in the next few days?'

Jimmy shook his head. He knew what Roy was on about, but ignored him, as Roy sat there thinking that if he was capable of love he had to love all of Jimmy now, at this moment.

It was imperative, though, that he clear his mind for Munday.

The drug got him moving. He fetched a jersey and clean socks for Jimmy, thrust Jimmy's old clothes into a plastic bag, and, holding them at arm's length, pushed them deep into the rubbish. He showered, got changed, opened the windows and prepared coffee.

It was only when Munday, who was ten years younger than he and Jimmy and far taller, came through the door, that Roy realized how spaced he and Jimmy were. Fortunately Clara had said she'd be out that evening, and Munday, who had just got off the plane, wanted to relax and talk.

Roy forced his concentration as Munday explained his latest good news. His business, for which Roy had made many music videos, was in the process of being sold to a conglomerate. Munday would make more films than at present, and with bigger budgets. He would be managing director and rich.

'Excellent,' said Roy.

'In some ways,' Munday said.

'What do you mean?'

'Let's have another drink.'

'Yes, we must celebrate.' Roy got up. 'I won't be a moment.'

At the door he heard Jimmy say, 'You might be interested to hear that I myself have attempted a bit of writing in my time . . . '

It was that 'I myself' that made him leave.

Roy went to buy champagne. He was hurrying around the block. Powerful forces were keeping him from his house. His body ached and fluttered with anxiety; he had Aids at least, and cancer, without a doubt. A heart attack was imminent. On the verge of panic, he was afraid he might run yelling into the road but was, at that moment, unable to take another step. He couldn't, though, stay where he was for fear he might lie down and weep. He went into a pub and ordered a half but took only two sips. He didn't know how long he'd been sitting there, but he didn't want to go home.

Munday and Jimmy were sitting head to head. Jimmy was telling him a 'scenario' for a film about a famous ageing film director and a drifting young couple who visit him, to pay homage. After they've eaten with him, praised his percipience and vision, admired his awards and heard his Brando stories, they

234

enquire if there is anything they can do for him. The director says he wants to witness the passion of their lovemaking, hear their conversation, see their bodies, hear their cries and look at them sleeping. The girl and her earnest young man cooperate until . . . They become his secretaries; they take him prisoner; maybe they murder him. Jimmy couldn't remember the rest. It was written down somewhere.

'It's a decent premise,' said Munday.

'Yes,' agreed Jimmy.

Munday turned to Roy, who had rejoined them. 'Where's this guy been hiding?'

He was durable and unsubtle, Munday; and, in spite of his efforts, his kindness and concern for others were obvious.

'In the pub,' said Roy.

'Artist on the edge,' said Jimmy.

'Right,' said Munday. 'Too much comfort takes away the hunger. But I'll do this . . . ' he said.

He would advance Jimmy the money to prepare a draft.

'How much?' asked Jimmy.

'Sufficient.'

Jimmy raised his glass. 'Sufficient. Brilliant—don't you think, Roy?'

Roy said he had to talk to Munday in the kitchen.

'OK,' said Munday. Roy closed the door behind them. Munday said, 'Terrific guy.'

'He used to be remarkable,' said Roy in a low voice, realizing he'd left the champagne in the pub. 'Shame he's so fucked now.'

'He has some nice ideas.'

'How can he get them down? He's been dried out three times but always goes back on.'

'Anyhow, I'll see what I can do for him.'

'Good.'

'I meet so few interesting people these days. But I'm sorry to hear about your condition.'

'Pardon?'

'It happens to so many.'

'What happens?'

235

'I see. You don't want it to get around. But we've worked together for years. You're safe with me.'

'Is that right? Please tell me,' Roy said, 'what you're talking about.'

Munday explained that Jimmy had told him about Roy's addiction to cocaine as well as alcohol.

'You don't believe that, do you?' Roy said.

Munday put his arm around him. 'Don't fuck about, pal, you're one of my best directors. It's tough enough as it is out.'

'But you don't, do you?'

'He predicted you'd be in denial.'

'I'm not in fucking denial!'

Munday's eyes widened. 'Maybe not.'

'But I'm not—really!'

Nevertheless, Munday wouldn't stop regarding him as if he were contriving to fit these startling new pieces into the puzzle that Roy had become.

He said, 'What's that white smear under your nose? And the blade on the table? You will always work, but not if you lie to my face. Roy, you're degrading yourself! I can't have you falling apart on a shoot. You haven't been giving one hundred per cent and you look like shit.'

'Do I?'

'Sure you feel OK now? Your face seems to be twitching. Better take some of these.'

'What are they?'

'Vitamins.'

'Munday—'

'Go on, swallow.'

'Please—'

'Here's some water. Get them down. Christ, you're choking. Lean forward so I can smack you on the back. Jesus, you won't work for me again until you've come out of the clinic. I'll get the office to make a booking tonight. Just think, you might meet some exciting people there.'

'Who?'

'Guitarists. Have you discussed it with Clara?'

'Not yet.'

'If you don't, I will.'

'Thank you. But I need to know what's happening with the film.'

'Listen up then. Just sip the water and concentrate—if you can.'

Later, at the front door, Munday shook Jimmy's hand and said he'd be in touch.

He said, 'You guys. Sitting around here, music, conversation, bit of dope. I'm going back to the airport now. Another plane, another hotel room. I'm not complaining. But you know.'

The moment Munday got in his Jag and started up the street Roy slammed his fist into the table and screamed. Jimmy covered his face, swearing, through his sobs, that he couldn't recall what he'd told Munday. Roy turned away. There was nothing to grasp or punish in Jimmy.

They stopped at an off-licence and drank on a bench in Kensington High Street. A young kid calling himself a traveller sat beside them and gave them a hit on some dope. Roy considered how enjoyably instructive it could be to take up such a position in the High Street, and how much one noticed about people, whereas to passers-by one was invisible, pitied or feared. After a while they went morosely into a pub where the barman served everyone else first and then was rude.

Roy's film would be delayed for at least eighteen months, until Munday was in a stronger position to argue for 'unconventional' projects. Roy doubted it would happen now.

For most of his adult years he'd wanted success and thought he knew what it was. But now he didn't. He would have to live with himself as he was, without the old hope. Within it would be bitter; he would detest himself. Clara, too, would be irked and probably ashamed of him. As his financial burdens increased, his resources had, in a few minutes, shrunk.

As the dark drew in, the street lights came on, and people rushed through the tube stations; he and Jimmy walked about, stopping here and there: in London there seemed to be a pub on every corner. Occasionally they passed restaurants where, in the old days, Roy had been greeted warmly and had passed much time—sometimes four or five hours—with business acquaintances, now forgotten. Soon Roy was lost, fleeing with the energy of the frustrated and distressed, while Jimmy moved beside him, coughing, stumbling and giggling, fuelled by the elation of unaccustomed success.

At one point Jimmy pulled Roy suddenly towards a phone box. Jimmy ran in, waited crouching, and shot out again, pulling Roy by his jacket across the road where they shrank down beside a hedge.

'What are you doing?'

'We were going to get beaten up.' Though shuddering and looking about wildly, Jimmy didn't slop his drink. 'Didn't you hear them swearing at us? Poofs, poofs, they said.'

'Who, who?'

'Don't worry. But keep your head down!' After a while he said, 'Now come on. This way!'

Roy couldn't believe that anyone would attempt such a thing on the street, but how would he know? He and Jimmy hastened through crowds of young people queuing for a concert who, mostly, stepped aside for them; and along streets lined with posters advertising groups and comedians whose names he didn't recognize.

There was a burst of laughter behind him. He wheeled round, but there was no one. It was coming from a parked car; no, from across the road. Then it seemed to disappear down the street like the tail of a typhoon. Now his name was being called. Assuming it was a spook, he pressed on, only to see a young actor he'd given work to, and to whom he'd promised a part in the film. Roy was aware of his swampy loafers and stained jacket that stank of pubs. Jimmy stood beside him, leaning on his shoulder, and they regarded the boy insolently.

'I'll wait to hear, shall I?' said the actor after a time.

They settled in a pub from which Roy refused to move. At last he was able to tell Jimmy what Munday had said, and explain what it meant. Jimmy listened. There was a silence.

'Tell me something, man,' Jimmy said. 'When you prepared your shooting scripts and stuff—'

'I suppose you're a big film writer now.'

'Give me a chance. That guy Munday seemed OK.'

'Did he?'

'He saw something good in me, didn't he?'

'Yes, yes. Perhaps he did.'

'Right. It's started, brother. I'm on the up. I need to get a room—a bedsitter with a table—to get things moving in the literary department. Lend me some money until Munday pays me.'

'There you go.'

Roy laid a twenty-pound note on the table. It was all the cash he had now. Jimmy slid it away.

'What's that? It's got to be a grand.'

'A grand?'

Jimmy said, 'That's how expensive it is—a month's rent in advance, a deposit, phone. You've avoided the real world for ten years. You don't know how harsh it is. You'll get the money back—at least from him.'

Roy shook his head. 'I've got a family now and I haven't got an income.'

'You're a jealous bastard—an' I just saved your life. It's a mistake to begrudge me my optimism. Lend me your pen.' Jimmy made a note on the back of a bus ticket, crossed it out and rejigged it. 'Wait and see. Soon you'll be coming to my office an' asking me for work. I'm gonna have to examine your CV to ensure it ain't too low-class. Now, do you do it every day?'

'Do what?'

'Work.'

'Of course.'

'Every single day?'

'Yes. I've worked every day since I left university. Many nights too.'

'Really?' Jimmy read back what he'd scrawled on the ticket, folded it up and stuck it in his top pocket. 'That's what I must do.' But he sounded unconvinced by what he'd heard, as if, out of spite, Roy had made it sound gratuitously laborious.

Roy said, 'I feel a failure. It's hard to live with. Most people do it. I s'pose they have to find other sources of pride. But what? Gardening? Christ. Everything's suddenly gone down. How am I going to cheer myself up?'

Hanif Kureishi

'Pride?' Jimmy sneered. 'It's a privilege of the complacent, a stupid illusion.'

'You would think that.'

'Why would I?'

'You've always been a failure. You've never had any expectations to feel let down about.'

'Me?' Jimmy was incredulous. 'But I have.'

'They're alcoholic fantasies. They were never going to happen because you can't begin to do anything. Even you can see that.'

Jimmy was staring at him. 'You cunt! You've never had a kind word for me or my talents!'

'Lifting a glass isn't a talent.'

'You could encourage me! You don't know how indifferent people can be when you're down.'

'Didn't I pick you up and invite you to stay in my house?'

'But you were trying to shove me out. Everything about me is wrong or despised. I tell you, you're shutting the door on everyone. It's bourgeois snobbery and it's ugly.'

'You're difficult, Jimmy.'

'At least I'm a friend who loves you.'

'You don't give me anything but a load of trouble.'

'I've got nothing, you know that! Now you've stolen my hope! Thanks for robbing me!' Jimmy finished his drink and jumped up. 'You're safe. Whatever happens, you ain't really going down, but I am!'

Jimmy walked out. Roy had never before seen Jimmy leave a pub so decisively. Roy sat there another hour, until he knew Clara would be home.

He opened the front door and heard voices. Clara was showing the house to two couples, old friends, and was describing the conservatory she wanted built. Roy greeted them and made for the stairs.

'Roy.'

He joined them at the table. They drank wine and discussed the villa near Perugia they would take in the summer. He could visualize them there wearing old linen and ancient straw hats, fanning themselves haughtily.

240

He tilted his head to get different perspectives, rubbed his forehead and studied his hands, which were trembling, but couldn't think of anything to say. Clara's friends were well-off, and of unimaginative and unchallenged intelligence. About most things, by now, they had some picked-up opinion, sufficient to aid party conversation. Set and protected. Roy couldn't imagine them overdosing on their knees, howling.

The problem was: at the back of Roy's world view lay the Rolling Stones and the delinquent dream of his adolescence—the idea that vigour and spirit existed in excess, authenticity and the romantic unleashed self: a bourgeois idea that was strictly anti-bourgeois. It had never, finally, been Roy's way, though he'd played at it. But Jimmy had lived it to the end, for both of them.

The complacent talk made Roy weary. He went upstairs. As he undressed, a cat tripped the security lamps, and he could see the sodden garden. He'd barely stepped into it, but there were trees and grass and bushes out there. Soon he would get a table and chairs for the lawn. With the kid in its pram, he'd sit under the tree, brightened by the sun, eating Vignotte and sliced pear. What did one do when there was nothing to do?

He'd fallen asleep; Clara was standing over him, hissing. She ordered him to come down. He was being rude; he didn't know how to behave; he had 'let her down'. But he needed five minutes to think. The next thing he heard was her saying goodnight at the door.

He awoke abruptly. The front-door bell was ringing. It was six in the morning. Roy tiptoed downstairs with a hammer in his hand. Jimmy's stringy body was soaked through, and he was coughing uncontrollably. He had gone to Kara's house, but she'd been out, so he'd decided to lie down in her doorway until she returned. At about five there had been a storm, and he'd realized she wasn't coming back.

Jimmy was delirious, and Roy persuaded him to lie on the sofa, where he covered him up. When he brought up blood, Clara called the doctor. An ambulance took him away not long after, fearing a clot on the lung.

Roy got back into bed beside his wife and rested his drink on her hard stomach. Clara went to work, but Roy couldn't get up. He stayed in bed all morning, feeling he'd never sleep enough to recover. At lunchtime he walked around town, lacking even the desire to buy anything. In the afternoon he visited Jimmy in the hospital.

'How you feeling, pal?'

A man in his pyjamas can only seem disabled. No amount of puffing up can exchange the blue and white stripes for the daily dignity which has been put to bed with him. Jimmy hardly said hello. He was wailing for a drink and a cigarette.

'It'll do you good, being here,' Roy patted Jimmy's hand. 'Time to sort yourself out.'

Jimmy almost leapt out of bed. 'Change places!'

'No thanks.'

'You smug bastard—if you'd looked after me I wouldn't be in all this shit.'

A fine-suited consultant, haughty and pursued by white-coated disciples, entered the ward. A nurse drew the curtain across, hiding Jimmy's wounded face.

'Make no mistake, I'll be back!' Jimmy cried.

Roy walked past the withered, ashen patients and towards the lift. Two men in lightweight uniforms were pushing a high bed to the doors on their way to the operating theatre. Roy slotted in behind them as they talked across a dumb patient who blinked up at the roof of the lift, discussing where they'd go drinking later. Roy hoped Jimmy wouldn't want him to return the next day.

Downstairs the wide revolving door swept people into the hospital and pushed him out into the town. From the corner of the building, where dressing-gowned patients had gathered to smoke, Roy turned to make a farewell gesture at the building where his friend lay, and saw the girl in the leopard-skin hat—Kara's friend.

He called out. Smiling, she came over, holding a bunch of flowers. He asked her if she was working, and when she shook her head, said, 'Give me your number. I'll call you tomorrow. I've got a couple of things on the go.'

He hadn't seen her in daylight. What, now, might there be time for?

She said, 'When's the baby due?'

'Any day now.'

'You're going to have your hands full.'

He asked her if she wanted a drink.

'Jimmy's expecting me,' she said. 'But ring me.'

Out on the street his spirit rose: Jimmy couldn't walk here, but he—Roy—could trip along light-headed, singing to himself, as if it were he who'd been taken to hospital, though at the last moment, as the anaesthetic was inserted into his hand, a voice had shouted, 'no, not him!' and he'd been reprieved.

Nearby was a coffee shop he used to visit. The manager waved at him and brought over hot chocolate and a cake, and, as usual, complained about how bored he was and how he wished he had a job like Roy's. When he'd gone, Roy opened his bag and extracted his newspaper, book, notebook and pens. But he just watched the passers-by. He couldn't stay long because he remembered that he and Clara had an antenatal class. He wanted to get back. Some people you couldn't erase from your life.  □

# BRAVE NEW FICTION

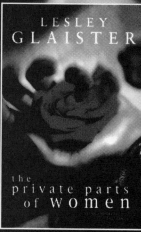

## THE PRIVATE PARTS OF WOMEN

BY LESLEY GLAISTER

'Spine-chilling... Lesley
Glaister has excelled herself'
- SUNDAY TELEGRAPH

£5.99

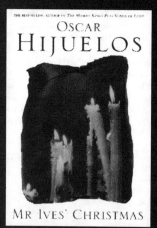

## MR IVES' CHRISTMAS

BY OSCAR HIJUELOS

'Moving, tender and
passionate' - INDEPENDENT

£5.99

**GRANTA**

# SIMON WINCHESTER
## THE LAST POST

## BRITISH IMPERIAL POSSESSIONS, SEPTEMBER 1944

| | | |
|---|---|---|
| Aden | Gold Coast | St Helena |
| Bahama Islands | Hong Kong | Sarawak |
| Barbados | India | Seychelles |
| Bermuda | Jamaica | Sierra Leone |
| British Guiana | Kenya | Singapore |
| British Honduras | Leeward Islands | Somaliland Protectorate |
| Brunei | Federation of Malaya | Tanganyika |
| Burma | Malta | Trinidad & Tobago |
| Ceylon | Mauritius | Uganda |
| Cyprus | Newfoundland | Western Pacific |
| Falkland Islands | Nigeria | Windward Islands |
| Fiji | North Borneo | Zanzibar |
| Gambia | Northern Rhodesia | |
| Gibraltar | Nyasaland Protectorate | *Total population 760,774,473* |

## BRITISH COLONIAL POSSESSIONS, JULY 1997

| | | |
|---|---|---|
| Anguilla | Falkland Islands | South Georgia |
| Bermuda | Gibraltar | Turks & Caicos Islands |
| British Virgin Islands | Montserrat | |
| Cayman Islands | Pitcairn Islands | |
| Diego Garcia | St Helena | *Total population 168,075* |

Near the very top of The Peak on the island of Hong Kong is one of the prettiest pathways that remain in the Empire. Lugard Road is about two miles long, and whenever I get back—after ten years there, now two years away—I like to try to stroll along it, particularly at dawn. I go not so much for what I can see—the views are always breathtaking, unforgettable—but more simply for what I am able to hear.

Sir Frederick Lugard is probably the only governor of the colony who deserves to be long remembered. He founded Hong Kong University, among other things, during his tenure, and then he set off in triumph to found Nigeria. It would be generous and brave of the Chinese if they were to leave his name rusting gently on the road signs that memorialize him. But I dare say they won't. Changing the names of places in China is powerful joss.

The path follows a roughly circular course along a contour line, eight hundred feet or so above the harbour level, a couple of hundred below the rounded summit of The Peak. It is cool up here, and the first few hundred yards seem like a dark tunnel through a forest of damp palm trees, with a Victorian, moss-covered wall on the left-hand side. Two tiny crystal streams gush from culverts in the wall; and from another outlet below a mansion clinging to the hill there is on most mornings, if I get there at the right time, a sudden rush of warm and perfumed water: I suspect it is the morning bathwater of the portly Chinese taipan who lives there.

Just beyond his palace and its garden full of sculptures, the palm trees on the right give way, and Lugard Road, here supported on a framework of stilts from the sheer wall of the cliff, opens on to one of the grandest views in all imperial creation. The scene is framed by the distant folds of the low blue hills of China; but it begins on their nearer slopes, which are etched with tens of thousands of buildings, toylike and tiny at this distance. A little closer, in front of a protective barrier of skyscrapers, there is the winding curve of the harbour, with hundreds of ships riding quietly at anchor, all of them perfectly aligned by the press of tide, anchor-chains stretched taut to the holding buoys. Not long ago the officials of the great British *hongs* would come up here each morning to count the waiting vessels.

A line of massive towers stretches across my entire field of vision: Kennedy Town and Possession Point, where the British first came in 1841, are directly ahead of me, the buildings' long shadows cast on the waters behind, breaking the sunlight that sparkles out towards Lantau; the twin, scarlet-banded towers of the Macau ferry terminal and the Victoria Hotel lie slightly to the fore, and then the grand glittering structures of Central—the banks, the clubs, the huge headquarters of Jardines and Swires, Hutchinson and Inchcape and the other British traders who made this place, who carved their presence on the island that Lord Palmerston once mocked as 'barren, and with hardly a house on it'.

Between where I stand and the great commercial monsters of Central, ranging up the slope towards me as though they are alive and clambering, are the vast blocks of flats where all the drones of the Empire live. Some are small-windowed and stained with tropical mould, some are salmon-pink and gleaming with excess and affluence. Air-conditioning motors whirr on their rooftops alongside groups of Chinese women with tinfoil swords glinting in the sun, performing their morning rituals of t'ai chi ch'uan.

It is the roar, however, that is most magnificent and daunting, the huge sound of the engine work of a great colony: the buzz of machines, snatches of conversation, the horns of angry taxis, the first jackhammerings, sirens, the scream of jet engines on the early planes dipping in from San Francisco and Singapore and Kao-hsiung, their thrust reversers roaring as they settle on to the runway at Kai Tak.

Any Briton who loves Hong Kong and who comes back to it with any frequency these days must feel the pangs of an impending loss. What is about to happen to Hong Kong is right and just and inevitable—but it is a small tragedy nevertheless. Yet the sight from this little pathway and the sound that washes over it remain encouraging, invigorating.

In the year that I was born, 1944, nearly 800 million people, Adenis to Zanzibaris, were enjoying the privilege or suffering the burden of being the subjects of George VI. Thirty years later, when I first visited Hong Kong, that number (of those then counted as subjects of the present Queen) had fallen to a paltry and scarcely believable eight million.

By the end of June next year, the smattering of those around the globe who will still officially look to London for guidance and the succour of imperial command—the forty-five people on Pitcairn, the three hundred fishermen on Tristan da Cunha, those on Gibraltar or in Bermuda and the others scattered half-forgotten among the eleven colonies that remain—will number just about 168,000. It is a grim arithmetic: in a little more than half a century the world's most fabulous empire will have shrunk to one fiftieth of one per cent of its former size—not even Charlemagne's realms declined so quickly.

The first formal announcement was made about the future of Hong Kong at a press conference in July 1984 in the comfortably suburban-sounding Beaconsfield House on Queen's Road. Six million people were being unceremoniously extracted from imperial rule, and yet such Britons as were on hand to hear what history will probably judge as Sir Geoffrey Howe's only memorable pronouncement—that it was 'no longer reasonable to anticipate' that Britain would remain in administrative charge of Hong Kong after the end of June 1997—were casually dismissive. To them it was neither a surprise nor a blow. We were case-hardened to our colonial decline, inured.

To some of the Chinese in the room that afternoon, however, the words fell like thunderbolts. Irene Yau—a formidable ironclad of a civil servant who has held very senior positions in the government—burst into tears. The rest of us shifted uncomfortably away from her, not wanting to be a part of her misery. I think we were embarrassed and perplexed by it, and yet at the same time, and strangely, rather proud that our leaving—as we thought—had made her cry.

Now, with only months till the handover, it is interesting to see how both sides' attitudes have changed. The Chinese—or those Chinese at least who have been compelled to stay behind—appear largely to have made their peace with the situation. The Hong Kong Cantonese, many of them refugees who have known terrible hardships, are calm; those I know have all decided that, there being little by way of other choices, they will just make the best of the coming changes.

But for the British things have turned out rather differently.

249

Those who have clung on in the dying days of the colony, and those who have retired and retreated to Godalming and Cyprus and the Dordogne (vowing to return for the moment of farewell), have over these past twelve years become steadily more pensive and dismayed. The ebullience and sang-froid has all gone. There is an almost shamed aspect to them now. They seem like bewildered members of some shabby nobility waiting to leave the country house to which their former staff have taken title.

Perhaps the countdown to what is officially called the retrocession of the colony has been all too visible for them: the seconds ticking down on a digital clock on Tiananmen Square, the stopwatches blinking on the various Internet sites, the endless processions of visiting analysts and commentators. Perhaps they find it unnecessarily brutal, and it has made them strangely uneasy, robbing them of their old certitude and equanimity.

I spent some time recently with a battalion of the Gurkha Rifles, a British regiment of Nepalese soldiers. (Their particular loyalty has become legend: these were men of the same regiment that, back in the Arakan in 1944, had looked only slightly reluctant when told that they must jump into battle from eight hundred feet, but were much relieved—'their faces wreathed in smiles'—when reassured that, naturally, parachutes would be available.) These Gurkhas had been in Hong Kong for years, based in tidy cantonments tucked away up in the endless blue hills of the New Territories. On the day before this unit's departure all their Land-Rovers and armoured cars were lined up on the drill square, polished and ready for shipping; and in the officers' mess I came across a miserable-looking havildar watching as his men wrapped great solid silver centrepieces in newspaper and laid them softly in tea chests. The regiment was leaving and would then be decommissioned: it was a double blow, an officer said, a whole chapter of imperial soldiering was being closed, the retrocession of Hong Kong the central reason.

It was much the same over on Stonecutters Island, a place long off-limits to civilians officially because the Japanese had kept snakes there during the war for the making of antivenin, and had freed them into the jungle on the day of their surrender. The

British kept their ammunition stores on the island, in tunnels carved into the granite and lined with brick. For a hundred years they had been guarded by Sikhs, men whose religion forbade smoking, and who would watch as you deposited your pipe and Swan Vestas in red boxes at the tunnel entrances and then sign you in. But now these men have all been stood down and some perform humiliating work as security guards in the big hotels; the ammunition was taken out in three grey ships and sent home; it now sits in a big damp bunker near Carlisle.

I remember the Black Watch skirling out, their pipers playing a Highland dirge. And the Navy selling off its old charts. And the Air Force removing its last squadron of helicopters, packed up in great crates marked for Tilbury and Falmouth. The men who listened in on secrets left too, and dismantled their computers and their satellite dishes and took them off to Australia. The BBC, which had in a moment of naive madness built a great transmitting aerial in Hong Kong, realized it could hardly beam its truth from within the new China and so tore the structure down and took it to Thailand.

These were big things, imperial symbols of former might. But smaller things hurt just as much. I remember the otherwise unmemorable day that they unscrewed the weathered bronze crown from the wall of the General Post Office, and some old buffer walking by said he felt truly wounded to see it go. Then the Queen's head came off the coins, to be replaced by a bauhinia flower. Next, the Bank of China—the Communists' bankers, no less, and now based in an ugly, spiky new building looming menacingly over the territory—started issuing notes, a privilege that had once belonged only to the Hongkong & Shanghai Bank, and the Standard Chartered. Such things made people wince as well: evidence in their very pockets and wallets that something beyond their power to control was happening.

Until recently Britain's empire ran to sixteen colonial possessions, one in every ocean, so fashioned that the sun really never did set on Her Majesty's dominions. Colonial governments dotted around the globe stood ready to take in those with a few years of Hong Kong experience, or could offer to Hong

Kong in return some of their best and brightest staff. So the assistant director, home affairs, Hong Kong, might one day become director (acting), home affairs on Montserrat, say; or a district officer (Islands) in Hong Kong—an official whose job brings with it a pretty little brassbound boat called the *Sir Cecil Clementi* on which you could get good curry lunches—could move temporarily down to Tristan da Cunha, or to The Castle in Jamestown, St Helena, or even to Port Stanley in the Falkland Islands or to the cold of South Georgia. The pattern of work and the paperwork would be much the same; only the outside temperature and the look of one's secretary would be any different.

Now, though, the governments of these relict colonies are local people. The roundabout has almost stopped; the gravy train is edging in to the station; the civil servants from Central who are sailing back to Southampton on the *Canberra* (as many had contracts to do), or those constables and commissioners and clerks who are leaving because, with the Chinese coming, they have to, are all now bewildered, wondering what to do. 'When-I's' someone called them, with contempt: 'When I was in Hong Kong . . . ' They are doomed to be unemployable; before long they'll be insufferable.

All the great cities in China, like most of the world's great cities, stand where they do because of natural phenomena—at river-crossings, below mountain passes, close to mineral deposits. But Hong Kong is different: it is cut off by hills, isolated by distance, tucked away from the China for which, under British rule, she has seemed such an entrance. It was built in a hurry; it flourished for only a little over 150 years; how long can it last?

Not long, some say. Theory has it that a new map of China will be drawn in twenty or fifty years in which Beijing will be the country's Washington, as now; Shanghai, at the mouth of the Yangtze, will become its New York; and Hong Kong will wither in importance until it becomes, say, its New Orleans. An important southern city—architecturally interesting, gastronomically varied, popular with tourists and merchants—but in the grand celestial scheme of things not so important.

This is hardly a prospect that pleases those British who like to assume that they are leaving a 'legacy', as they did in most of the other colonial possessions. But the legacy may be barely significant: there will be no real democracy, no proper rule of law and perhaps not even the English language, which is spoken less competently in Hong Kong than almost anywhere Britain has ruled.

There is a fear among the British there that once they have left it will be as though they were never there at all. That is what happened in Port Edward, in north-eastern China, which Britain took as a possession back in 1898. It was a truly forlorn little colony, its one dreary town sandwiched between the Fitzgerald Range and the Seymour Range on the peninsular part of eastern Shantung. But it had the symbols of empire—a dockyard, a public-works department, large bungalows for the naval officers, a club and a gymkhana. In 1930 the British found themselves obliged to go. It was a very simple ceremony: two speeches, a band performance, two fifteen-gun salutes. The Chinese flag was raised alongside the Union Jack at sunset on the final night; and when the sun rose next morning, the British flag had gone and so had the governor. During the darkness he had been rowed silently out to a waiting battleship and, as the first morning breeze took hold of the Republic's flag on shore, he ordered the captain to give the Chinese three siren blasts of Godspeed! before setting sail.

Today in Weihai, as Port Edward is now known, there is scarcely a sign that the British were ever there. A few buildings have a vague familiarity to them, and there is a much overpainted Edwardian letterbox by the fish dock. But otherwise the town displays an aloof immunity to the once colonial presence.

During my last couple of years in Hong Kong I lived in a tiny Chinese village close to the border fence in a narrow fold of the rolling hills of the New Territories. It was a long way from anywhere and a good hour's drive home from the island. After I had been at a restaurant in Lan Kwai Fong, or at a party at a flat in the Mid-Levels, or at an improbably grand dinner at some mansion on The Peak—the three likeliest settings in the limited social spectrum of Hong Kong—I would look forward to driving back along progressively smaller roads and lanes, and into the dung-specked paths and utter quiet of the countryside. The only interruption, once in a while, was a roadblock of flashing blue lights and armoured cars, the police out looking for illegal immigrants or escaped Vietnamese boat people.

I would listen to the radio, usually to an old stager named Ray Cordeiro, who did the graveyard shift and played Ella Fitzgerald and Connie Francis numbers, dedicating them to night owls with pleasantly English-sounding names—Jenny and Clive on Conduit Road, Michael and Patricia in Happy Valley, or Warrant Officer Geoffrey Williams in camp at Blenheim Lines. I always thought it was like that old Sunday-lunchtime programme back home—*Family Favourites*: it was dated, soppy, nice.

The British Forces still have their own radio station in Hong Kong, as they do in all those few remaining places—Cyprus, Belize, the Falklands—where the army does imperial picket duty. The managers have said that towards the end of June next year they will move the studio from the barracks to a warship and broadcast their final few programmes from the harbour. Then, during the last hours of Monday 30 June, the ship will be directed out to sea, its course plotted so that at a few minutes before midnight it will pass below the old Victorian lighthouse on Waglan Island, the most distant of all the old Imperial Lighthouse Service structures—the Light, someone called it, at the End of the Empire.

Then there is only the territorial line before the bow, and beyond, the open sea. The transmitter will play one final song. It will probably not be triumphalist, not 'Rule Britannia', not Elgar, not Delius, not 'Hearts of Oak', but something much sadder and sweeter. Vera Lynn, perhaps: I heard someone up at one of the clubs call for 'The White Cliffs of Dover'. And then it will be midnight, and the ship will cross the invisible line in the ocean, and the radio transmitter will be turned off for ever. □

# NOTES ON CONTRIBUTORS

JOHN BANVILLE is literary editor of the *Irish Times* and the author of *Doctor Copernicus, Kepler, The Book of Evidence, Newton's Letter, Ghosts* and *Athena,* among other novels. His next novel, *The Untouchable,* from which 'The Enemy Within' is taken, will be published by Picador in March.

TIM BINDING is the author of two novels: *In the Kingdom of the Air* and *A Perfect Execution.*

PHILIP HENSHER spent five years as a parliamentary clerk. He is the author of two novels: *Other Lulus* and *Kitchen Venom.*

HANIF KUREISHI received an Oscar nomination for his first screenplay, *My Beautiful Laundrette,* in 1986. His novels include *The Buddha of Suburbia* and *The Black Album.*

NORMAN LEWIS is the author of thirteen novels and nine works of non-fiction. The latest volume of his autobiography, *The World The World,* was published earlier this year.

HILARY MANTEL's most recent novel, *An Experiment in Love,* won the 1996 Hawthornden Prize. Her next book, *The Giant, O'Brien,* is set in London in 1782 and will be published by Viking.

DUNCAN McLEAN was born in Aberdeenshire, lives in Orkney and dreams of Texas. He is the author of two novels and a collection of stories. *Lone Star Swing: on the trail of Bob Wills and his Texas Playboys,* which 'A Good Man is Hard to Find' is an extract from, will be published by Jonathan Cape next year.

JONATHAN MEADES's books include *Peter Knows What Dick Likes, Filthy English* and *Pompey.* He is working on two books: *Digging for Himmler* and *An Encyclopedia of Myself.*

FINTAN O'TOOLE is on the staff of the *Irish Times.* His books include *Black Hole, Green Card: the Disappearance of Ireland.* He lives in Dublin.

JEREMY SEABROOK's most recent book is *In the Cities of the South.*

SIMON WINCHESTER has worked as a foreign correspondent for the *Guardian* and the London *Sunday Times* in the United States and Asia. His next book, *The River at the Centre of the World: a journey up the Yangtze and back in Chinese Time,* will be published by Viking in February.

DONOVAN WYLIE was born in Belfast in 1971. He has published two books of photographs: *32 Countries* and *The Dispossessed* (with Robert Wilson).